The *Least* You Should Know
ABOUT ENGLISH

FORM *B* FIRST CANADIAN EDITION

Teresa Ferster Glazier

Paige Wilson

CANADIAN EDITOR: Kathleen A. Wagner
CAMBRIAN COLLEGE

THOMSON

NELSON

Australia   Canada   Mexico   Singapore   Spain   United Kingdom   United States

THOMSON

NELSON

The Least You Should Know about English, Form B, First Canadian Edition

by Teresa Ferster Glazier, Paige Wilson, and Kathleen A. Wagner

Editorial Director and Publisher:
Evelyn Veitch

Executive Editor:
Anne Williams

Marketing Manager:
Lisa Rahn

Senior Developmental Editor:
Mike Thompson

Permissions Coordinator:
Indu Ghuman

Senior Production Editor:
Bob Kohlmeier

Copy-Editor:
Sarah Robertson

Proofreader:
Margaret Crammond

Indexer:
Margaret Crammond

Production Coordinator:
Ferial Suleman

Creative Director:
Angela Cluer

Cover Design:
Ken Phipps

Cover Image:
Karen Beard/Photonica

Compositor:
Zenaida Diores

Printer:
Webcom Ltd.

National Library of Canada Cataloguing in Publication

Glazier, Teresa Ferster
The least you should know about English : form B / Teresa Ferster Glazier and Kathleen A. Wagner. — 1st Canadian ed.

Includes index.
ISBN 0-17-641575-0

1. English language—Rhetoric—Problems, exercises, etc. 2. English language—Grammar—Problems, exercises, etc. I. Wagner, Kathleen A. II. Title.

PE1413.G58 2004 808'.042
C2004-900560-X

This book is for students who need to review basic English skills and who may profit from a simplified "least you should know" approach. Parts 1 to 3 cover the essentials of spelling, sentence structure, and punctuation. Part 4 on writing teaches students the basic structures of the paragraph and the essay, along with the writing skills necessary to produce them.

Throughout the book, we try to avoid the use of linguistic terminology whenever possible. A conjunction is a connecting word; gerunds and present participles are *ing* words; an infinitive is the *to* ___ form of a verb. Students work with words they know instead of learning a vocabulary they may never use again.

There are abundant exercises, including practice with writing sentences and proofreading paragraphs—enough so that students learn to use the rules automatically and thus *carry over their new skills into their writing*. Exercises consist of sets of ten thematically related, informative sentences on such diverse subjects as Canadian sports heroes, the Juno Awards, the phenomenal success of Tim Hortons, and finding the perfect parking spot. Such exercises reinforce the need for coherence and details in student writing. With answers provided at the back of the book, students can correct their own work and progress at their own pace.

For this new edition, we have completely revised Part 4 on writing, which covers the writing process and which stresses the development of the student's written "voice." Writing assignments follow each discussion, and there are samples by both student and professional writers. Part 4 ends with a section designed to help students with writing assignments based on readings. It includes articles to read, react to, and summarize. Students improve their reading by learning to spot main ideas and their writing by learning to write meaningful reactions and concise summaries.

The Least You Should Know about English functions equally well in the classroom and at home as a self-tutoring text. The simple explanations, ample exercises, and answers at the back of the book provide students with everything they need to progress on their own. Students who have previously been overwhelmed by the complexities of English should, through mastering simple rules and through writing and rewriting simple papers, gain enough competence to succeed in further composition courses.

We all want to have our opinions heard, our thoughts understood, our input respected. Carefully crafting our messages according to universally accepted rules of grammar, spelling, and usage encourages readers to pay attention to what we have to say. In fact, in decoding our messages, members of our reading audience assume that we have followed the rules.

This textbook offers an upbeat yet comprehensive study of how to express your ideas well. If you have unhappy memories of "dangling participles" and "subordinate clauses," you will be delighted that *The Least You Should Know about English* guides readers through the maze of correct grammar and usage without the use of fancy terminology. As a result, the book's lessons are accessible and user-friendly. If you are willing to make an honest commitment to learning, you will feel a new sense of self-confidence in tackling writing tasks.

This book also uses refreshing approaches to upgrade language skills that have gotten a bit rusty over the years. If you once felt in control of your writing but are now less sure of your abilities, reading this book and completing its exercises will dust out the cobwebs caused by informal language use. You'll discover that recalling basic principles is not as difficult as you may have feared.

Qualified individuals in any career field know how to use the right tools to get a job done. Naturally, you will place a high importance on learning the tools of the trade for the career field you have chosen.

But regardless of where you see yourself headed in life, regardless of which occupation attracts you, the ability to communicate correctly and effectively will make a significant contribution to your professional and personal success.

For that reason, fine-tuning your language skills is just as important to your future as learning about the tools and procedures specific to your chosen career path.

Because words are the fundamental building blocks of communication, you need to understand how words work—what jobs they do—before you can comfortably and confidently build sentences, paragraphs, and longer written messages.

Think of this book as a language toolbox. It contains the word and communication tools you will need to build effective pieces of communication. Just as a carpenter carefully selects the right techniques to construct fine furniture, you should carefully apply the principles explained in this book to compose fine written messages.

Simple explanations, no complicated rules to memorize, plenty of opportunities for hands-on application of the principles, and even an answer key to check your work—it just doesn't get any better than this!

The Least You Should Know about English makes it easy to learn exactly what you need to know to avoid the most common writing mistakes. Turn the page and allow this book to be your tour guide on the road to effective communication.

Best wishes on your journey!

Kathleen A. Wagner
Sudbury, Ontario, Canada

ACKNOWLEDGMENTS

For their thoughtful commentary on the book, we would like to thank the following reviewers: Irene Badaracco, Fordham University; Cheryl Delk, Western Michigan University; Nancy Dessommes, Georgia Southern University; Donna Ross Hooley, Georgia Southern University; Sandra Jensen, Lane Community College; Anastasia Lankford, Eastfield College; Ben Larson, York College; Sue McKee, California State University at Sacramento; Karen McGuire, Pasadena City College; Kevin Nebergall, Kirkwood Community College; Peggy Porter, Houston Community College; and Anne Simmons, Olean Business Institute.

In addition, we would like to thank our publishing team: Steve Dalphin, Acquisitions Editor; Michell Phifer, Developmental Editor; Kathryn Stewart, Project Editor; James McDonald, Production Manager; and Garry Harman, Art Director.

We would also like to thank the following people for their contributions: Roman Dodson, Roberta Hales, Paul Miller, Pat Rose, Joseph Sierra, and Lillian Woodward.

Finally, we are indebted to Herb and Moss Rabbin, Kenneth Glazier, and the rest of our families and friends for their support and encouragement.

Teresa Ferster Glazier
Paige Wilson

The goal of Form B continues to be the fair representation of topics and perspectives of interest to Canadian readers. I am grateful to Arlene Davies-Fuhr, Grant MacEwan College; Patricia Hachey, Algonquin College; Gary McNeely, Brandon University; and Jane Walton, Nova Scotia Community College, for helping me to reach that objective through their thoughtful suggestions and review of the text.

As well, the book was made possible through the efforts of some dedicated individuals at Nelson: Anne Williams, Executive Editor (who persevered for nearly two years to acquire the Canadian rights); Mike Thompson, Senior Developmental Editor (who must have been a choreographer in a previous life); Bob Kohlmeier, Senior Production Editor; Sarah Robertson, copy-editor; Susan Calvert, Executive Production Editor; Joanne Buckley; and Margaret Crammond (whose eagle eye kept us all honest).

Finally, this book is dedicated to Nayda Schultz, a now retired colleague whose personal and professional mentorship ignited my passion for teaching English grammar.

Kathleen A. Wagner
Cambrian College, Sudbury, Ontario

Form B differs from Form A in that all of the exercises, and many of the examples, are new. The explanations remain the same.

A **Test Packet** with additional exercises and ready-to-photocopy tests accompanies this text and is available to instructors.

CONTENTS

What Is the Least You Should Know?

Most English textbooks try to teach you more than you need to know. This one will teach you the least you need to know—and still help you learn to write acceptably. You won't have to bother with grammatical terms like gerunds and modal auxiliary verbs and demonstrative pronouns and all those others you've been hearing about for years. You can get along without knowing these terms if you learn a few basic concepts thoroughly. You *do* have to know how to spell common words; you *do* have to recognize subjects and verbs to avoid writing fragments; you *do* have to know a few rules of sentence structure and punctuation—but rules will be kept to a minimum.

The English you'll learn in this book is sometimes called Standard Written English, and it may differ slightly or greatly from the spoken English you use. Standard Written English is the accepted form of writing in business and the professions. So no matter how you speak, you will communicate better in writing when you use Standard Written English. You might *say* something like "That's a whole nother problem," and everyone will understand, but you would probably want to *write,* "That's a completely different problem." Knowing the difference between spoken English and Standard Written English is essential in college and university, in business, and in life.

Unless you learn the least you should know, you'll have difficulty communicating in writing. Take this sentence for example:

I hope my application will be excepted by the hiring committee.

We assume the writer will not actually be happy to be overlooked by the committee but merely failed to use the right word. If the sentence had read

I hope my application will be *accepted* by the hiring committee.

then the writer would convey the intended meaning. Or take this sentence.

The manager fired Lee and Dave and I received a $100 raise.

The sentence needs a comma.

The manager fired Lee and Dave, and I received a $100 raise.

But perhaps the writer meant

The manager fired Lee, and Dave and I received a $100 raise.

Punctuation makes all the difference, especially if you are Dave. What you'll learn from this text is simply to make your writing so clear that no one will misunderstand it.

As you make your way through the book, it's important to master every rule as you come to it because many rules depend on previous ones. For example, unless you learn to pick out subjects and verbs, you'll have trouble with fragments, with subject-verb agreement, and with punctuation. The rules are brief and clear, and it won't be difficult to master all of them—*if you want to*. But you do have to want to!

How to Master the Least You Should Know

1. Study the explanation of each rule carefully.

2. Do the first exercise. Correct your answers using the answer section at the back of the book. If you miss even one answer, study the explanation again to find out why.

3. Do the second exercise and correct it. If you miss a single answer, go back once more and study the explanation. You must have missed something. Be tough on yourself. Don't just think, "Maybe I'll get it right next time." Go back and master the rules, and *then* try the next exercise. It's important to correct each group of ten sentences before going on so that you'll discover your mistakes while you still have sentences to practise on.

4. You may be tempted to quit after you do one or two exercises perfectly. Don't! Make yourself finish another exercise. It's not enough to *understand* a rule. You have to *practise* it.

If you're positive, however, after doing several exercises, that you've mastered the rule, take the next exercise as a test. If you miss even one answer, you should do all the rest of the questions. But if you again make no mistakes, move on to the proofreading and sentence writing exercises so that your understanding of the rule carries over into your writing.

Mastering the essentials of spelling, sentence structure, and punctuation will take time. Generally, community college and university students spend a couple of hours outside of class for each hour in class. You may need more. Undoubtedly, the more time you spend, the more your writing will improve.

P A R T   1

Spelling

Anyone can learn to spell better. You can eliminate most of your spelling errors if you want to. It's just a matter of deciding you're going to do it. If you really intend to learn to spell, study each of the seven parts of this section until you make no more mistakes in the exercises.

Your Own List of Misspelled Words

Words Often Confused (Sets 1 and 2)

Contractions

Possessives

Words That Can Be Broken into Parts

Rule for Doubling a Final Letter

Using a Dictionary

Study these seven parts, and you'll be a better speller.

Your Own List of Misspelled Words

On the inside cover of your English notebook or in some other obvious place, write correctly all the misspelled words in the papers handed back to you. Review them until you're sure of them.

Words Often Confused (Set 1)

Learning the differences between these often-confused words will help you overcome many of your spelling problems. Study the words carefully, with their examples, before trying the exercises.

a, an Use *an* before a word that begins with a vowel *sound* (*a, e, i,* and *o,* plus *u* when it sounds like *uh*) or silent *h*.

Note that it's not the letter but the *sound* of the letter that matters.

> an apple, an essay, an inch, an onion

> an umpire, an ugly design (the *u*'s sound like *uh*)

> an hour, an honest person (silent *h*)

Use *a* before a word that begins with a consonant sound (all the sounds except the vowels, plus *u* or *eu* when they sound like *you*).

> a chart, a pie, a history book (the *h* is not silent in *history*)

> a union, a uniform, a unit (the *u*'s sound like *you*)

> a European vacation, a euphemism (*eu* sounds like *you*)

accept, except   *Accept* means "to receive willingly."

> I *accept* your apology.

Except means "excluding" or "but."

> Everyone arrived on time *except* him.

advise, advice   *Advise* is a verb (pronounce the *s* like a *z*).

> I *advise* you to take your time finding the right job.

Advice is a noun (it rhymes with *rice*).

> My counsellor gave me good *advice*.

affect, effect   *Affect* is a verb and means "to alter or influence."

> All quizzes will *affect* the final grade.

> The happy ending *affected* the mood of the audience.

Effect is most commonly used as a noun and means "a result." If *a, an,* or *the* is in front of the word, then you'll know it isn't a verb and will use *effect*.

> The strong coffee had a powerful *effect* on me.

> We studied the *effects* of sleep deprivation in my psychology class.

all ready, already   If you can leave out the *all* and the sentence still makes sense, then *all ready* is the form to use. (In that form, *all* is a separate word and could be left out.)

We're *all ready* for the trip. (*We're ready for the trip* makes sense.)

The banquet is *all ready*. (*The banquet is ready* makes sense.)

But if you can't leave out the *all* and still have the sentence make sense, then use *already* (the form in which the *al* has to stay in the word).

They've *already* eaten. (*They've ready eaten* doesn't make sense.)

We have seen that movie *already*.

are, our   *Are* is a verb.

We *are* going to Saskatoon.

Our shows we possess something.

We painted *our* fence to match the house.

brake, break   *Brake* used as a verb means "to slow or stop motion." It's also the name of the device that slows or stops motion.

I had to *brake* quickly to avoid an accident.

Luckily I just had my *brakes* fixed.

Break used as a verb means "to shatter" or "to split." It's also the name of an interruption, as in "a coffee break."

She never thought she would *break* a world record.

Enjoy your spring *break*.

choose, chose   The difference here is one of time. Use *choose* for present and future; use *chose* for past.

I will *choose* a new area of study this semester.

We *chose* the wrong time of year to get married.

clothes, cloths   *Clothes* are something you wear; *cloths* are pieces of material you might clean or polish something with.

I love the *clothes* that characters wear in movies.

The car wash workers use special *cloths* to dry the cars.

coarse, course   *Coarse* describes a rough texture, or something crude or vulgar.

I used *coarse* sandpaper to smooth the surface of the board.

His *coarse* language offended some listeners.

Course is used for all other meanings.

Of *course* we saw the golf *course* when we went to Wasaga Beach.

complement, compliment

The one spelled with an *e* has to do with completing something or bringing it to perfection.

Use a colour wheel to find a *complement* for purple.

Juliet's personality *complements* Romeo's; she is practical, and he is a dreamer.

The one spelled with an *i* has to do with praise. Remember "*I* like compliments," and you'll remember to use the *i* spelling when you mean "praise."

My evaluation included a really nice *compliment* from my coworkers.

We *complimented* them on their new home.

conscious, conscience

Conscious means "aware."

They weren't *conscious* of any problems before the accident.

Conscience is a person's inner voice of right and wrong. The extra *n* in *conscience* should remind you of *No,* which is what your conscience often says to you.

My *conscience* told me to turn in the expensive watch I found.

dessert, desert

Dessert is the sweet one, the one you like two helpings of. So give it two helpings of *s.*

We had a whole chocolate cheesecake for *dessert.*

The other one, *desert,* is used for all other meanings and has two pronunciations.

I promise that I won't *desert* you.

The snake slithered slowly across the *desert.*

do, due

Do is a verb, an action. You *do* something.

I always *do* my best work at night.

But a payment or an assignment is *due;* it is scheduled for a certain time.

Our first essay is *due* tomorrow.

Due can also be used before *to* in a phrase that means "because of."

The outdoor concert was cancelled *due to* rain.

feel, fill   *Feel* describes *feel*ings.

Whenever I stay up late, I *feel* sleepy in class.

Fill describes what you do to a cup or a gas tank.

Did they *fill* the pitcher to the top?

fourth, forth   The word *fourth* has *four* in it. (But note that *forty* does not. Remember the word *forty-fourth*.)

This is our *fourth* quiz in two weeks.

My grandparents celebrated their *forty fourth* anniversary.

If you don't mean a number, use *forth*.

We wrote back and *forth* many times during my trip.

have, of   *Have* is a verb. Sometimes, in a contraction, it sounds like *of*. When you say *could've*, the *have* may sound like *of*, but it is not written that way. Always write *could have, would have, should have, might have*.

We should *have* planned our vacation sooner.

Then we could *have* used our coupon for a free one-way ticket.

Use *of* only in a prepositional phrase (see p. 55).

She sent me a box *of* chocolates for my birthday.

hear, here   The last three letters of *hear* spell "ear." You *hear* with your ear.

When I listen to a sea shell, I *hear* ocean sounds.

The other spelling *here* tells "where." Note that the three words indicating a place or pointing out something all have *here* in them: *here, there, where*.

I'll be *here* for three more weeks.

it's, its   *It's* is a contraction and means "it is" or "it has."

It's hot. (*It is* hot.)

It's been hot all week. (*It has* been hot . . .)

Its is a possessive. (Possessives such as *its, yours, hers, ours, theirs, whose* are already possessive and never need an apostrophe. See p. 31.)

The jury had made *its* decision.

The dog pulled at *its* leash.

knew, new
Knew has to do with knowledge (both start with *k*).

New means "not old."

They *knew* that she wanted a *new* bike.

know, no
Know has to do with knowledge (both start with *k*).

By Friday, I must *know* the names of all the past prime ministers.

No means "not any" or the opposite of "yes."

My boss has *no* patience. *No*, I need to work late.

E X E R C I S E S

Underline the correct word. Don't guess! If you aren't sure, turn back to the explanatory pages. When you've finished ten sentences, compare your answers with those at the back of the book. Correct each group of ten sentences before continuing so you'll catch your mistakes while you still have sentences to practise on.

Exercise 1

1. The (affects, effects) of caffeine on our society would be hard to measure.

2. Of (coarse, course), we were (all ready, already) comfortable with caffeine before trendy coffee houses were introduced in Canada in the early 1960s.

3. That's when Tim Horton, founder of the Canadian chain of coffee houses, introduced (a, an) assortment of donuts in Hamilton, Ontario.

4. (It's, Its) product line began with originals like the Apple Fritter and the Dutchie.

5. (Conscience, Conscious) of (it's, its) growing success, Tim Hortons has increased (it's, its) product line to include Timbits, now available in thirty-nine varieties.

6. With (are, our) love of (desserts, deserts) and socializing, Canadians were (all ready, already) for a store so specialized.

7. Canadians are famous for their high consumption of donuts, and they seemed to (fill, feel) immediately attracted by the concept.

8. By contrast, the American Starbucks chain had first to teach Americans to (accept, except) coffee as a (compliment, complement) to their lives instead of just something to drink on a (break, brake).

9. By 2004, four decades after the ex-hockey player (chose, choose) to start his business, over 2200 Tim Hortons donut shops have opened across Canada.

10. In 1995, the numbers expanded (do, due) to the company's merger with Wendy's, and now (a, an) number of locations can be found in Michigan, New York, Ohio, Kentucky, Maine, and West Virginia as well.

Source: http://www.timhortons.com

Exercise 2

1. I used to (hear, here) the expression "hobo" when I was growing up, but I didn't (know, no) what it meant.

2. Now after reading (a, an) obituary of Irving Stevens, the "King of the Hobos," I understand (it's, its) meaning better.

3. The word "hobo" was a shortened form of "hoe boy"; it described a man who would (do, due) temporary farm work and travel from place to place in open railway cars.

4. It was a life that people (choose, chose) to live rather than were forced to live, and it brought (it's, its) own kind of rewards.

5. Stevens, whose hobo nickname was Fishbones, became (conscience, conscious) of people's perceptions of hobos as worthless "bums."

6. Such negative stereotypes did not (affect, effect) Stevens' self-image or his love of the hobo lifestyle, and he prospered in spite of them.

7. Stevens' insights and stories, as well as some of his (advise, advice) for other hobos, (feel, fill) two books called *Dear Fishbones* and *Hoboing in the 1930s.*

8. He even invented (a, an) insect repellent sold under the name of Irving's Fly Dope, and he was especially proud of (it's, its) success.

9. Despite the original name "hoe *boy*," some women (choose, chose) to be hobos and were readily (accepted, excepted) by their male counterparts; Boxcar Bertha was one famous example.

10. Irving Stevens' own daughter, Connie Hall, became "Queen of the Hobos" at the end of her father's reign, and to her that was a real (complement, compliment).

Source: The Economist, May 15, 1999.

Exercise 3

1. Dinosaur footprints bring (fourth, forth) images of huge creatures and (feel, fill) us with wonder.

2. The fact that the footprints are still (hear, here) but the creatures aren't (affects, effects) us deeply.

3. These reactions (are, our) especially true when we see not one footprint but many in (a, an) unbroken row; scientists call them dinosaur "trackways."

4. Before 1995, the longest trackway that we (knew, new) of measured just under 150 metres long; (it's, its) located in Portugal.

5. That was (all ready, already) an incredible discovery, but then scientists found five new trackways between 180 and 300 metres long in Uzbekistan and Turkmenistan.

6. The tracks were made by megalosaurs, meat eaters a lot like *Tyrannosaurus rex,* (accept, except) that these dinosaurs lived earlier—more than 150 million years ago.

7. The tracks' sizes and shapes (complement, compliment) what we (all ready, already) (know, no) about the creatures of the late Jurassic period.

8. But the megalosaurs that made the tracks in Uzbekistan seem to (have, of) walked with their feet far apart.

9. Perhaps these creatures used to (feel, fill) up on dinosaur (desserts, deserts).

10. Their tracks reveal them to (have, of) been almost twelve metres long and a little wider than usual.

Source: Discover, Dec. 1995.

Exercise 4

1. I've lived on my own for two years, and I'm (all ready, already) tired of trying to decide what to (do, due) for dinner every night.

2. When I lived at home, I used to come home from school, change my (clothes, cloths), and (choose, chose) from all of the things my mom, dad, or siblings were eating for dinner.

3. I could take a plate of Dad's famous macaroni and cheese back to my room and then go downstairs later for a slice of Mom's lemon pie with (it's, its) fluffy meringue on top.

4. Now I have to come up with a main (coarse, course) and a (dessert, desert) all by myself.

5. (Do, Due) to my lack of cooking experience, dinners of my own are either burned or bought.

6. I'm beginning to (feel, fill) a little self-(conscience, conscious) about my limitations in the kitchen.

7. I could call my parents for (advise, advice), but I don't want them to worry about me.

8. Without a doubt, I should (have, of) paid more attention when both my parents were cooking, not just have (complemented, complimented) them on the results.

9. I guess I could take a cooking (coarse, course) or get a roommate to (do, due) the cooking for reduced rent.

10. I like everything about living away from home (accept, except) making my own dinner.

Exercise 5

1. There is (a, an) old, commonly held belief that if you (choose, chose) to wash your car today, it will rain tomorrow.

2. Of (coarse, course), that's just a saying; (it's, its) not true.

3. However, if you take my (advise, advice) and wash your car at home, it will save you considerable expense should this happen to you.

4. To avoid the undesirable (affect, effect) of clouding or streaking of the finish, never wash your car in direct sunlight.

5. But don't park your car under a tree to take advantage of (it's, its) shade, or you may be sorry later (do, due) to the possibility of sap falling from the tree.

6. Also, be sure that the (clothes, cloths) you use to wipe the surface are clean and have (know, no) (coarse, course) stitching or texture.

7. You don't want to (brake, break) your antenna, so it should be removed if possible.

8. Once your car is (all ready, already) to be washed, use circular motions and (feel, fill) the surface every now and then to be sure (it's, its) been cleaned.

9. Take the time to dry the whole surface of the car with a chamois if you want to get a lot of (complements, compliments) from your friends.

10. If you've done a thorough job, the (clothes, cloths) you are wearing will be wet, but your car will be dry and as shiny as it was the day you bought it.

PROOFREADING EXERCISE

Find and correct the ten errors contained in the following student paragraph. All of the errors involve Words Often Confused (Set 1).

I like all the classes I chose this semester accept my computing class. Its not what you might think. The teacher is nice, my classmates have a good attitude, and I enjoy learning software too. Its just that I don't no how to design a good web page. Everyone has given me advise, but I can't seem to make a web page that is attractive. I have learned HyperText Markup Language, or HTML, but I still have problems creating something easy to read. Now that everyone knows about my lack of talent, I fill very self-conscience whenever its part of the assignment to put something on the web. I guess I always new that I should of dropped this course and taken something else instead.

SENTENCE WRITING

The surest way to learn these Words Often Confused is to use them immediately in your own writing. Choose the five pairs or groups of words that you most often confuse from Set 1. Then use each of them correctly in a new sentence. No answers are provided at the back of the book, but you can see if you are using the words correctly by comparing your sentences to the examples in the explanations.

Words Often Confused (Set 2)

Study this second set of words carefully, with their examples, before attempting the exercises. Knowing all of the word groups in these two sets will take care of many of your spelling problems.

lead, led   *Lead* is the metal that rhymes with *head*.

Old paint is dangerous because it often contains *lead*.

The past form of the verb "to lead" is *led*.

What factors *led* to your decision?

I *led* our school's debating team to victory last year.

If you don't mean past time, use *lead*, which rhymes with *bead*.

I will *lead* the debating team again this year.

loose, lose	*Loose* means "not tight." Note how *l o o s e* that word is. It has plenty of room for two *o*'s.

My dog's tooth is *loose.*

Lose is the opposite of win.

If we *lose* this game, we will be out for the season.

passed, past	The past form of the verb "to pass" is *passed.*

She easily *passed* her math class.

The runner *passed* the baton to her teammate.

We *passed* your house twice before we saw the address.

Use *past* when it's not a verb.

We drove *past* your house. (the same as "We drove *by* your house")

I always use my *past* experiences to help me solve problems.

In the *past,* he had to borrow his brother's car.

personal, personnel	Pronounce these two correctly, and you won't confuse them—*per´son al, per son nel´.*

She shared her *personal* views as a parent.

Personnel means "a group of employees."

I had an appointment in the *personnel* office.

piece, peace	Remember "piece of pie." The one meaning "a *piece* of something" always begins with *pie.*

One child asked for an extra *piece* of candy.

The other one, *peace,* is the opposite of war.

The two gangs discussed the possibility of a *peace* treaty.

principal, principle	*Principal* means "main." Both words have *a* in them: princip*a*l, m*a*in.

The *principal* concern is safety. (main concern)

He lost both *principal* and interest. (main amount of money)

Also, think of a school's "princi*pal*" as your "*pal.*"

An elementary school *principal* must be kind. (main administrator)

A *principle* is a rule. Both words end in *le:*
princip*le,* ru*le*

I am proud of my high *principles.* (rules of conduct)

We value the *principle* of truth in advertising. (rule)

quiet, quite   Pronounce these two correctly, and you won't confuse them. *Quiet* means "free from noise" and rhymes with *diet.*

Tennis players need *quiet* in order to concentrate.

Quite means "very" and rhymes with *bite.*

It was *quite* hot in the auditorium.

right, write   *Right* means "correct" or "proper."

You will find your keys if you look in the *right* place.

It also means "in the exact location, position, or moment."

Your keys are *right* where you left them.

Let's go *right* now.

Write means "to compose sentences, poems, essays, and so forth."

I asked my teacher to *write* a letter of recommendation for me.

than, then   *Than* compares two things.

I am taller *than* my sister.

Then tells when (*then* and *when* rhyme, and both have *e* in them).

I always write a rough draft of an essay first; *then* I revise it.

their, there, they're   *Their* is a possessive, meaning "belonging to them."

Their cars have always been red.

There points out something. (Remember that the three words indicating a place or pointing out something all have *here* in them: *here, there, where.*)

I know that I haven't been *there* before.

There was a rainbow in the sky.

They're is a contraction and means "they are."

> *They're* living in Halifax. (*They are* living in Halifax now.)

threw, through *Threw* is the past form of "to throw."

> We *threw* snowballs at each other.

> I *threw* away my chance at a scholarship.

If you don't mean "to throw something," use *through*.

> We could see our beautiful view *through* the new curtains.

> They worked *through* their differences.

two, too, to *Two* is a number.

> We have written *two* papers so far in my English class.

Too means "extra" or "also," and so it has an extra *o*.

> The movie was *too* long and *too* violent. (extra)

> They are enrolled in that biology class *too*. (also)

Use *to* for all other meanings.

> They like *to* ski. They're going *to* the mountains.

weather, whether *Weather* refers to conditions of the atmosphere.

> Snowy *weather* is too cold for me.

Whether means "if."

> I don't know *whether* it is snowing there or not.

> *Whether* I travel with you or not depends on the weather.

were, wear, where These words are pronounced differently but are often confused in writing.

Were is the past form of the verb "to be."

> We *were* interns at the time.

Wear means to have on, as in wearing clothes.

> I always *wear* a scarf in winter.

Where refers to a place. (Remember that the three words indicating a place or pointing out something all have *here* in them: *here, there, where*.)

> *Where* is the mailbox? There it is.

Where are the closing papers? Here they are.

who's, whose   *Who's* is a contraction and means "who is" or "who has."

Who's responsible for signing the cheques? (*Who is* responsible?)

Who's been reading my journal? (*Who has* been . . . ?)

Whose is a possessive. (Possessives such as *whose, its, yours, hers, ours, theirs* are already possessive and never take an apostrophe. See p. 31.)

Whose keys are these?

woman,   The difference here is one of number: wo*man* refers to
women   one female; wo*men* refers to two or more females.

I know a *woman* who won $8000 on a single horse race.

I bowl with a group of *women* from my work.

you're, your   *You're* is a contraction and means "you are."

You're as smart as I am. (*You are* as smart as I am.)

Your is a possessive meaning "belonging to you."

I borrowed *your* lab book.

E X E R C I S E S

Underline the correct word. When you've finished ten sentences, compare your answers with those at the back of the book. Do only ten sentences at a time so you can teach yourself while you still have sentences to practise on.

Exercise 1

1. I don't know (weather, whether) I should (right, write) my own résumé or pay a service to do it for me.

2. I have a friend (who's, whose) just been hired at a law firm; he told me, "(You're, Your) crazy if you don't let an expert put together (you're, your) résumé."

3. Maybe he's (right, write); he's been (threw, through) the process already and was (quiet, quite) satisfied with the result.

4. He has never (lead, led) me astray before, and I'm not (two, too, to) sure I know how to (right, write) all of my (personal, personnel) information in a clear format.

5. For instance, I can't figure out how much of my (passed, past) experience I should include.

6. (Personal, Personnel) offices do have strict requirements about the length and styles of documents.

7. (Their, There, They're) often harder to get (passed, past) (than, then) the people on the hiring committees.

8. In fact, the one (woman, women) who helped me last time I tried to get a job told me that the (principal, principle) problem with my file was the poor quality of my résumé.

9. I think I'll ask my friend (were, wear, where) he got his résumé done and how much it cost.

10. I would rather (loose, lose) a little money (than, then) (loose, lose) another job opportunity.

Exercise 2

1. When most of us picture a (piece, peace) of ice, we think of little see-(threw, through) cubes of frozen water.

2. And we consider (their, there, they're) (principal, principle) job (two, too, to) be cooling our lemonade when the (weather, whether) gets hot.

3. Scientists, however, know less (than, then) they would like to about the behaviour of water when it freezes.

4. A few of them, including physicist William Harrison, have made the study of ice (their, there, they're) (personal, personnel) mission in life.

5. Harrison, (who's, whose) especially intrigued by the curious movements and emissions of glaciers, is not alone; George Ashton studies ice, (two, too, to), but he focuses on places (were, wear, where) ice forms on top of rivers and lakes.

6. One of the things ice experts are (quiet, quite) sure of already is that ice covers just under 10 percent of the earth's surface.

7. (Than, Then) there is the strange way that water acts when frozen; unlike other substances, it gets bigger rather (than, then) smaller.

8. And it melts instead of getting more solid when pressure is applied to it; a (piece, peace) of wire can be pulled (threw, through) a chunk of ice, and the ice will just freeze again behind it.

9. Minute pieces of ice in the atmosphere have also been discovered to play a part in the thinning of the earth's ozone layer (threw, through) (their, there, they're) interaction with chlorofluorocarbons.

10. If the ice now covering a tenth of the globe (were, wear, where) to melt, the oceans would rise between sixty and ninety metres, and we would (loose, lose) nearly all of the big cities in the world.

Source: Discover, June 1999.

Exercise 3

1. After my exercise class, my feet feel as heavy as (lead, led), and I can still hear my instructor saying, "(You're, Your) not lifting (you're, your) feet high enough!"

2. My (personal, personnel) goal is to (loose, lose) ten pounds.

3. Lately, the indicator on the scale has gone (passed, past) my ideal weight, and I'm not (two, too, to) happy about it.

4. I am (quiet, quite) sure that I don't want to (were, wear, where) only (loose, lose) clothes for the rest of my life.

5. Luckily, I'm taller (than, then) the other members of my family, and my recent weight gain has escaped (their, there, they're) notice so far.

6. But once the warm (weather, whether) arrives, my family will head for the lake.

7. (Than, Then) I won't be able (two, too, to) hide in baggy clothes.

8. My brother and (two, too, to) of my sisters love to water-ski (their, there, they're) at the lake.

9. They don't care (weather, whether) anybody joins them; (their, there, they're) a party all by themselves.

10. I just don't want to be the one (who's, whose) still wearing a T-shirt after everyone else is in the water just because of a ten-pound spare tire around my waist.

Exercise 4

1. Lately, it seems people have forgotten the (principal, principle) "Mind (you're, your) own business, and let other people mind theirs."

2. Private moments are becoming more public (than, then) ever, especially when it comes (two, too, to) marriage proposals.

3. In the (passed, past), people asked each other the big question in the secure setting of a home or perhaps in a (quiet, quite) corner of a restaurant.

4. Now a stadium full of baseball fans or the readership of a whole newspaper must be (their, there, they're) to witness the event.

5. One man decided to (right, write) a crossword puzzle that would spell out the question "Will you marry me?" for his beloved to discover.

6. The (woman, women) he wanted to marry did the puzzle in the paper every morning.

7. On the morning of the proposal, she went (threw, through) the clues, answered all of them correctly, and when she saw the proposal and her name spelled out in the puzzle, she looked up at her boyfriend and said, "Yes!"

8. Some men and (woman, women) don't think it's (right, write) to be put on the spot in public, however.

9. In one instance, the intended (threw, through) the ring overboard after being asked in front of the entire population of a cruise ship.

10. (Weather, Whether) it's other people's portable phone calls or marriage proposals, we (loose, lose)—or maybe we give away—a little more privacy every day.

Exercise 5

1. GenTech, based in British Columbia, is a project that is attempting to (right, write) the wrongs of the (passed, past).

2. GenTech has a website (were, wear, where) the (principal, principle) aim is to study how girls and women can be helped to learn new information technologies.

3. Studies show that girls (loose, lose) interest in science, math, and technology due (two, too, to) lack of attention by teachers and decreased access to computers.

4. Data compiled (threw, through) the years (quiet, quite) clearly show the results: girls' scores in math, science, and technology-related subjects have been consistently lower (than, then) boys' scores.

5. (Lead, Led) by female colleagues at Simon Fraser University and the University of British Columbia, GenTech aims to harness young women's willingness to learn and (their, there, they're) ability to excel in school.

6. For their own (personal, personnel) reasons, young (woman, women) have traditionally avoided educational paths involving technology.

7. A female teacher (who's, whose) background in technology is extensive can inspire young women to pursue technology-based education and careers.

8. Studies on the relationship between gender and technology reveal more (then, than) a system that excludes women from technology programs: they show that women exclude themselves (threw, through) low enrolment in such programs.

9. (Weather, Whether) a young woman is studying information technologies or the arts, the researchers at GenTech would like to increase her opportunities to pursue an education.

10. Parents gain (piece, peace) of mind by exploring non-traditional career options available to (their, there, they're) daughters.

Source: http://www.educ.sfu.ca/gentech

PROOFREADING EXERCISE

See if you can correct the ten errors in this student paragraph. All errors involve Words Often Confused (Set 2).

Now that the whether is nice, my husband and I have decided to repaint the outside of our house. We are going to paint it ourselves. But it isn't going to be an easy job since many of the boards have come lose over the years. Sometime in the passed, the previous owners repainted the house but didn't scrape and sand it first; now the paint is peeling, and big flakes have started falling onto the grass. We worry that their is led in the old paint, but we can't decide weather to call in a professional. One of my husband's friends, a woman who's house was just remodelled, told him, "Your going to regret doing it yourselves. After what I've been threw, I would strongly recommend hiring a professional. That's the only way to guarantee your piece of mind."

SENTENCE WRITING

Write several sentences using any words you missed in doing the exercises for Words Often Confused (Set 2).

Sentence writing is a good idea not only because it will help you remember these words often confused, but also because it will be a storehouse for ideas you can later use in writing papers. Here are some topics you might consider writing your sentences about:

— Your study habits

— Your favourite musician or group

— One of your best qualities

— Something you would like to change

— Your favourite sport to watch on TV

Contractions

When two words are condensed into one, the result is called a contraction:

is not ·······➤ isn't   you have ·······➤ you've

The letter or letters that are left out are replaced with an apostrophe. For example, if the two words *do not* are condensed into one, an apostrophe is put where the *o* is left out.

do not   don't

Note how the apostrophe goes in the exact place where the letter or letters are left out in these contractions:

I am	I'm
I have	I've
I shall, I will	I'll
I would	I'd
you are	you're
you have	you've
you will	you'll
she is, she has	she's
he is, he has	he's
it is, it has	it's

we are	we're
we have	we've
we will, we shall	we'll
they are	they're
they have	they've
are not	aren't
cannot	can't
do not	don't
does not	doesn't
have not	haven't
let us	let's
who is, who has	who's
where is	where's
were not	weren't
would not	wouldn't
could not	couldn't
should not	shouldn't
would have	would've
could have	could've
should have	should've
that is	that's
there is	there's
what is	what's

One contraction does not follow this rule: *will not* becomes *won't.*

In all other contractions that you're likely to use, the apostrophe goes exactly where the letter or letters are left out. Note especially *it's, they're, who's,* and *you're.* Use them when you mean two words. (See pp. 31–32 for the possessive forms—*its, their, whose,* and *your*—which don't have an apostrophe.)

E X E R C I S E S

Put an apostrophe in each contraction. Then compare your answers with those at the back of the book. Be sure to correct each group of ten sentences before going on so you'll catch your mistakes while you still have sentences to practise on.

Exercise 1

1. Weve all seen images of and heard stories about Cleopatra VII, the incredibly beautiful and powerful queen of Egypt.

2. The facts of Cleopatra's life dont need to be exaggerated to be intriguing and fantastic.

3. There isnt any disagreement that her appearance was stunning and her manner mesmerizing.

4. However, the picture on a coin shes said to have commissioned portrays her as more of a ruler than a lover; this coin is the closest thing weve got to a photograph of Cleopatra, and its on display at the British Museum in London.

5. Cleopatra certainly wasnt ordinary: she knew as many as eight languages, understood science and philosophy, and wrote scholarly works.

6. Theres also the famous story of Cleopatra rolling herself up in a rug or some blankets to be delivered to Julius Caesar; hes said to have been very impressed.

7. For political reasons, shed wanted to meet with Caesar in private, but she couldnt do so without attracting the attention of possible enemies.

8. This bold move and a longer, more complicated alliance with Marc Antony dont touch the surface of Cleopatra's accomplishments.

9. And scholars cant explain all of the evidence following Cleopatra's famous suicide.

10. Although weve been led to believe she used an asp, there werent any marks on her dead body, and the snake was never found.

Source: Smithsonian, Feb. 1997.

Exercise 2

1. My friends and I needed some extra money for a trip wed planned, so we decided to have a group yard sale.

2. I didnt think that Id find very many items to sell in my own house.

3. But I couldnt believe how much stuff I discovered that I hadnt ever used.

4. There wasnt any reason to hang on to an old exercise bicycle, for instance.

5. And I knew I didnt want to keep the cat-shaped clock that hung in my room when I was a kid.

6. My parents werent willing to part with the clock, though; I guess theyre more sentimental than I am right now.

7. It isnt easy to get rid of some things, and my friends didnt have any better luck with their parents than Id had.

8. Still, since there were so many of us, we ended up with a yard full of merchandise.

9. We spent the weekend selling a cup here and a bike there until wed made over $200.

10. Now were convinced that without our yard-sale profits, we couldnt have had such a fun-filled trip.

Exercise 3

1. Leonardo da Vinci's mural *The Last Supper* hasnt been treated well over the years.

2. If hed known in the 1490s when he created the mural that it would suffer so, da Vinci mightve reconsidered doing it at all.

3. In the past, its been painted over and even covered with glue in unsuccessful efforts to preserve it.

4. Often there wasnt any attempt to protect the mural; at one time, the room containing the masterpiece was even used as a stable for horses.

5. Napoleon's soldiers didnt treat it any better; in fact, theyre known to have vandalized it on purpose.

6. Although the room hasnt held horses or soldiers recently, its been filled with the exhaust from nearby cars and moisture from the breath of too many visitors.

7. In the late 1970s, Italy decided that it wouldnt allow the mural to suffer any further abuse.

8. The Italian government enlisted a team of experts to clean and repair da Vinci's famous painting, and theyd been working for more than twenty years on the project before it was finished in 1999.

9. Whats on the wall now that theyve finished hasnt been universally well received.

10. Its hard to tell how much of da Vinci's work remains after layers and chunks of grime and coverings have been removed.

Source: Newsweek, June 7, 1999.

Exercise 4

1. Every semester, theres a blood drive at my school, and usually I tell myself Im too busy to participate.

2. But this time, Ive decided to give blood with a couple of my friends.

3. Weve all wanted to donate before, but individually we havent had the nerve.

4. Well visit the "blood-mobile" together and support each other if any of us cant do it.

5. My friend Carla has donated before, so shes the one weve asked about how it feels.

6. She described the whole process and assured us that its easy and painless.

7. First, a volunteer asks us some questions and takes a small blood sample from one of our fingers to see if we are or arent able to give blood.

8. Once were cleared to donate, well be asked to lie down and have one of our arms prepared for the actual donation.

9. Thats the part Ill be dreading, but Carla says its just the first little jab that stings a bit.

10. After that, she says that theres no sensation at all except the satisfaction of helping with such a worthy cause.

Exercise 5

1. People who are unfamiliar with Canadian film might ask, "Whos David Cronenberg?"

2. Ive just watched one of his films, and hes definitely someone people whove a taste for the offbeat would appreciate.

3. They mightnt recognize his name, but they probably wouldve seen his work.

4. At the 2003 Genie Awards, Cronenberg was named best director for the psychologically complex *Spider;* its adapted from the novel by Patrick McGrath.

5. Cronenberg's most controversial film, *Crash,* was a hit at Cannes, but it wasnt very successful at the box office.

6. Cronenberg wrote and directed *eXistenZ,* a science-fiction thriller thats popular with fans of cyberspace.

7. Over the years, its been impossible to ignore Cronenberg's audacity and innovation, qualities that earned him the Jury Prize at Cannes.

8. Cronenbergs even made a movie based on a William S. Burroughs novel that many thought unfilmable.

9. Other movies have been equally sensational; theyve included *Dead Ringers* and *The Fly*, movies thatve helped to build an international audience for Cronenberg's work.

10. In his films, hes explored themes ranging from the intrusion of technology to the psychology of delusion.

PROOFREADING EXERCISE

Can you correct the ten errors in this student paragraph? They could be from any of the areas studied so far.

I cant even think of a roller coaster anymore without being afraid. I used to look forward to the warm whether and frequent trips to our local amusement parks. I loved everything about the rides—the speed, the dips, the turns, the loops. Then I was in a minor car accident wear I injured my knee after crashing into the rear end of another car. It was'nt to bad, and only my knee was hurt. I thought that a sore knee would be the only negative affect. I was wrong. For some reason, since the accident, I've become really frightened of going fast. I found out the hard way, by going threw the most terrifying minutes of my life on a coaster that Id been on several times in the passed. I guess its time for me to find new ways of having fun.

SENTENCE WRITING

Doing exercises helps you learn a rule, but even more helpful is using the rule in writing. Write ten sentences using contractions. You might write about your reaction to the week's big news story, or you can choose your own subject.

Possessives

The trick in writing possessives is to ask yourself the question, "Who (or what) does it belong to?" (Modern usage has made *who* acceptable when it comes first in a sentence, but some people still say, "*Whom* does it belong to?" or even "*To whom* does it belong?") If the answer to your question doesn't end in *s*, then add an apostrophe and *s*. If the answer to your question ends in *s*, add an apostrophe. Then you must see if you need another sound to make the possessive clear. If you need another *s* sound, add the apostrophe and another *s* (as in the last of the following examples).

one girl (uniform)	Who does it belong to?	girl	Add *'s*	girl's uniform
two girls (uniforms)	Who do they belong to?	girls	Add *'*	girls' uniforms
a man (coat)	Who does it belong to?	man	Add *'s*	man's coat
men (hats)	Who do they belong to?	men	Add *'s*	men's hats
children (game)	Who does it belong to?	children	Add *'s*	children's game
a month (pay)	What does it belong to?	month	Add *'s*	month's pay
Brahms (Lullaby)	Who does it belong to?	Brahms	Add *'*	Brahms' Lullaby
my boss (office)	Who does it belong to?	boss	Add *'s*	boss's office

This trick will always work, but you must ask the question every time. Remember that the key word is *belong*. Who (or what) does it belong to? If you ask the question another way, you may get an answer that won't help you. Also, if you just look at a word without asking the question, you may think the name of the owner ends in *s* when it really doesn't.

To Make a Possessive

1. Ask "Who (or what) does it belong to?"
2. If the answer doesn't end in *s*, add an apostrophe and *s*.
3. If the answer ends in *s*, add just an apostrophe *or* an apostrophe and *s* if you need the extra sound to show a possessive (as in *boss's office*).

EXERCISES

Follow the directions carefully for each of the following exercises. Because possessives can be tricky, explanations follow some exercises to help you understand them better.

Exercise 1

Cover the right column and see if you can write the following possessives correctly. Ask the question "Who (or what) does it belong to?" each time. Don't look at the answer before you try!

1. the women (soccer team) _____ the women's soccer team

2. an umpire (decisions) _____ an umpire's decisions

3. Phyllis (career) _____ Phyllis' or Phyllis's career

4. Anthony (new dog) _____ Anthony's new dog

5. the Porters (mailbox) _____ the Porters' mailbox

6. Ms. Ross (picture) _____ Ms. Ross's picture

7. parents (responsibilities) _____ parents' responsibilities

8. a butterfly (wings) _____ a butterfly's wings

9. two butterflies (wings) _____ two butterflies' wings

10. a lawsuit (success) _____ a lawsuit's success

(Sometimes you may see a couple of choices when the word ends in *s*. *Phyllis' career* may be written *Phyllis's career*. That is also correct, depending on how you want your reader to say it. Be consistent when given such choices.)

NOTE: Don't assume that any word that ends in *s* is a possessive. The *s* may indicate more than one of something, a plural noun. Make sure the word actually possesses something before you add an apostrophe.

A few commonly used words are already possessive and don't need apostrophes. Memorize this list:

our, our   its

your, yours   their, theirs

his, her, hers   whose

Note particularly *its, their, whose,* and *your.* They are already possessive and don't take an apostrophe. (These words sound just like *it's, they're, who's,* and *you're,* which are *contractions* that use an apostrophe in place of their missing letters.)

Exercise 2

Cover the right column below and see if you can write the correct form. The answer might be a *contraction* or a *possessive.* If you miss any, go back and review the explanations.

1. (There) someone here to see you.	There's
2. (They) lease runs out next month.	Their
3. Are these keys (you) or hers?	yours
4. Let me know when (it) time to begin.	it's
5. (Who) taking you to the mall?	Who's
6. The car is so old that (it) paint is fading.	its
7. (We) looking for a new apartment.	We're
8. (Who) textbook is this?	Whose
9. (She) the one who called the radio station.	She's
10. Are you sure that (you) right?	you're

Exercise 3

Here's another chance to check your progress with possessives. Cover the right column again as you did in Exercises 1 and 2, and add apostrophes to the possessives. Each answer is followed by an explanation.

1. My cousins spent the weekend at my parents mountain cabin.	parents' (You didn't add an apostrophe to *cousins,* did you? The cousins don't possess anything.)
2. The border guard collected all of the tourists passports.	tourists' (Who did the passports belong to?)
3. I attended my sisters graduation.	sister's (if it is one sister), sisters' (two or more sisters)
4. Two of my friends borrowed the camp directors boat.	director's (The friends don't possess anything.)
5. Patricks salad was larger than hers.	Patrick's (*Hers* is already possessive and doesn't take an apostrophe.)

6. After a moments rest, the dog wagged its tail again.

moment's (*Its* is already possessive and doesn't take an apostrophe.)

7. Overnight, someone covered the Smiths house with tissue.

Smiths' (The house belongs to the Smiths.)

8. Childrens shoe sizes differ from adults sizes.

children's, adults' (Did you use the "Who do they belong to" test?)

9. The sign read, "Buses only."

No apostrophe, no possessive.

10. A toothpastes flavour affects its sales.

toothpaste's (*Its* is already possessive and doesn't take an apostrophe.)

Exercises 4 and 5

Now you're ready to put the apostrophe in each possessive that follows. But be careful. *First,* make sure the word really possesses something; not every word ending in *s* is a possessive. *Second,* remember that certain words are already possessive and don't take an apostrophe. *Third,* remember that even though a word ends in *s,* you can't tell where the apostrophe goes until you ask the question, "Who (or what) does it belong to?" Check your answers at the back of the book after the first set.

Exercise 4

1. One of Pablo Picassos famous paintings was recently vandalized at a museum in Amsterdam.

2. Before the incident, the painting, *Woman Nude in Front of the Garden,* was worth approximately $6 million (U.S.), but to the art world it was priceless.

3. A man who had been treated for psychological problems destroyed the masterpieces monetary and artistic value in a single moment.

4. When a museum guards back was turned, the deranged man used a kitchen knife to carve a huge hole in the paintings centre.

5. He effectively removed the womans image and the canvas behind her.

6. Art historians know that Picasso put three days effort into creating the painting in 1956.

7. But its life was cut short at forty-three; and unfortunately, the museums security team did not catch the attacker in the act.

8. Later, the vandal made the authorities job easier when he told his story to one of Amsterdams newspapers; the mans criminal record included an airline hijacking attempt in the late 1970s.

9. The future of Picassos *Woman Nude in Front of the Garden* is uncertain.

10. According to museum experts, the painting can be restored—but never to its unharmed state.

Source: U.S. News & World Report, May 31, 1999.

Exercise 5

1. Most Canadians know about the Canadian film industrys awards, the Genies.

2. At the 2003 awards ceremony, Atom Egoyans film *Ararat* won the Genie for best motion picture.

3. Arsinée Khanjian, who happens to be Egoyans wife, was named best actress for her role in *Ararat.*

4. That movies achievements in music and costume design were also recognized.

5. Sheila Copps contribution to the arts in Canada was acknowledged with a special award at the 2003 Genie Awards ceremony.

6. The Genie Awards inaugural program took place in 1980; since then, the Academys Cinema Division members have been invited to volunteer for the nominee selection jury.

7. The Genie statue was created by renowned Canadian sculptor Sorel Etrog; Etrogs career has spanned more than forty years.

8. Sorel Etrogs sculpture has played a significant role in the development of Canadian art; in 1967, he was commissioned by Expo in Montreal to create two large sculptures for the Worlds Fair.

9. A special Genie prize, awarded since 1993, is named after Quebec director Claude Jutra; Jutras best-known works are *Mon Oncle Antoine* and *Kamouraska.*

10. In the same way that the Oscar has highlighted Hollywoods efforts, the
Genie has raised Canadian films profile around the world.

Source: http://www.genieawards.ca

PROOFREADING EXERCISE

Find the five errors in this student paragraph. All of the errors involve possessives.

You might not know of Marion Donovans claim to fame. She invented
something most parents use thousands of times. When her babys' crib became
wet each night, Donovan used a shower curtain to create the worlds first plastic
diaper cover. After patenting her device and calling it the "Boater," Donovans'
business sense guided her to sell the idea, for which she received $1 million (U.S.)
in 1951. The Boater design led to the birth of the disposable diaper, and its' sales
currently bring in nearly $5 billion (U.S.) a year.

Source: People, Dec. 7, 1998.

SENTENCE WRITING

Write ten sentences using the possessive forms of the names of members of your
family or the names of your friends. You could write about a recent event where
your family or friends got together. Just tell the story of what happened that day.

REVIEW OF CONTRACTIONS AND POSSESSIVES

Here are two review exercises. First, add the necessary apostrophes to the following sentences. Try to get all the correct answers. Don't excuse an error by saying, "Oh, that was just a careless mistake." A mistake is a mistake. Be tough on yourself.

1. Although Laura Secords name is inextricably linked to chocolate in Canada, the historical figure has no connection with the companys origins.

2. Frank O'Connor, mayor of Toronto in 1913, is responsible for its beginnings long after Secords death.

3. Laura Secords name is remembered in Canadian history because of its association with loyalty and courage.

4. Although the Canadian stores bear Lauras name (her portraits no longer used), shes an American by birth.

5. Despite her American origins, she lived in Upper Canada and remained loyal to Britains forces in the War of 1812.

6. Legend has it that she saved Lieutenant James Fitzgibbons troops at the Battle of Beaver Dams in 1813.

7. Apparently, she set out to St. David's to warn the troops on behalf of her half-brother, Charles, who wasnt well enough to make the journey himself.

8. Lauras thirty-kilometre trek was successful, even though she arrived exhausted and barefoot.

9. In 1827, James Fitzgibbon mentioned Lauras courage in a letter.

10. In 1860, after reading Lauras account of her journey, the Prince of Wales sent her one hundred pounds sterling in recognition of her heroism.

Sources: http://la.essortment.com/laurasecord_raee.htm; *The Canadian Encyclopedia* (McClelland & Stewart, 1999).

Second, correct any errors in apostrophe use that you find in the following short student essay.

Home Is Where Your Stomach Is

For Shania Twain, its dill pickle potato chips, but weve all got our weaknesses when it comes to junk food. The attraction of many such foods is that they remind us of our parents traditions or our provinces special charm—especially when we're away, eating them makes us feel as though were at home.

Whether its Newfoundlands scruncheons or B.C. Ferries infamous Sunshine Breakfast or Northern Ontario's *poutine,* each regional "junk food" carries with it some powerful memories. That's why each regional specialty, from pickled pigs feet to the Nanaimo bar, is our's to crave. In fact, if our own regions' food is considered disgusting by large groups' in the rest of the country, were even more proud.

Source: Maclean's, July 1, 2003.

Words That Can Be Broken into Parts

Breaking words into their parts will often help you spell them correctly. Each of the following words is made up of two shorter words. Note that the word then contains all the letters of the two shorter words.

chalk board	chalkboard	room mate	roommate
over due	overdue	home work	homework
super market	supermarket	under line	underline

Becoming aware of prefixes such as *dis, inter, mis,* and *un* is also helpful. When you add a prefix to a word, note that no letters are dropped, either from the prefix or from the word.

dis appear	disappear	mis represent	misrepresent
dis appoint	disappoint	mis spell	misspell
dis approve	disapprove	mis understood	misunderstood
dis satisfy	dissatisfy	un aware	unaware
inter act	interact	un involved	uninvolved

inter active	interactive	un necessary	unnecessary
inter related	interrelated	un sure	unsure

Have someone dictate the above list for you to write, and then mark any words you miss. Memorize the correct spellings by noting how each word is made up of a prefix and a word.

Rule for Doubling a Final Letter

Most spelling rules have so many exceptions that they aren't much help. But here's one worth learning because it has only a few exceptions.

Double a final letter [consonants only] when adding an ending that begins with a vowel (such as *ing, ed, er*) if all three of the following are true:

1. the word ends in a single consonant,

2. which is preceded by a single vowel (the vowels are *a, e, i, o, u*),

3. and the accent is on the last syllable (or the word only has one syllable).

This is not, however, always the Canadian preference. Sometimes the final letters *l, p, s, t* are doubled when the accent in a word with more than one syllable is *not* on the last syllable (travelled, worshipped). When in doubt, look up the first choice in a Canadian dictionary. The main rule here is to be consistent, whichever choice you make.

We'll try the rule on a few words to which we'll add *ing, ed,* or *er.*

begin **1.** It ends in a single consonant — *n,*
   2. is preceded by a single vowel — *i,*
   3. and the accent is on the last syllable — *be gin ́.*
   Therefore we double the final consonant and write *beginning, beginner.*

stop **1.** It ends in a single consonant — *p,*
   2. is preceded by a single vowel — *o,*
   3. and the accent is on the last syllable (there is only one).
   Therefore we double the final consonant and write *stopping, stopped, stopper.*

filter **1.** It ends in a single consonant — *r,*
   2. is preceded by a single vowel — *e,*
   3. but the accent isn't on the last syllable. It's on the first — *fil ́ter.*
   Therefore we don't double the final consonant. We write *filtering, filtered.*

keep **1.** It ends in a single consonant — *p,*
   2. but it isn't preceded by a single vowel. There are two *e*'s.
   Therefore we don't double the final consonant. We write *keeping, keeper.*

NOTE: Be aware that *qu* is treated as a consonant because *q* is almost never written without *u*. Think of it as *kw*. In words like *equip* and *quit,* the *qu* acts as a consonant. Therefore *equip* and *quit* both end in a single consonant preceded by a single vowel, and the final consonant is doubled in *equipped* and *quitting*.

E X E R C I S E S

Add *ing* to these words. Correct each group of ten before continuing so you'll catch any errors while you still have words to practise on.

Exercise 1

1. eat	**6.** confer
2. cut	**7.** clap
3. slip	**8.** trim
4. talk	**9.** quiz
5. weed	**10.** mop

Exercise 2

1. snap	**6.** cancel
2. tear	**7.** prefer
3. heal	**8.** dream
4. flop	**9.** drip
5. suggest	**10.** transmit

Exercise 3

1. pat	**6.** brush
2. span	**7.** gather
3. feed	**8.** knot
4. alarm	**9.** offer
5. occur	**10.** hog

Exercise 4

1. dig	**6.** unhook
2. review	**7.** run
3. deal	**8.** push
4. clog	**9.** aim
5. click	**10.** deliver

Exercise 5

1. mourn	**6.** wish
2. dress	**7.** cook
3. pass	**8.** construct
4. button	**9.** polish
5. sit	**10.** lead

Progress Test

This test covers everything you've studied so far. One sentence in each pair is correct. The other is incorrect. Read both sentences carefully before you decide. Then write the letter of the incorrect sentence in the blank. Try to isolate and correct the error if you can.

1. ___ **A.** This years' roses are the most beautiful I've ever seen.

   B. The men's team will travel more than the women's team this season.

2. ___ **A.** I don't know how to play chess, but I want to learn.

   B. We could of gone to the movies last weekend.

3. ___ **A.** We submited our names to the scholarship committee for consideration.

   B. Classes were cancelled because of the heavy snowfall.

4. ___ **A.** I always loose my car keys, especially when I'm running late.

   B. The dog next door loves to put its paws up on the fence and watch us swim.

5. ___ **A.** The flavours of beans and rice complement each other perfectly.

   B. I would like to complement you on your choice of major.

6. ___ **A.** Do you know were Yellowknife is?

   B. We've seen that video several times, and I'm tired of it.

7. ___ **A.** Our suitcases were all ready on the plane when we heard the announcement.

   B. We were all ready to go on our trip to the Bahamas.

8. ___ **A.** Blooming plants and trees have no affect on my husband.

   B. But they do affect me, especially in the summer.

9. ___ **A.** Firefighters worried that someone was inside the empty building.

   B. Their principle goal was to save lives.

10. ___ **A.** We bought an umbrella that would last for many years.

    B. It was made of an unique material developed by NASA.

Using a Dictionary

Some dictionaries are more helpful than others. A tiny pocket-sized dictionary or one that fits on a single sheet in your notebook might help you find the spelling of very common words, but for all other uses, you will need a complete, recently published dictionary. For Canadian preferences in spelling and usage, use an up-to-date Canadian dictionary, such as the *Gage Canadian Dictionary, The Canadian Oxford Dictionary,* or the *ITP Nelson Canadian Dictionary.* A good Canadian dictionary will also include Canadian idioms, proper names, and geographic designations. Note that dictionaries may not always agree on the Canadian standard.

Work through the following thirteen exercises using a good dictionary. Then you will understand what a valuable resource it is.

1. Pronunciation

Look up the word *generic* and copy the pronunciation here.

_____

_____

_____

_____

Now under each letter with a pronunciation mark over it, write the key word having the same mark. You'll find the key words at the bottom of one of the two dictionary pages open before you. Note especially that the upside-down *e* (ə) always has the sound of *uh* like the *a* in *ago* or *about*. Remember that sound because it's found in many words.

Next, pronounce the key words you have written, and then slowly pronounce *generic,* giving each syllable the same sound as its key word.

Finally, note which syllable has the heavy accent mark. (In most dictionaries, the accent mark points to the stressed syllable, but in one dictionary it is in front of the stressed syllable.) The stressed syllable is *ner.* Now say the word, letting the full force of your voice fall on that syllable.

When more than one pronunciation is given, the first is more common. If the complete pronunciation of a word isn't given, look at the word above it to find the pronunciation.

Look up the pronunciation of these words, using the key words at the bottom of the dictionary page to help you pronounce each syllable. Then note which syllable has the heavy accent mark, and say the word aloud.

depot   sibilant   ambivalent   chorister

2. Definitions

The dictionary may give more than one meaning for a word. Read all the meanings for each italicized word and then write a definition appropriate to the sentence.

1. The woman left her *stole* in the taxi. _____

_____

2. At the museum, I always find the *period* furniture most interesting. _____

_____

3. They were taught how to *thread* the needle of a sewing machine. _____

_____

4. Artistic *licence* allows for the expansion of creativity. _____

_____

3. Spelling

By making yourself look up each word you aren't sure how to spell, you'll soon become a better speller. When two spellings are given in the dictionary, the first one (or the one with the definition) is preferred. In a Canadian dictionary, the first spelling shown is the Canadian preference.

Use a dictionary to find the preferred spelling for each of these words.

travelled, traveled	canceling, cancelling
millennium, millenium	judgment, judgement

4. Compound Words

If you want to find out whether two words are written separately, written with a hyphen between them, or written as one word, consult your dictionary. For example:

half brother	is written as two words
sister-in-law	is hyphenated
stepchild	is written as one word

Write each of the following correctly:

week end _____   care free   _____

off season _____   half truth   _____

5. Capitalization

If a word is capitalized in the dictionary, that means it should always be capitalized. If it is not capitalized in the dictionary, then it may or may not need a capital, depending on how it is used (see p. 186). For example, *Asian* is always capitalized, but *high school* is capitalized or not, according to how it is used.

>   Last year, I graduated from high school.

>   Last year, I graduated from Lester B. Pearson High School.

Write the following words as they're given in the dictionary (with or without a capital) to show whether they must always be capitalized or not. Take a guess before looking them up.

métis   _____   spanish   _____

dyslexia   _____   earth   _____

6. Usage

Just because a word is in the dictionary doesn't mean that it's in standard use. The following labels indicate whether a word is used today and, if so, where and by whom.

obsolete	no longer used
archaic	not now used in ordinary language but still found in some biblical, literary, and legal expressions
colloquial, informal	used in informal conversation but not in formal writing
dialectal, regional	used in some localities but not everywhere
slang	popular but nonstandard expression
nonstandard, substandard	not used in Standard Written English

Look up each italicized word and write the label indicating its usage for the meaning used in the sentence. Dictionaries differ. One may list a word as slang whereas another will call it colloquial. Still another may give no designation, thus indicating that that particular dictionary considers the word in standard use.

1. One of Joan's neighbours gives her the *creeps*. _____

2. Did she get the boss's *okay*? _____

3. I borrowed a thousand *bucks* from my brother—he's *loaded!* _____

4. The class hamster was a *goner* as soon as the teacher brought him through the door. _____

5. Are they *privy* to your thoughts? _____

7. Derivations

The derivations or stories behind words will often help you remember the current meanings. For example, if you read that someone is *narcissistic* and you consult your dictionary, you'll find that *narcissism* is a condition named after Narcissus, who was a handsome young man in Greek mythology. One day Narcissus fell in love with his own reflection in a pool, but when he tried to get closer to it, he fell in the water and drowned. A flower that grew nearby is now named for Narcissus. And *narcissistic* has come to mean "in love with oneself."

Look up the derivation of each of these words. You'll find it in square brackets either just before or just after the definition.

Cheddar _____

milquetoast _____

caesarean section _____

amphora _____

8. Synonyms

At the end of a definition, a group of synonyms is sometimes given. For example, at the end of the definition of *injure,* you'll find several synonyms, such as *damage* or *harm.* And if you look up *damage* or *harm,* you'll be referred to the same synonyms listed under *injure.*

List the synonyms given for the following words.

vapid _____

educate _____

cover _____

9. Abbreviations

Find the meaning of the following abbreviations.

R.S.V.P. _____   mg _____

SRO _____   cc _____

10. Names of People

The names of famous people will be found either in the main part of your dictionary or in a separate biographical names section at the back.

Identify the following famous people.

Pablo Casals   _____

Sappho   _____

Frank Gehry   _____

Ernest Shackleton   _____

11. Names of Places

The names of places will be found either in the main part of your dictionary or in a separate geographical names section at the back.

Identify the following places.

Sable Island   _____

Lake of the Woods   _____

Port Said   _____

Sandwich   _____

12. Foreign Words and Phrases

Find the language and the meaning of the italicized expressions.

   1. Jason committed a real *faux pas* when he forgot his host's name. _____

   2. For a modern example of *deus ex machina,* just watch the end of that new movie. _____

   3. We used *trompe l'œil* to paint a doorway on the garden wall. _____

   4. The two fighters went at it *mano a mano.* _____

13. Miscellaneous Information

See if you can find these miscellaneous bits of information in a dictionary.

   1. Would you put a *valence* or a *valance* at the top of your window? _____

   2. Where would you expect to see an example of *stichomythia*? _____

   3. What seasoning is used in *goulash*? _____

   4. How long did the *Trojan War* last? _____

   5. How often is *biweekly*? _____

PART 2

Sentence Structure

Sentence structure refers to the way sentences are built using words, phrases, and clauses. Words are single units, and words link up in sentences to form clauses and phrases. Clauses are word groups *with* subjects and verbs, and phrases are word groups *without* subjects and verbs. Clauses are the most important because they make statements—they tell who did what (or what something is) in a sentence. Look at the following sentence, for example:

We bought oranges at the farmer's market on Queen Street.

It contains ten words, each playing its own part in the meaning of the sentence. But which of the words together tell who did what? *We bought oranges* is correct. That word group is a clause. Notice that *at the farmer's market* and *on Queen Street* also link up as word groups but don't have somebody (subject) doing something (verb). Instead, they are phrases to clarify *where* we bought the oranges.

Importantly, you could leave out one or both of the phrases and still have a sentence—*We bought oranges.* However, you cannot leave the clause out. Then you would just have *At the farmer's market on Queen Street.* Remember, every sentence needs at least one clause that can stand by itself.

Learning about the structure of sentences helps you control your own. Once you know more about sentence structure, then you can understand writing errors and learn how to correct them.

Among the most common errors in writing are fragments, run-ons, and awkward phrasing.

Here are some fragments:

Wandering around the mall all afternoon.

Because I tried to do too many things at once.

By interviewing the applicants in groups.

These groups of words don't make complete statements—not one has a clause that can stand by itself. Who was *wandering?* What happened *because you tried to do too many things at once?* What was the result of *interviewing the applicants in groups?* These incomplete sentence structures fail to communicate a complete thought.

In contrast, here are some run-ons:

Computer prices are dropping they're still beyond my budget.

The forecast calls for rain I'll wait to wash my car.

A truck parked in front of my driveway I couldn't get to school.

Unlike fragments, run-ons make complete statements, but the trouble is they make *two* complete statements; the first *runs on* to the second without correct punctuation. The reader has to go back to see where there should have been a break.

So fragments don't include enough information, and run-ons include too much. Another problem occurs when the information in a sentence just doesn't make sense.

Here are a few sentences with awkward phrasing:

The problem from my grades started to end.

It was a time at the picnic.

She won me at chess.

Try to find the word groups that show who did what, that is, the clauses. Once you find them, then try to put the clauses and phrases together to form a precise meaning. It's difficult, isn't it? You'll see that many of the words themselves are misused or unclear, such as *from, it,* and *won.* These sentences don't communicate clearly because the clauses, phrases, and even words don't work together. They suffer from awkward phrasing.

Fragments, run-ons, awkward phrasing, and other sentence structure errors confuse the reader. Not until you get rid of them will your writing be clearer and easier to read. Unfortunately there is no quick, effortless way to learn to avoid errors in sentence structure. First, you need to understand how clear sentences are built. Then you will be able to avoid common errors in your own writing.

This section will describe areas of sentence structure one at a time and then explain how to correct errors associated with the different areas. For instance, we start by helping you find subjects and verbs and understand dependent clauses; then we show you how to avoid fragments. You can go through the whole section yourself to master all of the areas. Or your teacher may assign only parts based on errors the class is making.

Finding Subjects and Verbs

The most important words in a sentence are those that make up its independent clause, the subject and the verb. When you write a sentence, you write about *something* or *someone.* That's the subject. Then you write what the subject *does* or *is.* That's the verb.

<u>Lightning</u> <u>strikes</u>.

The word *Lightning* is the something you are writing about. It's the subject, and we'll underline it once. *Strikes* tells what the subject does. It shows the action in the sentence. It's the verb, and we'll underline it twice. But most sentences do not include only two words—the subject and the verb. However, these two words still make up the core of the sentence even if other words and phrases are included with them.

<u>Lightning</u> <u>strikes</u> back and forth from the clouds to the ground very quickly.

Often <u>lightning</u> <u>strikes</u> people on golf courses or in boats.

When many words appear in sentences, the subject and verb can be hard to find. Because the verb often shows action, it's easier to spot than the subject. Therefore, always look for it first.

The neighbourhood cat folded its paws under its chest.

Which word shows the action? <u>Folded</u>. It's the verb. Underline it twice. Now ask yourself who or what folded? <u>Cat</u>. It's the subject. Underline it once.

Study the following sentences until you understand how to pick out subjects and verbs.

Tomorrow our school celebrates its fiftieth anniversary. (Which word shows the action? <u>Celebrates</u>. It's the verb. Underline it twice. Who or what celebrates? <u>School</u>. It's the subject. Underline it once.)

The team members ate several boxes of chocolates. (Which word shows the action? <u>Ate</u>. Who or what ate? <u>Members</u> <u>ate</u>.)

Internet users crowd the popular services. (Which word shows the action? <u>Crowd</u>. Who or what crowd? <u>Users</u> <u>crowd</u>.)

Often the verb doesn't show action but merely tells what the subject *is* or *was.* Learn to spot such verbs—*is, am, are, was, were, seems, feels, appears, becomes, looks,* and so forth. (For more information on these verbs, see the discussion of sentence patterns on pp. 123–25.)

Sasha is a neon artist. (First spot the verb <u>is</u>. Then ask who or what is? <u>Sasha</u> <u>is</u>.)

The bread appears mouldy. (First spot the verb appears. Then ask who or what appears? Bread appears.)

Sometimes the subject comes after the verb.

In the audience were two reviewers from *The Globe and Mail*. (Who or what were in the audience? Reviewers were.)

There was a fortuneteller at the carnival. (Who or what was there? Fortune-teller was there.)

There were name tags for all the participants. (Who or what were there? Name tags were there.)

Here are the worksheets. (Who or what are here? Worksheets are here.)

NOTE: Remember that *there* and *here* (as in the last three sentences) are not subjects. They simply point to something.

In commands, often the subject is not expressed. It is *you* (understood).

Sit down. (You sit down.)

Place flap A into slot B. (You place flap A into slot B.)

Meet me at 7:00. (You meet me at 7:00.)

There may be more than one subject in a sentence.

Toys and memorabilia from the 1950s are high-priced collectibles.

Celebrity dolls, board games, and even cereal boxes from that decade line the shelves of antique stores.

There may also be more than one verb.

Water boils at a consistent temperature and freezes at another.

The ice tray fell out of my hand, skidded across the floor, and landed under the table.

As you pick out subjects in the following exercises, you may wonder whether you should say the subject is, for example, *memories* or *childhood memories*. It makes no difference so long as you get the main subject, *memories,* right. In the answers at the back of the book, usually—but not always—the single word is used. Don't waste your time worrying whether to include an extra word with the subject. Just make sure you get the main subjects right.

E X E R C I S E S

Underline the subjects once and the verbs twice. When you've finished ten sentences, compare your answers carefully with those at the back of the book.

Exercise 1

1. Pleasant childhood memories are often quite vivid.

2. We remember special places, people, and things from our youth.

3. The image of our first house stays in our minds, for instance.

4. There are the neighbourhood children to recall.

5. Such memories include favourite furniture and decorative objects.

6. Think back to your childhood now.

7. Most likely, it brings back a flood of memories.

8. Perhaps colours and smells seemed brighter and sweeter then.

9. Such sensations strike most of us at some point in our lives.

10. At these times, we cherish the past and look forward to the future.

Exercise 2

1. The sperm business has an unfortunate history of mistrust.

2. Until recently, the system denied patients any choice at all.

3. The sperm simply came from the nearest willing medical student.

4. There were many health problems as a result.

5. In the 1980s, donor semen infected several women with HIV.

6. Only a decade ago, a doctor from the state of Virginia, Cecil Jacobson, went to prison.

7. Without telling his patients, Jacobson fathered as many as seventy-five children using his own sperm.

8. An internal audit at a Hamilton, Ontario, clinic sparked a two-year government probe of Canada's sperm business.

9. New stringent semen regulations came into effect in 1996.

10. As a result, the Canadian government now keeps track of donor semen and ensures proper screening for sexually transmitted and infectious diseases.

Source: "Offspring: One Man's Search for Family," *Witness*, CBC-TV, Oct. 10, 2000.

Exercise 3

1. Amateur talent shows celebrate the performer or "ham" in all of us.
2. Schools and charities organize these events and raise funds for their organizations.
3. There are singers, dancers, comics, and acrobats in nearly every community.
4. They are not always good singers, dancers, comics, and acrobats, however.
5. In fact, crowds often love the worst performers in talent shows.
6. A sense of humour in the audience and the performers helps enormously.
7. Otherwise, participants feel embarrassment instead of encouragement.
8. Laughing with someone is not the same as laughing at someone.
9. Amateur performers need courage and support.
10. Every celebrity started somewhere, perhaps even in a talent show.

Exercise 4

1. The word *toast* has a couple of different meanings.
2. We toast pieces of bread and eat them with butter and jam.

3. People also make toasts to the bride and groom at weddings.

4. There are Old French and Latin word roots for *toast*.

5. Both *toster* (Old French) and *torrere* (Latin) refer to cooking and drying.

6. *Toast* as the word for cooked bread slices arrived in the 1400s.

7. The story of *toast*'s other meaning makes sense from there.

8. In the 1600s, there was a tradition in taverns.

9. Revellers placed spicy croutons in their drinks for added flavour.

10. Then they drank to the health of various ladies and invented the other meaning of *toast*.

Source: Dictionary of Word Origins (Arcade Publishing, 1990).

Exercise 5

1. Canada's tourism industry suffered during the SARS outbreak of 2003.

2. Canoeing on the French River in Northern Ontario is an exhilarating experience for tourists.

3. Halifax hosts an annual festival that celebrates the talents of more than eighty of the world's finest street performers.

4. Though memorably named, Eyebrow, Saskatchewan, is a little-known tourist destination.

5. Fringe festivals are a popular attraction in cities like Edmonton.

6. Springbank Gardens in London, Ontario, is a beloved destination for children.

7. Nanaimo's annual bathtub races attract international attention.

8. Bernard Callebaut produces high-quality chocolate products at its factory in downtown Calgary.

9. Chefs throughout Canada admire the work of Michael Smith, co-owner of the Inn at Bay Fortune in Prince Edward Island.

10. Newfoundland's attractions include Signal Hill, a site rich in historical connections.

PARAGRAPH EXERCISE

Underline the subjects once and the verbs twice in the following student paragraph.

My aunt and uncle have an incredible cookie jar collection. At the moment, they own about eight hundred jars and get new ones every day. Some of their cookie jars date back to the late 19th century. But others commemorate more current cartoon or movie characters. Celebrity cookie jars bring my aunt special happiness and add to the glamour of the collection. There are Elvis, Marilyn Monroe, and James Dean jars and even ones depicting The Grateful Dead's bus and The Beatles' psychedelic car. I really appreciate my aunt and uncle's collection and hope for one of my own someday.

SENTENCE WRITING

Write ten sentences about any subject—your favourite movie or sport, for instance. Keeping your subject matter simple in these sentence-writing exercises will make it easier to find your sentence structures later. After you have written your sentences, go back and underline your subjects once and your verbs twice.

Locating Prepositional Phrases

Prepositional phrases are among the easiest structures in English to learn. Remember that a phrase is just a group of words (at least two) without a subject and a verb. And don't let a term like *prepositional* scare you. If you look in the middle of that long word, you'll find a familiar one—*position*. In English, we tell the *positions* of people and things in sentences using prepositional phrases. Look at the following sentence with its prepositional phrases in parentheses:

Our field trip (to the mountain) begins (at 6:00) (in the morning) (on Friday).

One phrase tells where the field trip is going (*to the mountain*), and three phrases tell when the trip begins (*at 6:00, in the morning,* and *on Friday*). As you can see, prepositional phrases show the position of someone or something in space or in time.

Here is a list of prepositions that can show positions in space:

above	behind	in	past
across	below	inside	through
against	between	near	to
among	beyond	on	under
around	by	outside	without
at	from	over	

Here are prepositions that can show positions in time:

after	by	in	throughout
at	during	past	until
before	for	since	within

These lists include only individual words, *not phrases.* Remember, a preposition must be followed by an object—someone or something—to create a prepositional phrase. Notice that in the added prepositional phrases that follow, the position of the plane in relation to the object, *the clouds,* changes completely.

The passenger plane flew *above the clouds.*
below the clouds.
within the clouds.
between the clouds.
past the clouds.
around the clouds.

Now notice the different positions in time:

The plane landed *at 3:30.*
by 3:30.
past 3:30.
before the thunderstorm.
during the thunderstorm.
after the thunderstorm.

NOTE: A few words—such as *of, as, like,* and *except*—are prepositions that do not fit neatly into either the space or time category, yet they are very common prepositions (box *of candy,* note *of apology,* type *of bicycle;* act *as a substitute,* use *as an example,* as happy *as my little brother;* vitamins *like A, C, and E,* shaped *like a watermelon,* moved *like a snake;* everyone *except Gilbert,* the whole house *except the upstairs washroom,* all knobs *except the red one).*

By locating prepositional phrases, you will be able to find subjects and verbs more easily. For example, you might have difficulty finding the subject and verb in a long sentence like this:

> After the rainy season, one of the windows in the attic leaked at the corners of its moulding.

But if you put parentheses around all the prepositional phrases like this

> (After the rainy season), <u>one</u> (of the windows) (in the attic) <u>leaked</u> (at the corners) (of its moulding).

then you have only two words left—the subject and the verb. Even in short sentences like the following, you might pick the wrong word as the subject if you don't put parentheses around the prepositional phrases first.

> <u>Many</u> (of the characters) <u>survived</u> (in that movie).

> The <u>waves</u> (around the ship) <u>looked</u> real.

NOTE: Don't mistake *to* plus a verb for a prepositional phrase. For example, *to quit* is not a prepositional phrase because *quit* is not the name of something. It's a form of verb.

E X E R C I S E S

Locate and put parentheses around the prepositional phrases in the following sentences. Be sure to start with the preposition itself (*in, on, to, at, of* . . .) and include the word or words that go with it (*in the morning, on our sidewalk, to St. John's* . . .). Then underline the subjects once and the verbs twice. Remember that subjects and verbs are never inside prepositional phrases. Review the answers given at the back for each group of ten sentences before continuing.

Exercise 1

1. My family and I live in a house at the top of a hilly neighbourhood in Vancouver.
2. On weekday mornings, nearly everyone drives down the steep winding roads to their jobs or to school.
3. In the evenings, they all come back up the hill to be with their families.
4. For the rest of the day, we see only an occasional delivery van or compact school bus.

5. But on Saturdays and Sundays, there is a different set of drivers on the road.

6. Then tourists in minivans and prospective home buyers in convertibles cram the narrow streets.

7. On these weekend days, most of the neighbourhood residents stay at home.

8. Frequently, drivers unfamiliar with the twists and turns of the roads up here cause accidents.

9. The expression "Sunday driver" really means something to those of us on the hill.

10. And we could add "Saturday driver" to the list as well.

Exercise 2

1. In England, Bob Martin is a man with a very strange claim to fame.

2. The seventy-year-old Martin lives in Eastleigh, a town approximately 160 kilometres south of London.

3. For ten years, he travelled by train to London hundreds of times for one specific purpose.

4. During these trips, Martin attended 625 performances of *Cats*, the long-running musical by Andrew Lloyd Webber.

5. Martin became interested in the show upon listening to the original cast album.

6. This devoted *Cats* fan always sat in the orchestra section, but not always in the same seat.

7. Many of the actors and crew members in the productions befriended Bob Martin over the years.

8. In the eyes of his extended family, Martin is just a happy eccentric.

9. Without a wife or children to think about, Martin indulged his interest in *Cats*.

10. As a result, he travelled more than 160,000 kilometres over the rails and spent more than $20,000 (U.S.) on tickets to see the same play over and over again.

Source: People, Aug. 2, 1999.

Exercise 3

1. Canadian musicians of every kind are honoured annually at the Juno Awards.

2. One glance at the Juno Awards website will convince you of the overwhelming variety of Canadian musicians.

3. Fans of pop music will recognize Avril Lavigne as a newly risen star of Canadian music.

4. Besides pop, rap, country, and rock, the Juno Awards celebrate works of contemporary jazz, classical compositions, and alternative musical genres such as Aboriginal and gospel.

5. One distinctive feature of the Juno Awards is their dedication to promoting both English and French vocalists.

6. Now a singer of international stature, Céline Dion was once a relative unknown nominated for Francophone Album of the Year.

7. Performers like Shania Twain and Diana Krall have become better known around the world because of the promotional endeavours of the Juno Awards.

8. In the last few decades, with renowned singer-songwriters like Gordon Lightfoot and Joni Mitchell, Canadians have come to dominate pop music to a fair extent.

9. In an eclectic range of categories, the Junos salute everyone from Alanis Morissette to Fred Penner.

10. Regardless of your taste, there is something in Canadian music for your CD collection.

Source: http://www.junoawards.ca

Exercise 4

1. Louis Riel, a leader of his people in their resistance against the Canadian government, is perhaps the most controversial figure in Canadian history.

2. Riel was born in the Red River Settlement, in what is now Manitoba, in 1844.

3. He emerged as a leader among the Métis of the Red River.

4. His provisional government negotiated the Manitoba Act with the Canadian government.

5. Riel was the leader of the short-lived 1885 Rebellion.

6. Increasingly, he believed himself chosen to lead the Métis people.

7. Riel was forced to surrender to Canadian forces and to stand trial for treason.

8. At his trial, he demonstrated his gifts as a speaker.

9. Judged sane, he was sentenced to death in 1885.

10. Riel was hanged in Regina on November 16, 1885, despite Quebec's opposition to his sentencing.

Exercise 5

1. Gorgons have been extinct for 250 million years.
2. These creatures lived and died millions of years before dinosaurs.
3. They perished along with almost all life on the planet in a huge cataclysmic event.
4. In fact, dinosaurs met a similar fate of their own.
5. Gorgons were beasts with both lion-like and lizard-like qualities.
6. Recently, scientists discovered a full-size fossilized skeleton of a gorgon in South Africa.
7. At 2.1 metres long, the fossil tells a lot about these animals.
8. They had eyes in the sides of their nearly one-metre-long heads.
9. And they hunted successfully with the help of their ten-centimetre-long teeth.
10. The gorgons' extreme physical features reveal the harshness of their prehistoric surroundings.

Source: Discover, Apr. 1999.

PARAGRAPH EXERCISE

Put parentheses around the prepositional phrases in this paragraph.

Do you know about Lucy Maud Montgomery's phenomenal success in Japan? For some reason, the Japanese are enamoured of her first novel, *Anne of Green Gables,* along with its seven sequels, and they travel thousands of kilometres to visit Cavendish Beach. Many of the Japanese tourists arrange to be married in Prince Edward Island or to honeymoon there. As a consequence, many Japanese-language tours are organized in the province to accommodate these visitors. Despite the immense popularity of Montgomery in Japan and in other countries, no one has yet, to my knowledge, tried to analyze exactly why the books in the Anne series are so appealing to people from a completely different culture.

SENTENCE WRITING

Write ten sentences on the topic of your favourite snack—or choose any topic you like. When you go back over your sentences, put parentheses around your prepositional phrases and underline your subjects once and your verbs twice.

Understanding Dependent Clauses

All clauses contain a subject and a verb; however, there are two kinds of clauses: independent and dependent. An independent clause has a subject and a verb and can stand alone as a sentence. A dependent clause has a subject and a verb but can't stand alone because it begins with a dependent word (or words) such as

after	since	where
although	so that	whereas
as	than	wherever
as if	that	whether
because	though	which
before	unless	whichever
even if	until	while
even though	what	who
ever since	whatever	whom
how	when	whose
if	whenever	why

Whenever a clause begins with one of these dependent words, it is a dependent clause (unless it's a question, which would be followed by a question mark). If we take an independent clause such as

<u>We</u> ate dinner together.

and put one of the dependent words in front of it, it becomes a dependent clause and can no longer stand alone:

After we ate dinner together . . .

Although we ate dinner together . . .

As we ate dinner together . . .

Before we ate dinner together . . .

Since we ate dinner together . . .

That we ate dinner together . . .

When we ate dinner together . . .

While we ate dinner together . . .

With the added dependent words, these do not make complete statements. They leave the reader expecting something more. Therefore, these clauses can no longer stand alone. Each would depend on another clause—an independent clause—to make a sentence. We'll place a broken line beneath the dependent clauses.

After we ate dinner together, we went to the evening seminar.

We went to the evening seminar *after* we ate dinner together.

The speaker didn't know *that* we ate dinner together.

While we ate dinner together, the restaurant became crowded.

Note that in the examples above, *when a dependent clause comes at the beginning of a sentence, it is followed by a comma*. Often the comma prevents misreading, as in the following sentence:

When he returned, the video was almost over.

Without a comma after *returned,* the reader would read *When he returned the video* before realizing that this was not what the author meant. The comma prevents misreading. Sometimes if the dependent clause is short and there is no danger of misreading, the comma can be left off, but it's safer simply to follow the rule that a dependent clause at the beginning of a sentence is followed by a comma.

You'll learn more about the punctuation of dependent clauses on page 166, but right now just remember this rule.

Note that sometimes the dependent word is the subject of the dependent clause:

Theirs is the house that was remodelled last month.

The children understood what was happening.

Sometimes the dependent clause is in the middle of the independent clause:

The house that was remodelled last month is theirs.

The events that followed were confusing.

And sometimes the dependent clause is the subject of the entire sentence:

What you do also affects me.

Whichever they choose will be best for them.

How it looks doesn't mean anything.

Also note that sometimes the *that* of a dependent clause is omitted.

I know *that* you can tell the difference between red and green.

I know you can tell the difference between red and green.

Did everyone get the classes *that* they wanted?

Did everyone get the classes they wanted?

The word *that* doesn't always introduce a dependent clause. It may be a pronoun and serve as the subject of the sentence.

That was a big mistake.

That is my book.

That can also be a descriptive word.

That movie makes me cry every time.

I will take him to that restaurant tomorrow.

E X E R C I S E S

Underline the subjects once and the verbs twice in both the independent and the dependent clauses. Then put a broken line under the dependent clauses. Some sentences may have no dependent clauses, and others may have more than one.

Exercise 1

1. If you want to spend your vacation in Canada, there are many wonderful places to visit in the Atlantic provinces or Ontario.

2. If you crave adventure, you should visit Newfoundland's Signal Hill, where Marconi received the first transatlantic radio signal in 1901.

3. If you like tall ships, you should travel to Lunenburg, Nova Scotia.

4. Because they have a rich history, places like Lunenburg are often used as backdrops for Hollywood movies.

5. The Citadel is a military fort that stands on a high point of land overlooking Halifax Harbour.

6. The fort, which was built in 1856, today houses exhibits of early military life.

7. After a cannon is fired at noon each day, soldiers in military dress conduct precision drills.

8. If you have children, be sure to take them to Santa's Village in Bracebridge, Ontario.

9. African Lion Safari, which is located in Rockton, Ontario, will appeal to children who like monkeys and other exotic wildlife.

10. As these tourist sites demonstrate, the Atlantic provinces and Ontario have much to offer Canadians who prefer to vacation in their own country.

Exercise 2

1. On June 8, 1924, two British men, George Mallory and Andrew Irvine, disappeared as they were climbing to the top of Mount Everest.

2. When a reporter earlier asked Mallory why he climbed Everest, his response became legendary.

3. "Because it is there," Mallory replied.

4. No living person knows whether the two men reached the summit of Everest before they died.

5. Nine years after Mallory and Irvine disappeared, English climbers found Irvine's ice ax.

6. But nothing else of Mallory's or Irvine's was found until a Chinese climber spotted their bodies in 1975.

7. He kept the news of his sighting secret for several years but finally decided to tell a fellow climber on the day before he died himself in an avalanche on Everest.

8. In May 1999, a team of mountaineers searched the area where the Chinese man had seen something, and they found George Mallory's frozen body still intact after seventy-five years.

9. After they took DNA samples for identification, the mountaineers buried the famous climber on the mountainside where he fell.

10. Mallory and Irvine were the first climbers to try to get to the top of Everest, and the question remains whether they were on their way up or on their way down when they met their fate.

Source: Newsweek, May 17, 1999.

Exercise 3

1. If you ever plan a trip to Bangkok, be sure to visit the Royal Dragon restaurant.

2. Somchai T. Amornrat designed the Royal Dragon so that it would break the record for the largest restaurant in the world.

3. Since the previous record-holding restaurant was also in Bangkok, Amornrat did some research and made his restaurant even bigger.

4. The Royal Dragon covers 4.8 hectares and is so sprawling that servers must wear roller skates to get around.

5. As many as ten thousand people a day eat at the Royal Dragon or Mangkorn Luang, as it is called in Thai.

6. After customers enter the huge park-like complex, they dine at tables that encircle a large reflecting pool.

7. And once every evening, a waitress entertains the diners as she flies from the top of a Pagoda that is seven stories high to a stage in the middle of the pool.

8. Before the flying waitress takes off, speakers play the theme song from *Mission: Impossible.*

9. If guests want to make their own music, they can visit one of the Royal Dragon's fifty karaoke bars.

10. The one thousand people who cook and serve the food and who do the dishes afterward never worry about being late to work since most of them live in the restaurant complex.

Source: Avenues, Nov./Dec. 1998.

Exercise 4

1. Roch Carrier, a French-Canadian author, is best known for his novel *La Guerre, Yes Sir!* and for a touching story called "The Hockey Sweater."

2. This story is about a Francophone mother in a Quebec village who tries to order her son a hockey sweater from Eaton's.

3. The order forms are in English, a language that proves difficult for her.

4. The child's hero is Maurice "Rocket" Richard, who played for the Montreal Canadiens.

5. Because the boy expects a Montreal Canadiens sweater, he is bitterly disappointed when Eaton's mistakenly sends him a blue-and-white Toronto Maple Leafs sweater.

6. "The Hockey Sweater" illustrates the split between French and English Canada, though ironically the two solitudes are united by a common love of hockey.

7. Critics have suggested that the story is autobiographical.

8. Carrier's work provides insight into rural Quebec in the 1940s and 1950s.

9. As he relates in the story's first two lines, the lives of young children revolved around the church, the school, and the skating rink.

10. The proof of the story's relevance to Canadian nationalism is that the first two lines of "The Hockey Sweater" appear on the new Canadian five-dollar bill.

Source: http://www.ualberta.ca/~gsm2/EnglishThroughCanadianStudies

Exercise 5

1. The National Ballet of Canada was founded in 1951 by English dancer Celia Franca, who performed in *Les Sylphides* that year.

2. In 1964, the National Ballet moved to Toronto's O'Keefe (later Hummingbird) Centre, where it will remain until the opening of the Four Seasons Centre for the Performing Arts.

3. The National Ballet first toured Europe in 1972, when it showcased Rudolf Nureyev's production of *The Sleeping Beauty*.

4. The company's North American tour in 1973 culminated in a triumphant debut at the Metropolitan Opera House in New York.

5. After Alexander Grant became artistic director in 1976, many new works by British choreographer Frederick Ashton were added to the repertoire.

6. In 1979, the National Ballet made its debut at the Royal Opera House, Covent Garden, in London.

7. After Erik Bruhn took over as artistic director in 1983, the company expanded its repertoire to include more works from modern dance.

8. Perhaps Canada's best-known ballerina is Karen Kain, who retired in 1997 after twenty-eight years with the National Ballet.

9. Since he became artistic director in 1996, James Kudelka has premiered many of his own and other choreographers' works.

10. In 2001, the National Ballet celebrated its fiftieth anniversary as an integral part of Canadian culture.

Sources: http://www.national.ballet.ca; *The Canadian Encyclopedia* (McClelland & Stewart, 1999).

PARAGRAPH EXERCISE

Underline the subjects once, the verbs twice, and put a broken line under the dependent clauses in these paragraphs from *The Sense of Wonder,* by Rachel Carson.

If the moon is full and the night skies are alive with the calls of bird migrants, then the way is open for [an] adventure with your child, if he [or she] is old enough to use a telescope or a good pair of binoculars. The sport of watching migrating birds pass across the face of the moon has become popular and even scientifically important in recent years, and it is as good a way as I know to give an older child a sense of the mystery of migration.

Seat yourself comfortably and focus your glass on the moon. You must learn patience, for unless you are on a well-travelled highway of migration you may have to wait many minutes before you are rewarded. In the waiting periods you can study the topography of the moon, for even a glass of moderate power reveals enough detail to fascinate a space-conscious child. But sooner or later you should begin to see the birds, lonely travellers in space glimpsed as they pass from darkness into darkness.

SENTENCE WRITING

Write ten sentences about your morning routine (getting up, getting ready for school or work, eating breakfast, etc.). Try to write sentences that contain both independent and dependent clauses. Then underline your subjects once, your verbs twice, and put a broken line under your dependent clauses.

Correcting Fragments

Sometimes a group of words looks like a sentence—with a capital letter at the beginning and a period at the end—but it is missing a subject or a verb or both. Such incomplete sentence structures are called fragments. Here are a few examples:

> Just ran around hugging everyone in sight. (no subject)

> Paul and his sister with the twins. (no verb)

> Nothing to do but wait. (no subject and no verb)

To change these fragments into sentences, we must make sure each has a subject and an adequate verb:

> The sweepstakes winner just ran around hugging everyone in sight. (We added a subject.)

> Paul and his sister reconciled with the twins. (We added a verb.)

> We had nothing to do but wait. (We added a subject and a verb.)

Sometimes we can simply attach such a fragment to the sentence before or after it.

> I want to find a fulfilling job. A career like teaching, for example.

> I want to find a fulfilling job, a career like teaching, for example.

Or we can change a word or two in the fragment and make it into a sentence.

> A teaching career is one example.

PHRASES

Phrases by definition are word groups without subjects and verbs, so whenever a phrase is punctuated as a sentence, it is a fragment. Look at this example of a sentence followed by a phrase fragment beginning with *hoping* (see pp. 112–13 for more about verbal phrases).

> I waited outside the director's office. Hoping to have a chance for an audition.

We can correct this fragment by attaching it to the previous sentence.

> I waited outside the director's office, hoping to have a chance for an audition.

Or we can change it to include a subject and a real verb.

I waited outside the director's office. I hoped to have a chance for an audition.

Here's another example of a sentence followed by a phrase fragment:

The actor's profile was striking. Sketched on an envelope by a famous artist.

Here the two have been combined into one complete sentence:

The actor's striking profile was sketched on an envelope by a famous artist.

Or a better revision might be

A famous artist sketched the actor's striking profile on an envelope.

Sometimes, prepositional phrases are also incorrectly punctuated as sentences. Here a prepositional phrase follows a sentence, but the word group is a fragment— it has no subject and verb of its own. Therefore, it needs to be corrected.

I have lived a simple life so far. With my family on our farm in Saskatchewan.

Here is one possible correction:

I have lived a simple life so far with my family on our farm in Saskatchewan.

Or it could be corrected this way:

My family and I have lived a simple life on our farm in Saskatchewan.

DEPENDENT CLAUSES

Dependent clauses punctuated as sentences are still another kind of fragment. A sentence needs a subject, a verb, *and* a complete thought. As discussed in the previous section, a dependent clause has a subject and a verb, but it begins with a word that makes its meaning incomplete, such as *after, while, because, since, although, when, if, where, who, which,* and *that* (see p. 60 for a full list). To correct such fragments, you need to remove the word that makes the clause dependent *or* add an independent clause.

FRAGMENT
While some of us worked on our journals.

CORRECTED

Some of us worked on our journals.

or

While some of us worked on our journals, the fire alarm rang.

FRAGMENT

Which kept me from finishing my journal entry.

CORRECTED

The fire alarm kept me from finishing my journal entry.

or

We responded to the fire alarm, *which* kept me from finishing my journal entry.

Are fragments ever permissible? Fragments are sometimes used in advertising and in other kinds of writing. But such fragments are used by professional writers who know what they're doing. These fragments are used intentionally, not in error. Until you're an experienced writer, stick with complete sentences. Especially in college and university writing, fragments should not be used.

E X E R C I S E S

Some—but not all—of the following word groups are sentences. The others suffer from incomplete sentence structure. Put a period after each of the sentences. Make any fragments into sentences by assuring that each has a subject and an adequate verb.

Exercise 1

1. Nellie McClung achieved fame as an advocate of women's rights in Canada

2. Her birth name being Helen Mooney

3. She wrote popular novels about rural life in pre–World War I Canada

4. Her novels recording the realities of prairie experience and the struggles of farming families

5. But today she is remembered as a political activist and essayist

6. Who became a reformer in the suffrage movement

7. As a reformer, protesting the harsh conditions of women's labour

8. Advancing the feminist cause by touring on behalf of the Political Equality League

9. In the courts and in Parliament, McClung arguing for women's right to be declared persons under the law

10. Due to her efforts, women in Manitoba getting the vote

Source: The Canadian Encyclopedia (McClelland & Stewart, 1999).

Exercise 2

1. In the 19th century, sculling a popular sporting event

2. Edward Hanlan regarded by some as the best sculler of all time

3. Born in Toronto, he sculled across Toronto Harbour every day to attend school

4. Hanlan competing in local regattas by age sixteen

5. Achieving a new world's record for sculling in 1878

6. Hanlan known for his eccentric style and flamboyant behaviour on the water

7. He won both the American and English titles—the latter by eleven lengths

8. Hanlan won the world professional championship in 1880 and went on to defend the title six times

9. A monument on the grounds of Toronto's Canadian National Exhibition honouring him as "the most renowned oarsman of any age"

10. Part of one of the Toronto Islands named Hanlan's Point

Source: The Canadian Encyclopedia (McClelland & Stewart, 1999).

Exercise 3

Correct each phrase fragment by changing or adding words or by attaching the phrase to the complete sentence nearby.

1. Finding a parking space on the first day of classes seems impossible. Driving endlessly around campus and looking for an empty spot.

2. With hope that the situation will improve. I always spend the $200 for a parking permit.

3. My old car's engine doesn't like the long periods of idling. Stalling a lot and not starting up again easily.

4. In order to get a space close to my first class. I always follow anyone walking through the parking lot closest to the science building.

5. I am usually disappointed by this method, however. Most people just walking through the parking lot to get to farther lots or to the bus stop.

6. I was really lucky on the first day of classes two semesters ago. Driving right into a spot vacated by a student from an earlier class.

7. Every morning, I see these early birds in their cars with their seats back. Sleeping there for hours before class but in a great spot.

8. Maybe I should get up before dawn myself. A foolproof way to secure a perfect parking place.

9. I don't think I can solve the problem this way. Finding it hard to get out of bed in the dark.

10. Due to the increase in college enrolment. Campus parking problems will most likely only get worse.

Exercise 4

Correct each dependent clause fragment by eliminating its dependent word or by attaching the dependent clause to the independent clause before or after it.

1. We were writing in our journals. When suddenly the fire alarm rang.

2. Everyone in the class looked at each other first and then at the teacher. Who told us to gather up our things and follow him outside.

3. The series of short bells continued. As we left the room and noisily walked out into the parking lot beside the main building.

4. The sunlight was very warm and bright compared to the classroom's fluorescent lights. Which make everything look more clinical than natural.

5. As we stood in a large group with students and teachers from other classes. We wondered about the reason for the alarm.

6. I have never taken part in a fire alarm. That was anything but a planned drill.

7. Without the danger of injury, a party atmosphere quickly develops. Since we all get a break from our responsibilities.

8. I've noticed that the teachers seem the most at ease. Because they don't have to be in control during these situations.

9. After we students and the teachers chatted for ten minutes or so. The final bell rang to signal the end of the drill.

10. When we sat down at our desks again. The teacher asked us to continue writing in our journals until the end of the hour.

Exercise 5

All the following word groups contain clauses. If the clause has a subject and a verb and *does not* begin with a dependent word (such as *when, while, after, because, since, although, where, if, who, which,* or *that*), put a period after it. If the clause has a subject and a verb and *does* begin with a dependent word (making it a dependent clause fragment), add an independent clause either before or after it to make it a sentence. Remember that if the dependent clause comes first, a comma should follow it. These ten clauses are not about the same topic.

1. That you know so much about the Canadian health-care system

2. While the jury deliberated

3. But that story sounds unbelievable

4. Be sure to send me a postcard

5. Harry Houdini promised to visit his wife after his death

6. Taking artistic photographs requires skill and patience

7. The restaurant where we first met

8. Until he noticed the price tag hanging from the side of the couch

9. A woman who travelled extensively during her childhood

10. When the blizzard stops

PROOFREADING EXERCISE

Correct the five fragments in the following paragraph.

Although Barbara Ann Scott won the Olympic gold medal in women's figure skating in 1948. No other Canadian woman has managed to follow in her footsteps. A fact that demonstrates her extraordinary talent. Winning many titles in her brief career, including North American and European championships and two world championships. Scott was known for her ability to overcome adverse conditions. An ability all the more remarkable because of her youth. Retiring from competition at the tender age of twenty-five.

SENTENCE WRITING

Write ten fragments and then revise them so that they are complete sentences. Or exchange papers with another student and turn your classmate's ten fragments into sentences.

Correcting Run-On Sentences

Any word group having a subject and a verb is a clause. As we have seen, the clause may be independent (able to stand alone) or dependent (unable to stand alone). If two independent clauses are written together without proper punctuation between them, the result is called a run-on sentence. Here are some examples.

Classical music is soothing I listen to it in the evenings.

I love the sound of piano therefore, Chopin is one of my favourites.

Run-on sentences can be corrected in one of four ways:

1. Make the two independent clauses into two sentences.

Classical music is soothing. I listen to it in the evenings.

I love the sound of piano. Therefore, Chopin is one of my favourites.

2. Connect the two independent clauses with a semicolon.

Classical music is soothing; I listen to it in the evenings.

I love the sound of piano; therefore, Chopin is one of my favourites.

When a connecting word such as

also	however	otherwise
consequently	likewise	then
finally	moreover	therefore
furthermore	nevertheless	thus

is used to join two independent clauses, the semicolon comes before the connecting word, and a comma usually comes after it.

Cellular phones are convenient; however, they can be intrusive.

Earthquakes scare me; therefore, I don't live in Los Angeles.

We travelled to London; then we took the "Chunnel" to Paris.

The college recently built a large new library; thus students have more quiet study areas.

NOTE: The use of the comma after the connecting word depends on how long the connecting word is. If it is only a short word, like *then* or *thus,* no comma is needed.

3. Connect the two independent clauses with a comma and one of the following seven words (the first letters of which create the word *fanboys*): *for, and, nor, but, or, yet, so.*

> Classical music is soothing, *so* I listen to it in the evenings.

> Chopin is one of my favourites, *for* I love the sound of piano.

Each of the *fanboys* has its own meaning (for example, *so* means "as a result," and *for* means "because").

> Swans are beautiful birds, *and* they mate for life.

> Students may register for classes by phone, *or* they may do so in person.

> I applied for financial aid, *but* (or *yet*) I was still working at the time.

> Beth doesn't know how to use a computer, *nor* does she plan to learn.

But before you put a comma before a *fanboys,* be sure there are two independent clauses. The first sentence that follows has two independent clauses. The second sentence is merely one independent clause with two verbs, so no comma should be used.

> The snow began falling at dusk, and it continued to fall through the night.

> The snow began falling at dusk and continued to fall through the night.

4. Make one of the clauses dependent by adding a dependent word (such as *since, when, as, after, while,* or *because* — see p. 60 for a full list).

> *Since* classical music is soothing, I listen to it in the evenings.

> Chopin is one of my favourites *because* I love the sound of piano.

WAYS TO CORRECT RUN-ON SENTENCES

> They learned a new routine. They needed to practise it. (two sentences)

> They learned a new routine; they needed to practise it. (semicolon)

> They learned a new routine; therefore, they needed to practise it. (semicolon + transition)

> They learned a new routine, so they needed to practise it. (comma + *fanboys*)

> Because they learned a new routine, they needed to practise it. (dependent clause first)

> They needed to practise because they learned a new routine. (dependent clause last)

Learn these ways to join two clauses, and you'll avoid run-on sentences.

E X E R C I S E S

Exercises 1 and 2

CORRECTING RUN-ONS WITH PUNCTUATION

Most—but not all—of the following sentences are run-ons. If the sentence has two independent clauses, separate them with correct punctuation. For the first two exercises, *don't create any dependent clauses*; use only a period, a semicolon, or a comma to separate the two independent clauses. Your answers may differ from those at the back of the book depending on how you choose to separate the clauses. Remember that a comma may be used only before the words *for, and, nor, but, or, yet, so.*

Exercise 1

1. Billy Bishop is a well-known Canadian war hero for he once fought the infamous Red Baron.

2. Bishop wrote his wartime memoirs in 1918 he was the most famous of all the Allied aces.

3. King George V awarded him the Victoria Cross for his solo raid on a German aerodrome.

4. Bishop shot down seventy-two enemy aircraft but missed the Red Baron.

5. That encounter took place in 1917 it ended in a draw.

6. In 1918, another Canadian, Captain Arthur Roy Brown, encountered the Red Baron and did succeed in shooting him down.

7. The Red Baron was buried in France with full military honours but his remains were later exhumed and returned to Germany.

8. Some people have questioned the authenticity of Billy Bishop's combat record.

9. Bishop was the most decorated Canadian in World War I but many of his combat reports cannot be confirmed.

10. The Billy Bishop Heritage Museum in Owen Sound, Ontario, is dedicated to preserving artifacts of Canadian aviation history more specifically, it displays materials documenting Bishop's achievements.

Source: http://www.theaerodrome.com

Exercise 2

1. Last week I decided to adopt a pet from an animal shelter so I visited the SPCA near my house.

2. There were lots of great potential pets there at first I couldn't choose between the dogs or the cats.

3. I imagined the changes in my life with the addition of each type of pet.

4. My house doesn't have a fenced yard so a dog would need to be walked in the mornings and evenings.

5. I like small dogs anyway and could easily envision myself taking a tiny terrier for a stroll.

6. But I am at work for most of the day it might bark and disturb the neighbours.

7. A cat, on the other hand, can stay inside and doesn't make any noise.

8. Cats are also independent therefore, a cat wouldn't miss me during the day.

9. By coincidence, the shelter had just received a litter of grey-and-white kittens I was lucky enough to have first choice and picked the best one.

10. I named her Dizzy for she loves to chase the white tip of her tail around.

Exercises 3 and 4

CORRECTING RUN-ONS WITH DEPENDENT CLAUSES

Most—but not all—of the following sentences are run-ons. Correct any run-on sentences by making one of the clauses dependent. You may change the words. Use a dependent word (such as *since, when, as, after, while, because* or the others listed on p. 60) to begin the dependent clause. In some sentences you will want to put the dependent clause first; in others you may want to put it last (or in the middle of the sentence). Since various words can be used to start a dependent clause, your answers may differ from those suggested at the back of the book.

Exercise 3

1. I've been learning about sleep in my psychology class I now know a lot more about it.

2. Sleep has five stages we usually go through all these stages many times during the night.

3. The first stage of sleep begins our muscles relax and mental activity slows down.

4. During stage one, we are still slightly awake.

5. Stage two takes us deeper than stage one we are no longer aware of our surroundings.

6. We spend about half our sleeping time in the second stage.

7. Next is stage three in it we become more and more relaxed and are very hard to awaken.

8. Stage four is the deepest in this stage we don't even hear loud noises.

9. The fifth stage of sleep is called REM (rapid-eye-movement) sleep our eyes move back and forth quickly behind our eyelids.

10. REM sleep is only about as deep as stage two we do all our dreaming during the REM stage.

Exercise 4

1. Lionel Conacher is not as well known as he should be his accomplishments are truly amazing.

2. He was an outstanding all-round athlete he was voted Canada's Athlete of the Half Century by the Canadian Press in 1950.

3. Not only did he excel at football, hockey, baseball, and lacrosse, but he ran the 100-yard dash in 10 seconds at a time when the world record was 9.8 seconds.

4. As Canada's light-heavyweight boxing champion, he fought Jack Dempsey he was the world heavyweight champion.

5. He was one of the National Hockey League's leaders in penalty minutes Conacher is widely regarded as one of the best defencemen in hockey.

6. He did not learn to skate until age sixteen he won two Stanley Cups.

7. He practically won the 1921 Grey Cup by himself he scored fifteen points during the Toronto Argonauts' 23–0 victory over the Edmonton Eskimos.

8. He retired from sports he became a member of Parliament.

9. In 1954, he died of a heart attack while playing a charity softball game.

10. Conacher was inducted into the Canadian Football Hall of Fame in 1963 he was nicknamed "The Big Train."

Source: The Canadian Encyclopedia (McClelland & Stewart, 1999).

Exercise 5

Correct the following run-on sentences using any of the methods studied in this section: adding a period, a semicolon, a semicolon + a transition word, a comma + a *fanboys,* or using a dependent word to create a dependent clause.

1. In 1999, the BBC released its documentary series called *The Life of Birds* Sir David Attenborough was the host.

2. The series took nearly three years to complete the crew filmed in more than forty countries they shot over three hundred kilometres of film.

3. The BBC spent $15 million (U.S.) making *The Life of Birds* the cost included Attenborough's travelling the equivalent of ten times around the world.

4. The BBC takes such shows very seriously this one about birds comes after the BBC's amazing documentary called *The Private Life of Plants.*

5. For the plant series, BBC filmmakers even invented new ways to film plants and record the sounds they make a lot of the filming had to take place under artificial conditions however, for the bird series, the BBC wanted a more realistic feeling.

6. All of the filming was done in the birds' own habitats it showed their natural behaviour some of this behaviour had never been seen or filmed before.

7. To capture these rare moments, filmmakers had to live with birds in the wild it was not a very safe environment at times.

8. A tree full of BBC filmmakers was struck by lightning in an Amazon rain forest they were covered with insects in Jamaica and Attenborough had to speak to the camera in total darkness in a cave in Venezuela.

9. Makers of the series were especially proud of their bird of paradise footage they shot it in New Guinea.

10. It turned out to be one of their biggest disappointments the priceless film was erased by an especially powerful X-ray machine at the airport.

Source: Christian Science Monitor, Aug. 3, 1999.

REVIEW OF FRAGMENTS AND RUN-ON SENTENCES

If you remember that all clauses include a subject and a verb but only independent clauses can be punctuated as sentences (since only they can stand alone), then you will avoid fragments in your writing. And if you memorize these six rules for the punctuation of clauses, you will be able to avoid most punctuation errors.

PUNCTUATING CLAUSES

I am a student. I am still learning.	(two sentences)
I am a student; I am still learning.	(two independent clauses)
I am a student; therefore, I am still learning.	(two independent clauses connected by a word such as *also, consequently, finally, furthermore, however, likewise, moreover, nevertheless, otherwise, then, therefore, thus*)
I am a student, so I am still learning.	(two independent clauses connected by *for, and, nor, but, or, yet, so*)
Because I am a student, I am still learning.	(dependent clause at beginning of sentence)
I am still learning because I am a student.	(dependent clause at end of sentence) The dependent words are *after, although, as, as if, because, before, even if, even though, ever since, how, if, in order that, since, so that, than, that, though, unless, until, what, whatever, when, whenever, where, whereas, wherever, whether, which, whichever, while, who, whom, whose, why.*

It is essential that you learn the italicized words in this table—know which ones come between independent clauses and which ones introduce dependent clauses.

PROOFREADING EXERCISE

Rewrite the following paragraph, making the necessary changes so there will be no fragments or run-on sentences.

Most people would not recognize the name Joseph Ignace Guillotin but they probably have heard of the machine named after him. The guillotine. The device used when many a king or queen said, "Off with his—or her—head!" The guillotine consists of a slanted blade the blade falls down a window-frame-shaped tower and can be reset after it does its job. Guillotin was a doctor in France during the French Revolution. He was not the inventor of the machine he did suggest that it be used to behead people quickly and easily. Guillotin's name was first associated with the device in 1793 now doctors everywhere also use the word *guillotine*. To describe cutting procedures that they perform during tonsillectomies and other surgeries.

Source: Dictionary of Word Origins (Arcade Publishing, 1990).

SENTENCE WRITING

Write a sample sentence of your own to demonstrate each of the six ways a writer can punctuate two clauses. You may model your sentences on the examples used in the preceding review chart.

Identifying Verb Phrases

Sometimes a verb is one word, but often the whole verb includes more than one word. These are called verb phrases. Look at several of the many forms of the verb *speak,* for example. Most of them are verb phrases, made up of the main verb (*speak*) and one or more helping verbs.

speak	is speaking	had been speaking
speaks	am speaking	will have been speaking
spoke	are speaking	is spoken
will speak	was speaking	was spoken
has spoken	were speaking	will be spoken
have spoken	will be speaking	can speak
had spoken	has been speaking	must speak
will have spoken	have been speaking	should have spoken

Note that words like the following are never verbs even though they may be near a verb or in the middle of a verb phrase:

already	ever	not	really
also	finally	now	sometimes
always	just	often	usually
probably	never	only	possibly

Jason has *never* spoken to his instructor before. She *always* talks with other students.

Two verb forms—*speaking* and *to speak*—look like verbs, but neither can ever be the verb of a sentence. No *ing* word by itself can ever be the verb of a sentence; it must be helped by another verb in a verb phrase. (See the discussion of verbal phrases on pp. 112–13.)

Natalie speaking French. (not a sentence because there is no complete verb phrase)

Natalie is speaking French. (a sentence with a verb phrase)

And no verb with *to* in front of it can ever be the verb of a sentence.

Ted to speak in front of groups. (not a sentence because there is no real verb)

<u>Ted</u> <u><u>hates</u></u> to speak in front of groups. (a sentence with *hates* as the verb)

These two forms, *speaking* and *to speak,* may be used as subjects, or they may have other uses in the sentence.

<u>Speaking</u> on stage <u>is</u> scary. <u>To speak</u> on stage <u>is</u> scary. <u>Ted</u> <u><u>had</u></u> a *speaking* part in that play.

But neither of them alone can ever be the verb of a sentence.

E X E R C I S E S

Underline the subjects once and the verbs or verb phrases twice. It's a good idea to put parentheses around prepositional phrases first. (See pp. 54–55 if you need help in locating prepositional phrases.) The sentences may contain independent *and* dependent clauses, so there could be several verbs and verb phrases.

Exercise 1

1. I have always wondered how an Etch-A-Sketch works.

2. This flat TV-shaped toy has been popular since it first came out in the 1960s.

3. Now I have discovered a website that answers questions like the following: "How does an Etch-A-Sketch work?"

4. An Etch-A-Sketch is filled with a combination of metal powder and tiny plastic particles.

5. This mixture clings to the inside of the Etch-A-Sketch screen.

6. When the pointer that is connected to the two knobs moves, the tip of it "draws" lines in the powder on the back of the screen.

7. The powder at the bottom of the Etch-A-Sketch does not fill in these lines because it is too far away.

8. But if the Etch-A-Sketch is turned upside down, the powder clings to the whole underside surface of the screen and "erases" the image again.

9. Although the basic Etch-A-Sketch has not changed since I was a kid, it now comes in several different sizes.

10. Best of all, these great drawing devices have never needed batteries, and I hope that they never will.

Exercise 2

1. In 1994, Toronto businessman Jack Rabinovitch founded the Giller Prize for Canadian fiction because he wanted to honour his late wife, Doris Giller.

2. The first winner of the Giller Prize was M.G. Vassanji, who has written extensively about issues of race and identity.

3. Vassanji became a two-time winner when he was awarded the 2003 Giller Prize for *The In-Between World of Vikram Lall.*

4. Other nominees for the 2003 prize included Ann-Marie MacDonald for *The Way the Crow Flies* and Margaret Atwood for *Oryx and Crake.*

5. Already popular in Canada, MacDonald became well known to American readers when her first novel, *Fall on Your Knees,* was chosen for Oprah's Book Club.

6. Atwood's ninth novel, *Alias Grace,* won the Giller in 1996.

7. Less well-known nominees in 2003 included John Bemrose, who has published a play, two poetry collections, and an earlier novel.

8. Also in the running was John Gould for *Kilter,* a collection of fifty-five very short stories that have been described as quirky gems.

9. Previous Giller winners have included Austin Clarke, Bonnie Burnard, Alice Munro, and Mordecai Richler.

10. The Giller Prize has helped to raise the profile of both established and emerging Canadian writers.

Source: http://www.thegillerprize.ca

Exercise 3

1. When we think of ancient structures, Stonehenge in England and the Great Pyramids of Egypt come to mind.

2. Fairly recently, Fred Wendorf discovered an arrangement of stones possibly a thousand years older than Stonehenge.

3. Wendorf uncovered the stone structures of Nabta Playa while he was researching nomadic people in Egypt.

4. Wendorf dug down to the level where eight huge stone tablets formed a circle.

5. He and other anthropologists believe that nomads must have created the site for astronomical purposes.

6. The slabs and their arrangement date back seven thousand years.

7. They were placed in groups of two and were aligned with different points of the compass.

8. Near the circle of stones was a tomb that had not been found before.

9. It had been used not for a dead king but for the nomads' cattle.

10. These nomadic people may have been the first citizens of the Nile Valley so many thousands of years ago.

Source: Discover, July 1998.

Exercise 4

1. During the last semester of high school, my English teacher assigned a special paper.

2. He said that he was becoming depressed by all the bad news out there, so each of us was assigned to find a piece of good news and write a short research paper about it.

3. I must admit that I had no idea how hard that assignment would be.

4. Finally, I found an article while I was reading my favourite magazine.

5. The title of the article was a pun; it was called "Grin Reaper."

6. I knew instantly that it must be just the kind of news my teacher was searching for.

7. The article explained that one woman, Pam Johnson, had started a club that she named The Secret Society of Happy People.

8. She had even chosen August 8 as "Admit You're Happy Day" and had already convinced more than fifteen governors in the United States to recognize the holiday.

9. The club and the holiday were created to support people who are happy so that the unhappy, negative people around them will not bring the happy people down.

10. As I was writing my essay, I visited the Happy People website and, for extra credit, signed my teacher up for their newsletter.

Source: People, Aug. 30, 1999.

Exercise 5

1. Last night I took my daughter to a performance by her favourite group.

2. The tickets were not too expensive, and I remembered how much fun I had had at concerts in my younger days.

3. I had not been to an open-air event for several years, however, and I was expecting the same kind of experience.

4. I should have considered the changes that have occurred since then.

5. The first difference was that, when we arrived, people were waiting in a long line in the hot sunshine to get into the stadium even though everyone had assigned seats.

6. I asked a staff member why they weren't spending time in their cars or in the cool shade.

7. He told me that they were hoping to get in first so that they could buy the best souvenirs.

8. Once we were inside the place, I saw what he meant; T-shirts with $50 price tags and every other kind of object with the group's name or picture on it were being bought by frantic fans.

9. I understood then why the tickets had been so inexpensive; as long as they brought the customers to the merchandise, they had done their job.

10. After three opening acts, my daughter's favourite group finally arrived on stage, overwhelmed the crowd with special effects, and left everyone with lots of souvenirs as memories.

REVIEW EXERCISE

To practise all the sentence structures we have studied so far, mark the following paragraph about Avril Lavigne. First, put parentheses around prepositional phrases. Then underline subjects once and verbs or verb phrases twice. Finally, put a broken line underneath any dependent clauses you find.

Avril Lavigne is a Canadian singer who became a star at the age of seventeen. Originally from Napanee, Ontario, where she was born on September 27, 1984, Lavigne has been adjusting to life in the big city. At sixteen, she was discovered by Arista Records and moved to Manhattan where she began work on her debut album, *Let Go*. She later relocated to Los Angeles.

Not long after Lavigne released *Let Go* in 2002, fans responded with enthusiasm to her dynamic spirit and fierce individuality. The Napanee native, who plays the guitar, explores her personal experiences of love and of life in songs like "Losing Grip." Although Lavigne was shut out of the Grammy Awards, she triumphed at the Junos where she won single of the year for the hit song "Complicated," album of the year and best pop album for *Let Go,* and best new artist.

In recent years, singers like Avril Lavigne and pop-country superstar Shania Twain have demonstrated the growing prominence of Canada in pop culture.

Source: http://www.avrilfans.com

Using Standard English Verbs

The next two discussions are for those who need practice in using Standard English verbs. Many of us grew up doing more speaking than writing. But in college and university, and in the business and professional world, the use of Standard Written English is essential.

The following charts show the forms of four verbs as they are used in Standard Written English. These forms might differ from the way you use these verbs when you speak. Memorize the Standard English forms of these important verbs. The first verb (*talk*) is one of the regular verbs (verbs that all end the same way according to a pattern); most verbs in English are regular. The other three verbs charted here (*have, be,* and *do*) are irregular and are important because they are used not only as main verbs but also as helping verbs in verb phrases.

Don't go on to the exercises until you have memorized the forms of these Standard English verbs.

REGULAR VERB: TALK

PRESENT TIME		PAST TIME	
I		I	
you	talk	you	
we		we	talked
they		they	
he, she, it	talks	he, she, it	

IRREGULAR VERB: HAVE

PRESENT TIME		PAST TIME	
I		I	
you	have	you	
we		we	had
they		they	
he, she, it	has	he, she, it	

IRREGULAR VERB: BE

PRESENT TIME		PAST TIME	
I	am	I	was
you		we	
we	are	you	were
they		they	
he, she, it	is	he, she, it	was

IRREGULAR VERB: DO

PRESENT TIME		PAST TIME	
I		I	
you		you	
we	do	we	did
they		they	
he, she, it	does	he, she, it	

Sometimes you may have difficulty with the correct endings of verbs because you don't hear the words correctly. Note carefully the *s* sound and the *ed* sound at the end of words. Occasionally the *ed* is not clearly pronounced, as in *They tried to help,* but most of the time you can hear it if you listen.

Read the following sentences aloud, making sure that you say every sound.

He seems satisfied with his new job.

She likes saving money for the future.

It takes strength of character to control spending.

Todd makes salad for every potluck he attends.

I used to know all their names.

They supposed that they were right.

He recognized the suspect and excused himself from the jury.

Susan sponsored Reina in the school's charity event.

Now read some other sentences aloud from this text, making sure that you sound all the s's and ed's. Reading aloud and listening to others will help you use the correct verb endings automatically.

E X E R C I S E S

Exercises 1 and 2

In these pairs of sentences, use the present form of the verb in the first sentence and the past form in the second. All the verbs follow the pattern of the regular verb *talk* except the irregular verbs *have, be,* and *do.* Keep referring to the tables if you're not sure which form to use. Correct your answers for each exercise before going to the next.

Exercise 1

1. (prepare)   She _____ people's taxes. She _____ my taxes last year.

2. (help)   I always _____ my roommate with the dishes. I _____ him with them yesterday.

3. (be)   They _____ happy with their new home. They _____ too crowded in their old home.

4. (have)   We _____ a lot of homework this weekend. We _____ no homework last weekend.

5. (do)   She _____ well on most quizzes. She _____ very well on yesterday's quiz.

6. (need)   My son _____ a new backpack. He _____ several new textbooks at the start of the semester.

7. (have)   Sue fixed up her car; now it _____ a sunroof and a CD player. It only _____ a cassette deck before.

8. (be)   He _____ a counsellor at the summer camp. He _____ a lifeguard last year.

9. (work)   She _____ too hard. Last week, she _____ without a day off.

10. (be)   I _____ finally qualified to tutor other students. I _____ not qualified to tutor them before.

Exercise 2

1. (be)   They _____ college students this semester. They _____ high-school students last year.

2. (do)   He _____ his best writing at night. He _____ not do well on the first in-class essay.

3. (have)   She _____ only two days left to submit her job application letter. She originally _____ two weeks, but she has been putting it off.

4. (open)   He _____ a new restaurant every year. He even _____ one in my neighbourhood recently.

5. (have)   I always _____ fun with my friend Norman. I _____ a great time in Cuba with him over spring break.

6. (count)   She _____ boxes at the factory part time. Yesterday she _____ boxes for six hours straight.

7. (be)   Many of us _____ left-handed. We _____ unsure at first which hand to use when we played tennis.

8. (do)   They _____ everything to make their grandmother's life easier. They _____ her shopping and her laundry yesterday.

9. (look)   You _____ like an adult now. You _____ like a kid when your hair was longer.

10. (be)   At the moment, she _____ the fastest cashier in the store. She _____ the second-fastest cashier when Carl still worked there.

Exercises 3 and 4

Underline the Standard English verb forms. All the verbs follow the pattern of the regular verb *talk* except the three irregular verbs *have, be,* and *do.* Keep referring to the tables if you are not sure which form to use.

Exercise 3

1. I recently (change, changed) my career plans; now I (want, wants) to be a chef.

2. Last year, I (have, had) my mind set on becoming a kindergarten teacher.

3. I (sign, signed) up for several early childhood education classes, and they all (turn, turned) out to be disappointing.

4. The class work (was, were) often too easy, and the reading assignments (was, were) too hard.

5. We (does, did) spend part of the semester working in a real daycare centre where we (was, were) able to observe just what the educator (do, does).

6. The educator that I (observes, observed) (have, had) twenty-seven children to look after.

7. I (watch, watched) her as she (help, helped) them learn their numbers and letters.

8. She (have, had) the children, their parents, and the daycare centre's staff to worry about all the time.

9. I never (imagine, imagined) that an early childhood educator (have, had) so many responsibilities.

10. A chef (need, needs) to worry about the food and the customers, and those (is, are) responsibilities that I (is, am) ready to take.

Exercise 4

1. My mother and I (watch, watches) the same game show every night.

2. She (watch, watches) it at her house, and I (watch, watches) it at my house.

3. I (is, am) better at answering the literature questions, and my mom (is, am) better at answering the questions on science and geography.

4. Mom and I (is, are) very competitive and proud of the information that we know.

5. But the show's final question usually (decide, decides) the outcome of our contest.

6. For that question, we (wager, wagers) all or part of our winnings so far.

7. After the show, we both (add, adds) up our scores, and then one of us (call, calls) the other to see who the champion (is, are).

8. We (love, loves) this tradition and (has, have) kept it going for eight years now.

9. Someday I (plan, plans) to try out for the show and surprise my mom one night.

10. She (like, likes) the show so much that she would probably faint if she saw me up there with the signalling button in my hand.

Exercise 5

Correct any of the following sentences that do not use Standard English verb forms.

1. Yesterday my English teacher assigns a research paper.

2. Now we have one week to finish a rough draft.

3. Before the assignment, he showed us two sample papers.

4. They was about holiday traditions in different families.

5. In one paper, the writer explain the tradition of Thanksgiving at her house.

6. I likes the part about making pies for the adults and candy for the kids.

7. The second paper outline the steps another family goes through to prepare for Chinese New Year.

8. That one have even more details about food and gifts for the children.

9. My teacher asked us to write about a family ritual of our own.

10. I start my rough draft last night; it's about my dad's obsession with Halloween.

PROOFREADING EXERCISE

Correct any sentences in the following paragraph that do not use Standard English verb forms.

I have a new piano teacher, Mr. Stevenson, who talk very softly and play the piano beautifully. When he wants to teach me a new song, he start by showing me the sheet music. Then he ask me to look it over. I am always nervous if it show a new hand position or a new dynamic sign. But then he calm me down with his soothing voice and patient manner. Once I figure the piece out by looking at it, I plays it through slowly. Mr. Stevenson don't do any of the annoying things my other piano teachers did. I like him a lot.

SENTENCE WRITING

Write ten sentences about a problem in your neighbourhood. Check your sentences to be sure that they use Standard English verb forms. Exchange papers with another student if possible.

Using Regular and Irregular Verbs

All regular verbs end the same way in the past form and when used with helping verbs. Here is a table showing all the forms of some regular verbs and the various helping verbs they are used with.

REGULAR VERBS				
BASE FORM	**PRESENT**	**PAST**	**PAST PARTICIPLE**	***ING* FORM**
(Use after can, may, shall, will, could, might, should, would, must, do, does, did.)			*(Use after have, has, had. Some can be used after forms of be.)*	*(Use after forms of be.)*
ask	ask *(s)*	asked	asked	asking
bake	bake *(s)*	baked	baked	baking
count	count *(s)*	counted	counted	counting
dance	dance *(s)*	danced	danced	dancing
decide	decide *(s)*	decided	decided	deciding
enjoy	enjoy *(s)*	enjoyed	enjoyed	enjoying
finish	finish *(es)*	finished	finished	finishing
happen	happen *(s)*	happened	happened	happening
learn	learn *(s)*	learned	learned	learning
like	like *(s)*	liked	liked	liking
look	look *(s)*	looked	looked	looking
mend	mend *(s)*	mended	mended	mending
need	need *(s)*	needed	needed	needing
open	open *(s)*	opened	opened	opening
start	start *(s)*	started	started	starting
suppose	suppose *(s)*	supposed	supposed	supposing
tap	tap *(s)*	tapped	tapped	tapping
walk	walk *(s)*	walked	walked	walking
want	want *(s)*	wanted	wanted	wanting

NOTE: When there are several helping verbs, the last one determines which form of the main verb should be used: they *should* finish soon; they should *have* finished an hour ago.

When do you write *ask, finish, suppose, use*? And when do you write *asked, finished, supposed, used*? Here are some rules that will help you decide.

Write *ask, finish, suppose, use* (or their *s* forms) when writing about the present time, repeated actions, or facts:

He *asks* questions whenever he is confused.

They always *finish* their projects on time.

I *suppose* you want me to help you move.

Birds *use* leaves, twigs, and feathers to build their nests.

Write *asked, finished, supposed, used*

1. When writing about the past:

He *asked* the teacher for another explanation.

She *finished* her internship last year.

They *supposed* that there were others bidding on that house.

I *used* to study piano.

2. When some form of *be* (other than the word *be* itself) comes before the word:

He was *asked* the most difficult questions.

She is *finished* with her training now.

They were *supposed* to sign at the bottom of the form.

My essay was *used* as a sample of clear narration.

3. When some form of *have* comes before the word:

The teacher has *asked* us that question before.

She will have *finished* all of her exams by the end of May.

I had *supposed* too much without any proof.

We have *used* many models in my drawing class this year.

All the verbs in the chart on page 94 are regular. That is, they're all formed in the same way—with an *ed* ending on the past form and on the past participle. But many verbs are irregular. Their past and past participle forms change spelling instead of just adding an *ed*. Here's a chart of some irregular verbs. Refer to this list when you aren't sure which verb form to use. Memorize all the forms you don't know.

IRREGULAR VERBS

BASE FORM	PRESENT	PAST	PAST PARTICIPLE	*ING* FORM
(Use after can, may, shall, will, could, might, should, would, must, do, does, did.*)*			*(Use after* have, has, had. *Some can be used after forms of* be.*)*	*(Use after forms of* be.*)*
be	am, is, are	was, were	been	being
become	become *(s)*	became	become	becoming
begin	begin *(s)*	began	begun	beginning
break	break *(s)*	broke	broken	breaking
bring	bring *(s)*	brought	brought	bringing
buy	buy *(s)*	bought	bought	buying
build	build *(s)*	built	built	building
catch	catch *(es)*	caught	caught	catching
choose	choose *(s)*	chose	chosen	choosing
come	come *(s)*	came	come	coming
do	do *(es)*	did	done	doing
draw	draw *(s)*	drew	drawn	drawing
drink	drink *(s)*	drank	drunk	drinking
drive	drive *(s)*	drove	driven	driving
eat	eat *(s)*	ate	eaten	eating
fall	fall *(s)*	fell	fallen	falling
feel	feel *(s)*	felt	felt	feeling
fight	fight *(s)*	fought	fought	fighting
find	find *(s)*	found	found	finding
forget	forget *(s)*	forgot	forgotten	forgetting
forgive	forgive *(s)*	forgave	forgiven	forgiving
freeze	freeze *(s)*	froze	frozen	freezing
get	get *(s)*	got	got *or* gotten	getting
give	give *(s)*	gave	given	giving
go	go *(es)*	went	gone	going
grow	grow *(s)*	grew	grown	growing
have	have *or* has	had	had	having
hang (suspend)	hang *(s)*	hung	hung	hanging
hang (execute)	hang *(s)*	hanged	hanged	hanging
hear	hear *(s)*	heard	heard	hearing
hold	hold *(s)*	held	held	holding
keep	keep *(s)*	kept	kept	keeping

BASE FORM	PRESENT	PAST	PAST PARTICIPLE	*ING* FORM
know	know *(s)*	knew	known	knowing
lay (to put)	lay *(s)*	laid	laid	laying
lead (pron. "leed")	lead *(s)*	led	led	leading
leave	leave *(s)*	left	left	leaving
lie (to rest)	lie *(s)*	lay	lain	lying
lose	lose *(s)*	lost	lost	losing
make	make *(s)*	made	made	making
meet	meet *(s)*	met	met	meeting
pay	pay *(s)*	paid	paid	paying
read (pron. "reed")	read *(s)*	read (pron. "red")	read (pron."red")	reading
ride	ride *(s)*	rode	ridden	riding
ring	ring *(s)*	rang	rung	ringing
rise	rise *(s)*	rose	risen	rising
run	run *(s)*	ran	run	running
say	say *(s)*	said	said	saying
see	see *(s)*	saw	seen	seeing
sell	sell *(s)*	sold	sold	selling
shake	shake *(s)*	shook	shaken	shaking
shine (give light)	shine *(s)*	shone	shone	shining
shine (polish)	shine *(s)*	shined	shined	shining
sing	sing *(s)*	sang	sung	singing
sleep	sleep *(s)*	slept	slept	sleeping
sneak	sneak *(s)*	sneaked *or* snuck	sneaked *or* snuck	sneaking
speak	speak *(s)*	spoke	spoken	speaking
spend	spend *(s)*	spent	spent	spending
stand	stand *(s)*	stood	stood	standing
steal	steal *(s)*	stole	stolen	stealing
strike	strike *(s)*	struck	struck	striking
swim	swim *(s)*	swam	swum	swimming
swing	swing *(s)*	swung	swung	swinging
take	take *(s)*	took	taken	taking
teach	teach *(es)*	taught	taught	teaching
tear	tear *(s)*	tore	torn	tearing
tell	tell *(s)*	told	told	telling
think	think *(s)*	thought	thought	thinking
throw	throw *(s)*	threw	thrown	throwing
wear	wear *(s)*	wore	worn	wearing
win	win *(s)*	won	won	winning
write	write *(s)*	wrote	written	writing

Sometimes verbs from the past participle column are used after some form of the verb *be* (or verbs that take the place of *be* like *appear, seem, look, feel, get, act, become*) to describe the subject or to say something in a passive, rather than active, way.

She is contented.

You appear pleased. (You are pleased.)

He seems delighted. (He is delighted.)

She looked surprised. (She was surprised.)

I feel shaken. (I am shaken.)

They get bored easily. (They are bored easily.)

You acted concerned. (You were concerned.)

He was thrown out of the game. (Active: *The referee threw him out of the game.*)

They were disappointed by the news. (Active: *The news disappointed them.*)

Often these verb forms become words that describe the subject; other times they still act as part of the verb of the sentence. What you call them doesn't matter. The only important thing is to be sure you use the correct form from the past participle column.

E X E R C I S E S

Write the correct form of the verb. Refer to the tables and explanations on the preceding pages if you aren't sure which form to use after a certain helping verb. Check your answers after each exercise.

Exercise 1

1. (practise)   I must _____ my violin at least once a day, or I feel guilty.

2. (practise)   After I have _____ for half an hour or so, I feel better.

3. (practise)   Sometimes when I am _____, I lose track of time.

4. (practise)   Then I can _____ for over an hour without realizing it.

5. (practise)   Once I had _____ for two hours, but it felt like only twenty minutes.

6. (practise)   My instructor says that he has similar experiences when he _____.

7. (practise)   I guess all musicians _____ in pretty much the same way.

8. (practise)   It isn't easy to ignore someone who is _____ a musical instrument.

9. (practise)   Especially when people are _____ the violin, their family and neighbours can become irritated.

10. (practise)   That is why I always _____ when my family is away from home.

Exercise 2

1. (try)   I must _____ to think of new ways to entertain my parrot, Rusty. If I don't keep him amused, then he _____ to run away.

2. (buy)   My mom _____ Rusty for my eighteenth birthday even though she usually _____ me a new CD or a shirt or something simple like that.

3. (be)   So I _____ really surprised when I saw a big green parrot sitting on a perch in my room when I got home from school on my birthday. I _____ not usually a big animal lover.

4. (think)   Mom must have _____ that I needed a new responsibility, but I didn't _____ so.

5. (grow)   Rusty has _____ a little since I got him. And I've _____ a lot since I've had to take care of him.

6. (leave)   Before I _____ for school each day, I give Rusty fresh food, treats, and water. Once I _____ the window open by mistake and found him in the tree outside my room when I came back.

7. (watch)   Parrots love to talk and be entertained, so Rusty _____ all the game shows and soap operas that are on TV during the day. Meanwhile I am _____ my teachers draw their notes on the chalkboard at school.

8. (hear)   He _____ what the game show hosts and soap opera stars say, and then I _____ the same expressions all night long because he repeats them over and over again.

9. (speak)   Sometimes Rusty _____ so clearly that it sounds exactly like words that are _____ by a human being.

10. (be)   At first, I _____ not sure I wanted Rusty, but now he _____ such a big part of my life that I can't imagine not having him.

Exercise 3

1. (take, suppose)   My sister Brenda _____ a day off last week even though she was _____ to be working.

2. (do, earn)   She _____ not feel sick exactly; she just felt that she had _____ a day of rest.

3. (call, tell, feel)   So Brenda _____ her office and _____ her boss that she did not _____ well enough to work that day.

4. (think, be)   She never _____ that she would get caught, but she _____ wrong.

5. (leave, drive, see)   Just as Brenda was _____ the house to buy some lunch, her coworker _____ by and _____ her.

6. (feel, know, tell)   She _____ such panic because she _____ that he would _____ their boss that she looked fine.

7. (try, go)   Brenda _____ to explain herself when she _____ back to the office the next day.

8. (be, undo)   The damage had _____ done, however, and nothing could _____ it.

9. (wish, take)   Now Brenda _____ that she could _____ back that day.

10. (use, call, do)   She _____ to have a great relationship with her boss, but since the day she _____ in sick, he _____ not trust her anymore.

Exercise 4

1. (use, put)   Many people _____ a direct deposit system that _____ their salary money directly into their bank account.

2. (do, do)   With such a system, the employer _____ not have to issue paycheques, and employees _____ not have to cash or deposit them.

3. (transfer, spend)   The employer's computer just _____ the money to the bank's computer, and the employee can _____ it as usual after that.

4. (be, like, choose)   Direct deposit _____ almost always optional, but so many people _____ the system that most people _____ it.

5. (do, want)   My dad _____ not trust such systems; he _____ to have complete control over his money.

6. (trust, be)   He barely even _____ banks to keep his money safe for him, so he _____ definitely suspicious of computers.

7. (imagine, make)   I can _____ him as a pioneer in an old western movie sleeping on a mattress stuffed with all of the money he has ever _____ .

8. (talk, ask, worry)   I was _____ to my dad about money the other day, and I _____ him why he always _____ about it so much.

9. (look, say, understand)   He just _____ at me and _____ , "You'll _____ some day."

10. (trust, be)   I _____ my dad's experiences; he has never _____ wrong before.

Exercise 5

1. (lie, fall)   I was _____ out in the sun last Sunday, and I _____ asleep.

2. (be, do)   That _____ the worst thing I could have _____ .

3. (wear, shield)   I was _____ a pair of big dark sunglasses, which _____ my eyes from the light.

4. (lie, wake, realize, happen)   I must have _____ there for over an hour before I _____ up and _____ what had _____ .

5. (feel, start)   At first I _____ fine, but then my skin _____ to feel really tight and thin.

6. (pass, turn, begin)   As the minutes _____ , my skin _____ bright red, and the pain _____ .

7. (describe, experience)   I can't even _____ how much pain I _____ .

8. (be, feel, see)

Almost   worse   than   the   pain _____   the embarrassment I _____ as I _____ my face in the mirror.

9. (look, tape, be, protect, wear)

Around my eyes, it _____ as if someone had _____ the shape of white glasses to my face, but   that _____   just   the   skin   that   had   been _____ by the sunglasses I was _____ .

10. (have, feel)

The people at work _____ a big laugh the next day at my expense, but then they just _____ sorry for me.

Progress Test

This test covers everything you've learned in the Sentence Structure section so far. One sentence in each pair is correct. The other is incorrect. Read both sentences carefully before you decide. Then write the letter of the incorrect sentence in the blank. Try to name the error and correct it if you can.

1. ___ **A.** After taking a nap for several hours in the afternoon.

B. I was able to work past midnight without stopping.

2. ___ **A.** We have taken many classes together.

B. Last semester we enrol in the same math class.

3. ___ **A.** He likes every movie that we see.

B. Whenever we go to see a new movie.

4. ___ **A.** Karen use to take the bus to school.

B. Now she car-pools with her friend.

5. ___ **A.** Their camping location was far into the mountains.

B. Because Tim was driving his mother worried all night.

6. ___ **A.** I need to stop procrastinating.

B. I will write in my journal every day, and will turn in all my work on time.

7. ___ **A.** My brother and I were suppose to help with the garage sale.

   B. He forgot to pick me up.

8. ___ **A.** He had already finish his dinner by the time I came home.

   B. I ate my dinner while I watched television alone.

9. ___ **A.** I looked everywhere for the plane tickets before I found them.

   B. They were laying on the dining-room table.

10. ___ **A.** Packing for a long trip is difficult.

   B. Especially not knowing how hot or cold the weather will be.

Maintaining Subject/Verb Agreement

As we have seen, the subject and verb in a sentence work together, so they must always agree. Different subjects need different forms of verbs. When the correct verb follows a subject, we call it subject/verb agreement.

The sentences below illustrate the rule that *s* verbs follow most singular subjects but not plural subjects.

One turtle walks.	Three turtles walk.
The baby cries.	The babies cry.
A good leader listens to the people.	Good leaders listen to the people.
One child plays.	Many children play.

And the following sentences show how forms of the verb *be* (*is, am, are, was, were*) and helping verbs (*be, have,* and *do*) are made to agree with their subjects.

This puzzle is difficult.	These puzzles are difficult.
I am amazed.	You are amazed.
He was sleeping.	They were sleeping.
That class has been cancelled.	Those classes have been cancelled.
She does not want to participate.	They do not want to participate.

The following words are always singular and take an *s* verb or the irregular equivalent (*is, was, has, does*):

"ONE" WORDS	"BODY" WORDS	
one	anybody	each
anyone	everybody	either
everyone	nobody	neither
no one	somebody	
someone		

<u>Someone</u> <u>feeds</u> my dog in the morning.

<u>Everybody</u> <u>was</u> at the party.

<u>Each</u> <u>does</u> her own homework.

Remember that prepositional phrases often come between subjects and verbs. You should ignore these interrupting phrases, or you may mistake the wrong word for the subject and use a verb form that doesn't agree.

<u>Someone</u> from the apartments <u>feeds</u> my dog in the morning. (*Someone* is the subject, not *apartments*.)

<u>Everybody</u> on the list of celebrities <u>was</u> at the party. (*Everybody* is the subject, not *celebrities*.)

<u>Each</u> of the twins <u>does</u> her own homework. (*Each* is the subject, not *twins*.)

However, any word that represents a part or portion can be singular or plural, depending on the words that follow it in a prepositional phrase. Examples of part or portion words are *some, any, half, all, most,* and *none.*

<u>Some</u> of the *pie* <u>is</u> gone.

<u>Some</u> of the *cookies* <u>are</u> gone.

<u>Is</u> <u>any</u> of the paper still in the supply cabinet?

<u>Are</u> <u>any</u> of the pencils still in the supply cabinet?

All of her work has been published.

All of her poems have been published.

None of the jewellery is missing.

None of the clothes are missing.

On July 1st, most of the country celebrates.

On July 1st, most of the citizens celebrate.

When a sentence has more than one subject joined by *and,* the subject is plural:

The teacher and the tutors eat lunch at noon.

A glazed doughnut and an onion bagel were sitting on the plate.

However, when two subjects are joined by *or,* then the subject closest to the verb determines the verb form:

Either the teacher *or* the tutors eat lunch at noon.

Either the tutors *or* the teacher eats lunch at noon.

A glazed doughnut *or* an onion bagel was sitting on the plate.

In most sentences, the subject comes before the verb. However, in some cases, the subject follows the verb, and subject/verb agreement needs special attention. Study the following examples:

Over the building flies a solitary flag. (flag flies)

Over the building fly several flags. (flags fly)

There is a good reason for my actions. (reason is)

There are good reasons for my actions. (reasons are)

E X E R C I S E S

Underline the verbs that agree with the subjects of the following sentences. Remember to ignore prepositional phrases, unless the subjects are part or portion words (*some, any, half, all, none,* or *most*). Check your answers ten at a time.

Exercise 1

1. Since September 11th, the Canadian and U.S. governments (has, have) toughened security laws.
2. Even before that date, there (was, were) calls for improvements in security.
3. Canada's Anti-Terrorism Act (make, makes) terrorism a punishable offence under the Criminal Code.
4. The new law (include, includes) a definition for terrorism, as well as punishment guidelines for people convicted of terrorism.
5. It also (give, gives) police more freedom to use wiretaps and make arrests.
6. Privacy advocates (is, are) concerned that the law goes too far.
7. Some of these advocates (use, uses) the Internet to protest the new legislation.
8. One of the reasons for their concern (is, are) that the American government (has, have) used similar legislation to hold foreign-born citizens for indefinite periods without charging them.
9. They also (fear, fears) that political demonstrations, like the antiglobalization protests held around the world, will be seen as terrorist activity.
10. Few citizens (is, are) eager to see people's right to protest disappear.

Source: http://www.cbc.ca/witness/security/world.html

Exercise 2

1. There (is, are) new risks for kids in this technological age; these risks primarily (involve, involves) their wrists.
2. Many adults already (suffer, suffers) from carpal tunnel syndrome.
3. And now children (is, are) also coming down with similar conditions, called repetitive stress injuries (RSIs).
4. From the use of computers and video games (come, comes) unnatural body positions that (lead, leads) to health problems.

5. The child's wrists, neck, and back (start, starts) to hurt or feel numb after he or she (work, works) or (play, plays) on the computer for a long time.

6. The problem (start, starts) with computer furniture.

7. The chairs, desks, and screens (is, are) usually not at the proper height to be used comfortably by children.

8. Straining and repetition often (cause, causes) reduced circulation and even nerve damage.

9. Often RSI damage to the wrists (is, are) irreversible.

10. Experts in the field of RSI (warn, warns) parents to teach children how to avoid these injuries.

Source: U.S. News & World Report, July 5, 1999.

Exercise 3

1. The Governor General's Literary Awards (was, were) inaugurated in 1937 when Governor General Lord Tweedsmuir honoured the best books of the previous year.

2. The Canada Council for the Arts (administer, administers) the awards, a responsibility it (has, have) assumed since 1959.

3. Each of the award winners (take, takes) home $15,000 and a specially bound copy of his or her award-winning book.

4. Publishers of winning books (receive, receives) $3000 to help promote sales.

5. The awards ceremony (is, are) held in November to coincide with the holiday book-buying season.

6. The Bank of Montreal (sponsor, sponsors) the awards and (has, have) done so since 1988.

7. In the past, awards (was, were) presented only for fiction, nonfiction, poetry, and drama in English and French.

8. Today, there (is, are) prizes in fourteen categories, including translation and children's literature.

9. The aim of the Governor General's Awards (is, are) to support Canada's publishers and booksellers by raising the profile of Canadian literature.

10. Some of the attention once reserved for the Governor General's Awards (is, are) being redirected to the recently established Giller Prize.

Source: http://www.canadacouncil.ca

Exercise 4

1. Everyone in my drawing class (is, are) supposed to finish a drawing a week.

2. But each of us (has, have) a different way of beginning.

3. One of my classmates always (start, starts) by humming and rocking back and forth in front of his easel.

4. Another one just (put, puts) dots in the places where she (want, wants) her figures to go.

5. Jennifer, my best friend, (like, likes) to draw really light circles wherever the faces will be.

6. In the past, I (has, have) usually started by drawing a continuous line until it (look, looks) like something.

7. In other words, I (let, lets) the drawing tell me what it (want, wants) to be.

8. But Jennifer and my other classmates (has, have) taught me something.

9. It (help, helps) to have a plan; their drawings often (turn, turns) out better than mine.

10. Either they or I (am, are) right, but I don't know which it (is, are) yet.

Exercise 5

1. When an American (picture, pictures) Canada, a balmy summer scene (do, does) not usually come to mind.

2. But heat and humidity (is, are) just what Americans often find when they (travel, travels) north of the border.

3. Canadians routinely joke about American tourists who (expect, expects) to ski in Canada in July.

4. But "sleeping with an elephant"—as Pierre Trudeau described Canada's relationship to the United States—(creates, create) more serious problems.

5. Canadians like publisher Mel Hurtig (has, have) discovered that our knowledge of our own country is sadly lacking.

6. (Do, does) your classmates know who served as prime minister during World War II?

7. In the 1970s, schools in our country (was, were) using American textbooks and teaching American literature, rather than the Canadian equivalent.

8. At one Canadian university in 1971, there (was, were) a strike because students (was, were) unhappy about the lack of Canadian content.

9. At colleges and universities in the past thirty years, there (has, have) been a push to hire people born in Canada.

10. How many members of the faculty at your local college or university (is, are) Canadian?

PROOFREADING EXERCISE

Find and correct the ten subject/verb agreement errors in the following paragraph.

All of the students in my drama club has chosen the play *Cyrano de Bergerac* for our next production. There is actually two famous Cyrano de Bergeracs. One of them is the title character of the play, and the other is the real person who had that name. Both of these men is famous for their large noses and for their writing. But only the fictional Cyrano loves Roxane. The tragic story of Cyrano and Roxane were written by Edmond Rostand. In it, Cyrano believe that Roxane could never love an ugly man. She thinks that she love Christian, Cyrano's fellow soldier who is extremely handsome. But she really love Cyrano, who writes all of the love letters that Christian gives Roxane. In those letters are the soul that Roxane admire, but she finds out too late. It's a very sad and dramatic story, and I hope that either my friend Lisa or I gets the part of Roxane.

SENTENCE WRITING

Write ten sentences in which you describe the shoes you are wearing. Use verbs in the present time. Then go back over your sentences—underline your subjects once, underline your verbs twice, and be sure they agree.

Avoiding Shifts in Time

People often worry about using different time frames in writing. Let common sense guide you. If you begin writing a paper in past time, don't shift back and forth to the present unnecessarily; and if you begin in the present, don't shift to the past without good reason. In the following paragraph, the writer starts in the present then shifts to the past, and then shifts again to the present:

> In the novel *Anne of Green Gables,* Anne Shirley is an eleven-year-old orphan who is adopted by a couple living in Avonlea, Prince Edward Island. Marilla and Matthew Cuthbert, a rather stern middle-aged couple, expected a boy and were quite surprised to receive a red-haired girl! Initially, the Cuthberts were unsure about keeping her. However, because of her winsome nature, good heart, and spirit, Anne won their love and helped create the family that she has always wanted.

All the verbs should be in the present:

> In the novel *Anne of Green Gables,* Anne Shirley is an eleven-year-old orphan who is adopted by a couple living in Avonlea, Prince Edward Island. Marilla and Matthew Cuthbert, a rather stern middle-aged couple, expect a boy and are quite surprised to receive a red-haired girl! Initially, the Cuthberts are unsure about keeping her. However, because of her winsome nature, good heart, and spirit, Anne wins their love and helps create the family that she has always wanted.

This sample paragraph discusses only the events that happen within the novel's plot, so it needs to maintain one time frame—the present, which we use to write about literature and repeated actions.

However, sometimes you will write about the present, the past, and even the future together. Then it may be necessary to use these different time frames within the same paragraph, each for its own reason. For example, if you were to give biographical information about Lucy Maud Montgomery, author of *Anne of Green Gables,* within a discussion of the novel and its influence, you might need to use all three time frames:

> Lucy Maud Montgomery was born in Clifton (now New London), Prince Edward Island, and she based elements in the book on experiences from her childhood. Montgomery was raised by her grandparents in Prince Edward Island after the death of her mother and the departure of her father to Saskatchewan. Like Anne's entry into the Cuthbert household, Montgomery's arrival into her grandparents' home may have been tenuous at first. However, from the story's ending, one can conclude that Montgomery grew to love her grandparents immensely. *Anne of Green Gables* is Montgomery's most famous work and will

be 100 years old in the year 2008. Today it is considered a classic in children's literature.

Sources: 1) http://encarta.msn.com/find/Concise.asp?ti=06DB6000
            2) http://w3.one.net/~wilmhoff/ginny/aboutlmm.htm

This paragraph uses past (*was born, based, was raised, may have been, grew*), present (*is*), and future (*will be*) in the same paragraph without committing the error of shifting. Shifting occurs when the writer changes time frames inconsistently or for no reason, confusing the reader (as in the first example given).

PROOFREADING EXERCISES

Which of the following student paragraphs shift *unnecessarily* back and forth between time frames? In those that do, change the verbs to maintain one time frame, thus making the entire paragraph read smoothly. (First, read the paragraphs to determine whether unnecessary shifting takes place. One of the paragraphs is correct.)

1. Adrienne Clarkson was born in Hong Kong in 1939. She comes to Canada as a refugee with her parents during the war. She attended schools in Ottawa and goes on to obtain degrees in English literature from the University of Toronto. For almost twenty years, she worked as a host, writer, and producer for several influential CBC programs. Her career path takes a striking turn when she served as a diplomat in Paris and subsequently becomes president and publisher of McClelland & Stewart. She returned to broadcasting in 1988 and, a little more than a decade later, is sworn in as Governor General of Canada.

Source: The Canadian Encyclopedia (McClelland & Stewart, 1999).

2. I watched a documentary on the Leaning Tower of Pisa last night. I was amazed to find out that the tower began leaning before it was even finished. Workers over several centuries adjusted their materials as they built the tower to compensate for its increasing angle. That's why the tower is actually shaped a little like a banana. I'm surprised that the famous landmark is still standing after everything people have done to it since it was finished. In the 1930s, for instance, Mussolini thought that it should be straightened. So he had workers drill holes in the foundation and pour tons of concrete beneath it. Others tried digging out the earth around the sunken part. But that just caused flooding because they went below the soil's water table. The narrator of the documentary said that every time anyone tries to correct the tower, it leans a little more to the south. Now scientists are using special drilling techniques to extract enough soil deep beneath the tower to reverse its angle a little. If successful, this most recent correction will add three hundred years to the life of the Tower of Pisa.

3. I really enjoyed my summer vacation this year. It isn't long enough, of course, but I made the most of the time I have. My geology club took a trip to Baja, California. We didn't pack enough to eat, but the beautiful scenery takes my breath away. Once I'm back home, I always play a lot of tennis with my roommates. One night we stayed at the tennis court until after it closes. We are just hitting volleys in the dark with only the moon for lighting. It was an unplanned thing, and we could barely see the ball. It's fun to goof off with my friends on a summer evening. Overall, the trip to Baja and the after-hours tennis match are the highlights of my summer vacation.

Recognizing Verbal Phrases

We know (from the discussion on p. 82) that a verb phrase is made up of a main verb and at least one helping verb. But sometimes certain forms of verbs are used not as real verbs but as some other part of a sentence. Verbs put to other uses are called *verbals*.

A verbal can be a subject:

Skiing is my favourite Olympic sport. (*Skiing* is the subject, not the verb. The verb is *is*.)

A verbal can be a descriptive word:

His *bruised* ankle healed very quickly. (*Bruised* describes the subject, ankle. *Healed* is the verb.)

A verbal can be an object:

I like *to read* during the summer. (*To read* is the object. *Like* is the verb.)

Verbals link up with other words to form *verbal phrases*. To see the difference between a real verb phrase and a verbal phrase, look at these two sentences:

I was bowling with my best friends. (*Bowling* is the main verb in a verb phrase. Along with the helping verb *was*, it shows the action of the sentence.)

I enjoyed *bowling* with my best friends. (Here the real verb is *enjoyed*. *Bowling* is not the verb; it is part of a verbal phrase—*bowling with my best friends*—which is what I enjoyed.)

THERE ARE THREE KINDS OF VERBALS

1. *ing* verbs used without helping verbs (*running, thinking, baking . . .*)

2. verb forms that often end in *ed, en,* or *t* (*tossed, spoken, burnt . . .*)

3. verbs that follow *to* (*to walk, to eat, to cause . . .*)

Look at the following sentences using the previous examples in verbal phrases:

Running five kilometres a day is great exercise. (real verb = is)

She spent two hours *thinking of a title for her essay.* (real verb = spent)

We had such fun *baking those cherry vanilla cupcakes.* (real verb = had)

Tossed in a salad, artichoke hearts add zesty flavour. (real verb = add)

Sung in Italian, the opera sounds even more beautiful. (real verb = sounds)

The gourmet pizza, *burnt by a careless chef,* shrunk to half its normal size. (real verb = shrunk)

I like *to walk around the zoo by myself.* (real verb = like)

To eat exotic foods takes courage. (real verb = takes)

They actually wanted *to cause an argument.* (real verb = wanted)

E X E R C I S E S

Each of the following sentences contains at least one verbal or verbal phrase. Double underline the real verbs or verb phrases and put brackets around the verbals and verbal phrases. Remember to locate the verbal first (*running, wounded, to sleep . . .*) and include any word(s) that go with it (*running a race, wounded in the fight, to sleep all night*). Real verbs will never be inside verbal phrases. Complete the first set before going on to the next.

Exercise 1

1. Sending children to summer hockey camp is an increasingly common practice in Canada.

2. Many parents have decided to enrol their children in hockey camps instead of sending them to traditional camps.

3. Some families spend several months investigating hockey camps for their sons or daughters.

4. A good camp will help children to improve and broaden their hockey-playing skills.

5. Preparing children for junior hockey is the mandate of several hockey camps.

6. Most young hockey players want to have the opportunity to join a top team.

7. One camp in Manitoba has adopted a coeducational curriculum, allowing both boys and girls to attend.

8. Taking an advanced hockey course will benefit some players.

9. Concerned about education, a player may prefer to play college or university hockey.

10. Striking a healthy balance between school and sports is a difficult task.

Exercise 2

1. A Japanese company called Matsushita expects to offer fully interactive houses operated by computer network in the near future.

2. Getting ready for work in the morning will be very different.

3. The electronic toilet-of-the-future is designed to take care of everything—weighing you, checking your health through various tests, and even sending the data to your doctor if necessary.

4. Talking into your television's remote control will turn on the space-age TV screens of the future positioned in almost every room of the house.

5. Using a cell phone with its own video screen from your desk at work, you'll be able to check the contents of your refrigerator before shopping for groceries.

6. And once you return home with the food, you can update the fridge's contents using voice commands.

7. Glancing at monitors set up in key areas, you can check the status of your laundry room, living room, and kitchen simultaneously.

8. The rooms themselves will respond to your movements through the use of infrared sensors—lighting up, cooling off, or heating up as necessary.

9. A security system will be used to take the picture of anyone approaching the front door and to store the snapshot for twelve months.

10. Needless to say, the fully wired Japanese house of the 21st century will be expensive, costing nearly 5 percent more than an ordinary, old-fashioned one.

Source: U.S. News & World Report, June 7, 1999.

Exercise 3

1. The Fathers of Confederation, attending their first conference on the possibility of a Maritime union, met in Charlottetown in 1864.

2. Hearing of the planned conference, representatives proposed a larger union—that of British North America.

3. Adjourned on September 9, the meeting continued among delegates in Saint John, Fredericton, and Halifax.

4. An observing delegation from the Maritime provinces went to the second conference.

5. John A. Macdonald was a dominating presence at the conference, though Étienne-Paschal Taché was the official chair.

6. Following the second conference, a text called the Quebec Resolutions became the basis for the third conference.

7. To avoid angering the United States, representatives decided to call the new union a "dominion" instead of a "kingdom."

8. Lasting approximately four months, the final conference resulted in the British North America Act.

9. To be precise, Canada officially became a country on July 1, 1867.

10. Its new prime minister was John A. Macdonald, a practising lawyer born in Scotland.

Exercise 4

1. Canada East (also known as Quebec), Canada West (or Ontario), New Brunswick, and Nova Scotia joined Confederation in 1867.

2. Manitoba decided to become part of the union in 1870.

3. Separated from most of Canada, the land between British Columbia and the East was known as the Territories.

4. The sixth province to enter Confederation was British Columbia in 1871.

5. Prince Edward Island joined in 1873, bringing the total to seven.

6. Alberta and Saskatchewan came on board in 1905, frustrating Manitoba's plans to expand its borders west.

7. Newfoundland entered Confederation in 1949, becoming the last province to join.

8. Canada has three territories belonging to the union but not considered provinces.

9. Created in 1870 and 1898 respectively, the Northwest Territories and Yukon Territory have undergone a complicated evolution.

10. The Inuit advocated the establishment of a new political entity, resulting in the creation of Nunavut in 1999.

Exercise 5

1. Canadian places are often given unusual names, derived from a variety of languages.

2. Sighted by Leif Ericson, Baffin Island was named Helluland, meaning "Land of Flat Stones."

3. Jacques Cartier assigned the name Mont Royal to the city known as Hochelaga and destined to become Montreal.

4. Thinking them barriers to his path to China, Cartier named the Lachine Rapids.

5. Kanata, meaning "our village," became the name of the country explored: Canada.

6. A less accepted view is that the name Kanata is derived from the words *acada nada,* meaning "nothing here," written on a map by Portuguese explorers.

7. Located on the north shore of the St. Lawrence River, Quebec City was originally the site of an Indian village called Stadacona.

8. Originally named Bytown, Ottawa gets its name from the Algonquin word for "trade."

9. In December 1984, residents of Frobisher Bay voted to rename the place Iqaluit, meaning "place of fish."

10. Regina, named in honour of Queen Victoria, was originally called Pile of Bones.

PARAGRAPH EXERCISE

Double underline the real verbs or verb phrases and put brackets around the verbals and verbal phrases in the following paragraph.

Margaret Atwood, the author of more than thirty books of poetry, fiction, and nonfiction, was born in Ottawa in 1939 and grew up in northern Quebec and Ontario, as well as Toronto. Considered one of Canada's major contemporary writers, she has managed to achieve both popular and critical success, topping bestseller lists and garnering numerous awards, including the Booker Prize. Acclaimed internationally, her books have been published in over thirty-five countries and translated into more than thirty languages. Her novel *The Handmaid's Tale,* published in 1985, was made into a feature film starring Natasha Richardson and Robert Duvall. *Survival,* her groundbreaking study of Canadian literature, continues to shape the way Canadians look at themselves. Known for her keen interest in human rights, Atwood has been active in Amnesty International and International PEN, serving as president of the latter organization's Anglo-Canadian branch from 1984 to 1986. Adding to her many achievements, she was inducted into Canada's Walk of Fame in 2001.

Sources: http://www.web.net/owtoad/toc.html; *The Canadian Encyclopedia* (McClelland & Stewart, 1999).

SENTENCE WRITING

Write ten sentences that contain verbal phrases. Use the ten verbals listed here to begin your verbal phrases: *speaking, typing, driving, reading, to eat, to go, to chat, to cook, impressed, taken.* The last two are particularly difficult to use as verbals. There are sample sentences listed in the Answers at the back of the book. But first, try to write your own so that you can compare the two.

Correcting Misplaced or Dangling Modifiers

When we modify something, we often change whatever it is by adding something to it. We might modify a car, for example, by adding special tires. In English we call words, phrases, and clauses *modifiers* when they add information to part of a sentence. To do its job properly, a modifier should be in the right spot—as close to the word it describes as possible. If we put new tires on the roof of the car instead of where they belong, they would be misplaced. In the following sentence, the modifier is too far away from the word it modifies to make sense. It is a misplaced modifier.

Swinging from tree to tree, we watched the monkeys at the zoo.

Was it *we* who were swinging from tree to tree? That's what the sentence says because the modifying phrase *Swinging from tree to tree* is next to *we*. It should be next to *monkeys*.

At the zoo, we watched the monkeys swinging from tree to tree.

The next example has no word at all for the modifier to modify:

At the age of eight, my family finally bought a dog.

Obviously the family was not eight when it bought a dog. Nor was the dog eight. The modifier *At the age of eight* is dangling there with no word to attach itself to, no word for it to modify. We can get rid of the dangling modifier by turning it into a dependent clause. (See p. 60 for a discussion of dependent clauses.)

When I was eight, my family finally bought a dog.

Here the clause has its own subject and verb—*I was*—and there's no chance of misunderstanding the sentence. Here's another dangling modifier:

After a ten-minute nap, the plane landed.

Did the plane take a ten-minute nap? Who did?

After a ten-minute nap, I awoke just as the plane landed.

E X E R C I S E S

Carefully rephrase any of the following sentences that contain misplaced or dangling modifiers. Some sentences are correct.

Exercise 1

1. After checking out the online catalogue, my desire to spend grew.
2. I found many items surfing the Internet this afternoon.
3. Using my credit card, I paid for all my purchases.
4. Finding daily bargains on eBay, online shopping comes naturally to me.
5. I bid on a notebook computer with a wireless mouse, but I'll never do it again.
6. My friends send me advertisements from big box stores in e-mail.
7. This year I gave my parents a Christmas wish list of books and DVDs that are available at Amazon.ca.
8. After opening my presents, my parents were pleased with my reaction.
9. Running out of ideas, I bought gift certificates for many of my friends.
10. When surfing the Internet, impulse buying may be a problem.

Exercise 2

1. Getting ready for the fall, our clocks turned back one hour.
2. Lying in bed the next morning, I was grateful for the extra hour of sleep.
3. Forgetting to reset his clock, the adjustment was more difficult for my friend.
4. Setting the clocks ahead one hour in the spring, traffic accidents increase for about a week.
5. Yawning constantly, I fight to stay awake during my first class in the morning.
6. In the fall, I eat my bacon and eggs waiting for the sun to come up.
7. Feeling like a coal miner, the return home from work in the dark is depressing.
8. Ignoring the time changes, my cat's habit is to wake me at first light.
9. The time changes may be particularly hard to take for people suffering from depression.
10. Living near the equator, time changes are almost unknown.

Exercise 3

1. Born in Newmarket, Ontario, Norm Foster's plays are popular with audiences across Canada.

2. Often compared to Neil Simon, Foster's plays are noted for their light comic touch.

3. At the age of fifty-two, Foster and his wife toured as actors in his play *Here on the Flight Path.*

4. Admired for its insightful treatment of brothers, *The Melville Boys,* Foster's second play, won a major award.

5. Once a disc jockey in New Brunswick, Foster's plays are now produced across Canada and in the United States.

6. Known mainly for their comedic qualities, Foster's plays are not without their serious moments.

7. Working with Leslie Arden, a Canadian musician who studied with Stephen Sondheim, *The Last Resort* is a funny and touching musical comedy.

8. Raised in Toronto, Foster began a radio career that lasted twenty-five years.

9. Thinking that it is easy, comedy does not get the respect it deserves.

10. Written in 1990, *The Affections of May* was the most produced play in Canada in 1991.

Source: http://www.normfoster.com

Exercise 4

1. Margaret Atwood established her poetic reputation winning a Governor General's Award for *The Circle Game.*

2. She secured her international reputation with the publication of *The Handmaid's Tale,* a science-fiction novel that has been turned into both a movie and an opera.

3. Atwood completed a master's degree in English literature at the University of Toronto before deciding to become a writer.

4. Appearing in *The Globe and Mail,* I read the review of her eleventh novel, *Oryx and Crake.*

5. Nominated for a Governor General's Award, Atwood explored the death of a parent in a book of poetry entitled *Morning in the Burned House.*

6. Critics routinely praise Atwood for her writing at home and abroad.

7. Winning the Giller Prize, she fictionalized the life and times of a 19th-century domestic servant convicted of murder in *Alias Grace.*

8. Indifferently reviewed in Canada, Atwood won the 2000 Booker Prize for *The Blind Assassin.*

9. An early novel, *Surfacing,* explores the conflict between nature and technology by casting it in political terms.

10. Published in 1969, Atwood explores themes of women's alienation in *The Edible Woman.*

Sources: http://www.web.net/owtoad/toc.html; *The Canadian Encyclopedia* (McClelland & Stewart, 1999).

Exercise 5

1. Written by Dan Needles, the Wingfield plays have enjoyed box-office and critical success in theatres across Canada.

2. Before writing the Wingfield plays, a column in *Harrowsmith* magazine used to recount the adventures of a big-city fellow turned farmer in Persephone Township.

3. *Letters from Wingfield Farm,* the book version of the first three Wingfield plays, was short-listed for the Stephen Leacock Memorial Medal for Humour in 1989.

4. A talented raconteur, stories and songs dealing with life in rural Ontario have been performed by Needles.

5. A veteran of the Stratford Festival, Rod Beattie's name has become synonymous with the character of Walt Wingfield.

6. Walt is a retired stockbroker turned farmer who recounts his adventures in a series of letters to the editor on the farm.

7. Performed by Beattie, Walt made his American debut at the Cincinnati Playhouse in the Park in 1994.

8. Using a multitude of techniques, the Wingfield plays feature seventeen entertaining characters cleverly portrayed by Beattie.

9. Winner of a Dora Mavor Moore Award for his performances in the first three Wingfield plays, Beattie and his wife, actress Martha Henry, did an Ontario tour of *Love Letters*.

10. Spawning CDs and video/audio cassettes, the Wingfield plays prove that Canadian content and popular success are not mutually exclusive.

Source: http://www.wingfieldfarm.ca/bio.htm

PROOFREADING EXERCISE

Find and correct any misplaced or dangling modifiers in the following paragraphs.

A man in Edinburgh, Scotland, has invented a device, hoping to become famous and wealthy. The device is a variation on the centre-mounted brake light used in the design of many new cars, located just above the trunk and visible from behind. Instead of just a solid red brake light, however, this invention displays words to other drivers written in bold, red-lighted letters.

With simplicity in mind, the vocabulary the inventor gave the machine is limited to three words: "Sorry," "Thanks," and "Help." After making an aggressive lane change, the machine could apologize for us. Or after being allowed to go ahead of someone, the device could offer thanks to the considerate person responsible. Of course, at the sight of the "Help" display, we could summon fellow citizens for assistance.

And there is no need to worry about operating the device while driving. With three easy-to-reach buttons, the messages can be activated without taking our eyes off the road.

SENTENCE WRITING

Write five sentences that contain misplaced or dangling modifiers; then revise those sentences to put the modifiers where they belong. Use the examples in the explanations as models.

Following Sentence Patterns

Sentences are built according to a few basic patterns. For proof, rearrange each of the following sets of words to form a complete statement (not a question):

apples a ate raccoon the

the crashing beach were waves the on

your in am partner I life

been she school has to walking

you wonderful in look green

There are only one or two possible combinations for each due to English sentence patterns. Either *A raccoon ate the apples,* or *The apples ate a raccoon,* and so on. But in each case, the verb or verb phrase makes its way to the middle of the statement.

To understand sentence patterns, you need to know that verbs can do three things.

1. They can show actions.

A raccoon ate the apples.

The waves were crashing on the beach.

She has been walking to school.

2. They can link subjects with descriptive words.

I am your partner in life.

You look wonderful in green.

3. They can help other verbs form verb phrases.

The waves were crashing on the beach.

She has been walking to school.

Look at these sentences for more examples:

Mel grabbed a slice of pizza. (The verb *grabbed* shows Mel's action.)

His slice was the largest one in the box. (The verb *was* links *slice* with its description as *the largest one.*)

Mel had been craving pizza for a week. (The verbs *had* and *been* help the main verb *craving* in a verb phrase.)

Knowing what a verb does in a clause helps you gain an understanding of the three basic sentence patterns:

SUBJECT + ACTION VERB + OBJECT PATTERN

Some action verbs must be followed by a person or object that receives the action.

    S   **AV**   **OBJ.**

Sylvia completed the difficult math test. (*Sylvia completed* makes no sense without being followed by the object that she completed—*test.*)

Subject + Action Verb (+ No Object) Pattern

At other times, the action verb itself finishes the meaning and needs no object after it.

S   AV

She celebrated at home with her family. (*She celebrated* makes sense alone. The two prepositional phrases—*at home* and *with her family*—are not needed to understand the meaning of the clause.)

Subject + Linking Verb + Description Pattern

A special kind of verb that does not show an action but links a subject with a description is called a *linking verb*. It acts like an equal sign in a clause. Learn to recognize the most common linking verbs: *is, am, are, was, were, seem, feel, appear, become, look*.

S   LV   DESC.

Sylvia was always an excellent student. (*Sylvia* equals *an excellent student.*)

S   LV   DESC.

Sylvia has become very intelligent. (*Very intelligent* describes *Sylvia.*)

NOTE: We learned on page 82 that a verb phrase includes a main verb and its helping verbs. Helping verbs can be used in any of the sentence patterns.

S   AV

Sylvia is going to Vancouver for a vacation. (Here the verb *is* helps the main verb *going*, which is an action verb with no object followed by two prepositional phrases—*to Vancouver* and *for a vacation.*)

The following chart outlines the patterns using short sentences that you should memorize:

THE THREE BASIC SENTENCE PATTERNS

S + AV + Obj.	S + AV
They hit the ball.	They ran (quickly) (around the bases).
	not objects

S + LV +	Desc.
They are	amateur players.
They look	professional.

These are the three basic patterns of most of the clauses used in English sentences. Knowing them can help writers control their sentences and improve their use of words.

E X E R C I S E S

First, put parentheses around any prepositional phrases. Next, underline the subjects once and the verbs or verb phrases twice. Then mark the sentence patterns above the words. Remember that the patterns never mix together. For example, unlike an action verb, a linking verb will almost never be used alone (for example, "He seems."), nor will an action verb be followed by a description of the subject (for example, "She took tall."). And if there are two or more clauses, each one may have a different pattern. Check your answers after the first set of ten.

Exercise 1

1. My sister Belinda is allergic to many things.

2. She gets hives from mould and pollen.

3. Of course, milk upsets her stomach.

4. Strawberries and raspberries are many people's favourite fruits.

5. But they give Belinda a rash on her face and arms.

6. The doctor has made a list of Belinda's allergies.

7. Soon she'll be receiving allergy shots.

8. The shots should reduce Belinda's sensitivity to these substances.

9. Everyone in my family is hoping for the best.

10. With luck, Belinda will feel better soon.

Exercise 2

1. Scientists around the world are working on a new technology.

2. It is a special computer.

3. It will translate one language into another instantly.

4. People will carry the device with them in their travels.

5. They will ask a question in English, and the device will repeat the question in French, Spanish, German, or Japanese.

6. The traveller will hear the translation over a pair of headphones.

7. But computers still have some trouble in recognizing people's speech.

8. Ordinary ramblings usually include numerous interruptions, such as "um," "er," and "eh?"

9. Nobody has programmed totally accurate translating software yet.

10. But researchers are now closer than ever to using computers as translators.

Source: Discover, Nov. 1999.

Exercise 3

1. In 2003, a gala live performance commemorated the Queen's fiftieth year on the throne.

2. Sir Andrew Davis, who conducted the BBC Symphony Orchestra and Chorus, was among the performers.

3. Dame Kiri Te Kanawa, a soprano originally from New Zealand, also gave a performance, just as she did at Charles and Diana's wedding in St. Paul's Cathedral in 1981.

4. "The Party at the Palace" was a popular event at the gala.

5. At that event, pop singers like Sir Paul McCartney and Sir Elton John performed.

6. American bands like the Beach Boys were just as well received as British pop stars like Rod Stewart and Cliff Richard.

7. Dame Edna, also known as Barry Humphries, introduced the Queen as "the birthday girl" when Her Majesty arrived part way through the event.

8. Many people remember that Prince Charles called his mother "mummy" at the gala.

9. Despite some turbulent years, Queen Elizabeth II has become a much-respected figure during her reign.

10. Millions of people around the world watched the parades, processions, and performances staged in her honour.

Exercise 4

1. In Canada, we love our pets.

2. We own millions of them.

3. Most people in Canada live with pets.

4. Of these pet owners, most have chosen dogs as their favourites.

5. Many people, of course, prefer cats.

6. Pet food and supply companies in Canada are prospering at the moment.

7. Canadians are even buying health insurance for their pets.

8. In recent years, the average cost of pet medical treatment has soared.

9. Now people will spend thousands for pet-care measures.

10. The Canadian pet-care industry makes a great deal of money every year.

Exercise 5

1. One pet owner in my hometown tells a fascinating story about her dog.

2. She had a Chihuahua named Peppy.

3. Peppy hated mail carriers, and he even knew when they were coming.

4. Every day during the week, Peppy would bark at the window just before the mail carrier appeared.

5. Peppy was never wrong, even though the mail carrier was sometimes a bit late.

6. For some reason, the dog never barked on weekends.

7. We all wondered how on earth he knew the mail carrier's time of arrival.

8. Every weekday, Peppy's owner watched a soap opera.

9. Then the network changed the scheduling of the program, so that it aired an hour earlier every day.

10. The music of the soap opera had warned Peppy when the mail carrier was about to arrive, so the change in the program's schedule baffled him.

PARAGRAPH EXERCISE

Label the sentence patterns in the following paragraph. It helps to put parentheses around prepositional phrases first to isolate them from the words that make up the sentence patterns—the subjects, the verbs, and any objects after action verbs or any descriptive words after linking verbs (*is, was, were, seem, appear*, and so on).

Capital Cities

Most Canadians know that Ottawa is Canada's capital city. But they forget that the capital of British Columbia is beautiful Victoria. Some people assume that Vancouver, the larger city, is the provincial capital. Unlike many world capitals, however, provincial capitals are not always big cities; Charlottetown, for instance, has a population of only about 35,000. Some Canadians are more knowledgeable about capital cities in other countries, such as the United States, than about their own capitals. Quiz shows like *Jeopardy* demonstrate that Americans have limited knowledge of Canada in general.

SENTENCE WRITING

Write ten sentences describing the weather today and your feelings about it—make your sentences short and clear. Then go back and label the sentence patterns you have used.

Avoiding Clichés, Awkward Phrasing, and Wordiness

CLICHÉS

A cliché is an expression that has been used so often it has lost its originality and effectiveness. Whoever first said "light as a feather" had thought of an original way to express lightness, but today that expression is worn out. Most of us use an occasional cliché in speaking, but clichés have no place in writing. The good writer thinks up fresh new ways to express ideas.

Here are a few clichés. Add some more to the list.

the bottom line

older but wiser

last but not least

in this day and age

different as night and day

out of this world

white as a ghost

sick as a dog

tried and true

at the top of their lungs

the thrill of victory

one in a million

busy as a bee

easier said than done

better late than never

Clichés lack freshness because the reader always knows what's coming next. Can you complete these expressions?

the agony of . . .

breathe a sigh of . . .

lend a helping . . .

odds and . . .

raining cats and . . .

time flies when . . .

been there . . .

worth its weight . . .

Clichés are expressions too many people use too often. Try to avoid them in your writing.

AWKWARD PHRASING

Another problem—awkward phrasing—comes from writing sentence structures that *no one* else would use because they break basic sentence patterns, omit necessary words, or use words incorrectly. Like clichés, awkward sentences might *sound* acceptable when spoken, but as polished writing, they are usually unacceptable.

AWKWARD

There should be great efforts in terms of the cooperation between coaches and their athletes.

CORRECTED

Coaches and their athletes should cooperate.

AWKWARD

During the experiment, the use of key principles was essential to ensure the success of it.

CORRECTED

The experiment was a success. *or* We did the experiment carefully.

AWKWARD

My favourite was when the guy fell all the way down the ship.

CORRECTED

In my favourite scene, a man fell all the way down the deck of the sinking ship.

WORDINESS

Good writing is concise writing. Don't say something in ten words if you can say it better in five. "In today's society" isn't as effective as "today," and it's a cliché. "At this point in time" could be "presently" or "now."

Another kind of wordiness comes from saying something twice. There's no need to write "in the month of August" or "9 A.M. in the morning" or "my personal opinion." August *is* a month, 9 A.M. *is* morning, and anyone's opinion *is* personal. All you need to write is "in August," "9 A.M.," and "my opinion."

Still another kind of wordiness comes from using expressions that add nothing to the meaning of the sentence. "The point is that we can't afford it" says no more than "We can't afford it."

Here is a sample wordy sentence:

The construction company actually worked on that particular building for a period of six months.

And here it is after eliminating wordiness:

The construction company worked on that building for six months.

WORDY WRITING	**CONCISE WRITING**
advance planning	planning
an unexpected surprise	a surprise
ask a question	ask
at a later date	later
basic fundamentals	fundamentals
green in colour	green
but nevertheless	but (*or* nevertheless)
combine together	combine
completely empty	empty
down below	below
each and every	each (*or* every)
end result	result
fewer in number	fewer
free gift	gift
in order to	to
in spite of the fact that	although
just exactly	exactly
large in size	large
new innovation	innovation
on a regular basis	regularly
past history	history
rectangular in shape	rectangular
refer back	refer
repeat again	repeat
serious crisis	crisis
sufficient enough	sufficient (*or* enough)
there in person	there
two different kinds	two kinds
very unique	unique

E X E R C I S E S

Exercise 1

Rewrite the following sentences to eliminate clichés and awkward phrasing.

1. I know that practice makes perfect, but I just can't seem to get behind the idea of practising the piano.

2. I've been learning the ins and outs of piano playing for just about two years.

3. I thought it was a good idea at first, but in this day and age, it seems so old-fashioned to study all the notes and hand positions.

4. I mean, right now anyone can go into a store and buy keyboards that play music themselves.

5. That's what I did when I found out that owning a real piano is easier said than done.

6. I couldn't afford any of them; the prices were way over the top.

7. So I got one of the upright digital keyboards that is really close to the sound and feel of the real thing.

8. My music teacher has no idea that I spend hours not practising my fingering but having my keyboard play the demo songs.

9. All I have to do is push the right button, and the theme from *Star Wars* fills the air.

10. Of course, the sad truth is that I'll probably never learn to play the piano myself.

Exercise 2

Cross out words or rewrite parts of each sentence to eliminate wordiness. Doing these exercises can almost turn into a game to see how few words you can use without changing the meaning of the sentence.

1. After a lot of advance planning, we were recently able to hold a reunion where everybody in the family came together to celebrate my grandmother's birthday.

2. Of course, we wanted it to be a surprise so that Grandma wouldn't know about it ahead of time; we couldn't wait to see the happy look of joy on her face when she saw us all there in person.

3. Each and every one of us had to travel some distance to reach the campground where we were having the reunion since we have all spread out across the province and even the country in order to make our livings.

4. In spite of the fact that we all had to travel to get there, we made it at the exact time that we needed to be there so that Grandma could walk up and find us all there together already before she walked up.

5. My cousin Jeff was the one who was chosen to distract Grandma before the reunion.

6. He decided to take her shopping with him at the mall; he told her that he needed a new coat and that she was the one that he trusted the most to help him choose the right one.

7. She was flattered that he trusted her judgment, so she went with him to buy the coat.

8. To make a long story short, while they were shopping for the coat at the mall, Jeff pretended to suddenly remember that he told a friend that he would go camping with him, so Jeff drove Grandma to the campground.

9. When they drove up, we all kind of hid behind trees and tables so that we wouldn't be seen, and then we all jumped out together and yelled "Surprise!"

10. We sat Grandma down in a big chair somebody had brought and made her feel like the queen of a country; we waited on her and entertained her and made her feel special.

Exercises 3, 4, and 5

Revise the sentences in the remaining exercises to eliminate any clichés, awkward phrasing, or wordiness.

Exercise 3

1. I just got finished reading an article that explains that the ancient Egyptians used what we now call makeup in a lot of different ways, not just for beauty.

2. First of all, they used makeup to paint their faces in an effort to make themselves more attractive to other human beings.

3. Egyptians seemed to be just as hung up on staying young and gorgeous looking as we modern folks do.

4. And it was a big eye opener to me that the Egyptian men put makeup on their eyes and lips just like the Egyptian women.

5. French scientists and beauty experts have been studying the leftover contents that remain inside ancient vessels found inside the buried tombs of kings and queens of the Nile as far back in time as 2700 B.C.

6. From these leftover remains of ancient makeup, scientists have been able to identify the ingredients that the Egyptians used in their makeup concoctions.

7. The list of ingredients that the scientists discovered includes goose fat, lettuce, animal blood, crushed beetles, cinnamon, and some other ingredients that did not naturally occur in nature.

8. That means that the Egyptians had to know enough about chemistry to make artificial ingredients in the same way that we make artificial ingredients in this day and age.

9. Last but not least, the Egyptians seemed to have used makeup for medicinal rather than only cosmetic purposes.

10. Two of the substances that the Egyptians made artificially were laurionite and phosgenite, and these two ingredients may have helped to cure the eye problems that many Egyptians had due to the fact that the Nile river often flooded the valley and contained bacteria that commonly infected people's eyes.

Source: Discover, Sept. 1999.

Exercise 4

1. I was as happy as a clam when I found out a few days ago that I will be getting a tax return of $800 this year.

2. Before this, I used to do my own taxes myself.

3. I would wait for my T4 forms to get here in the mail and then fill out the short form that lets me get the whole thing over with quickly, even if I don't get a whole lot back from Canada Customs and Revenue.

4. Then my mom started giving me the old song and dance about that I'm getting old enough to do the right thing instead of taking the easy way out.

5. Well, that was all it took to make me wake up and smell the coffee.

6. I asked around at work to see if anyone knew a tax person to recommend, and my friend Jason said that he did, and he gave me her number.

7. I called the tax preparer that Jason used; her name was Helen.

8. After I went to see Helen, she explained to me that I should be the one to control the amount that gets taken out of my paycheque for taxes, not the other way around.

9. I never even had a clue that there was so much to know about being a "grownup," as my mom calls it.

10. And I bet I've just started to scratch the surface of what "real" grownups understand.

Exercise 5

1. One of the foods that Canadians like the most is pizza; we gobble it up like there's no tomorrow.

2. In fact, many of us order pizza at least once a week to be specific.

3. There is a lot of interest in the eating habits of Canadians on the part of those who produce and market fast food.

4. For many years, a pair of companies, namely Tim Hortons and Wendy's, have dominated—and continue to dominate—the industry that makes and sells fast food.

5. Tim Hortons and Wendy's went about forming a partnership, and the main reason for their union was, first and foremost, their desire to strengthen their position in the industry that produces fast food.

6. In a bid to increase sales of its products, Tim Hortons expanded operations by opening a bunch of new stores from coast to coast.

7. The company continues to establish more outlets in spite of the fact that there already seems to be a Tim Hortons on every corner.

8. It goes without saying that, when it comes to the highly competitive coffee wars, Tim Hortons and Starbucks are going at it hammer and tongs in the battle for first place.

9. A hard-and-fast rule of business in this day and age is that a company can survive only if there is sufficient consumer demand for its products.

10. Because of the high degree of competition, the bottom line is that if you work in the fast-food industry, you can expect to be busy as a bee.

PROOFREADING EXERCISE

Revise the sentences in the following paragraph to eliminate any clichés, awkward phrasing, or wordiness.

In my family, I don't think that you could call anybody in it "normal." In fact, every single member of my family is a bit of an oddball. The oddest one of all has to be my Uncle Crank. His real name is actually Frank, but ever since I was growing up, Uncle Frank told us kids to call him Uncle "Crank." That's because of his arm. Frank has an arm that is out of the ordinary because it doesn't bend the right way at the elbow. So you can go right up to it and turn it like a crank on an old car in the silent films. He is as proud as a peacock about the trick his arm can do. He is unique, all right, but I wish the doctors had fixed his elbow so that Uncle "Crank" could have been just a normal Uncle Frank. That way he wouldn't have to call attention to how different he is all the time.

SENTENCE WRITING

Go back to the sentences you wrote for the Sentence Writing exercise on p. 59 or p. 93, and revise them to eliminate any clichés, awkward phrasing, or wordiness.

Correcting for Parallel Structure

Your writing will be clearer and more memorable if you use parallel construction. That is, when you make any kind of list, put the items in similar form. If you write

> My favourite coffee drinks are lattes, mochas, and the ones with espresso.

the sentence lacks parallel structure. The items don't all have the same form. But if you write

> My favourite coffees are lattes, mochas, and espressos.

then the items are parallel. They are all single-word nouns. Or you could write

> I like drinks blended with milk, flavoured with chocolate, and made with espresso.

Again the sentence has parallel structure because all three descriptions are verbal phrases. Here are some more examples. Note how much easier it is to read the sentences with parallel construction.

LACKING PARALLEL CONSTRUCTION	**HAVING PARALLEL CONSTRUCTION**
I like to hike, to ski, and going sailing.	I like to hike, to ski, and to sail. (all "to ____" verbs)
The office has run out of pens, paper, ink cartridges, and we need more toner, too.	The office needs more pens, paper, ink cartridges, and toner. (all nouns)
They decided that they needed a change, that they could afford a new house, and wanted to move to Calgary.	They decided that they needed a change, that they could afford a new house, and that they wanted to move to Calgary. (all dependent clauses)

The supporting points in an outline should always be parallel. In the following brief outlines, the supporting points in the left-hand column are not parallel in structure. Those in the right-hand column are parallel.

NOT PARALLEL	**PARALLEL**
Food Irradiation	Food Irradiation
I. How is it good?	I. Benefits
A. Longer shelf life	A. Extends shelf life
B. Using fewer pesticides	B. Requires fewer pesticides
C. Kills bacteria	C. Kills bacteria

II. Concerns
    A. Nutritional value
    B. Consumers are worried
    C. Workers' safety

II. Concerns
    A. Lowers nutritional value
    B. Alarms consumers
    C. Endangers workers

Using parallel construction will make your writing more effective. Note the effective parallelism in these well-known quotations:

A place for everything and everything in its place.

Isabella Mary Beeton

I have been poor and I have been rich. Rich is better.

Sophie Tucker

The more the data banks record about each of us, the less we exist.

Marshall McLuhan

A Canadian I was born; a Canadian I will die.

John G. Diefenbaker

E X E R C I S E S

Most—but not all—of the following sentences lack parallel structure. In some, you will be able to cross out the part that is not parallel and write the correction above. Other sentences will need complete rephrasing.

Exercise 1

1. I was in Sudbury, Ontario, last fall, and that's when I paid a visit to Science North.

2. The educational features that the museum offers and the activities for children draw many visitors.

3. The late F. Jean MacLeod was the daughter of one of Sudbury's earliest pioneers, and established a trust that was used to fund Science North's butterfly gallery.

4. MacLeod's father worked as a geologist, assayer, prospector, and he was also a mining engineer.

5. Patients at the Northeastern Ontario Regional Cancer Centre can enter the butterfly gallery free of charge and benefit from its serene atmosphere.

6. Visitors to Science North find the exhibits informative, and they are also entertained.

7. Science North is famous for its visitor-friendly approach and exhibits that are interactive.

8. The museum is especially proud of its most popular attractions, such as the Climate Change Show, the 200-seat IMAX theatre, and something called the Virtual Voyages Adventure Ride.

9. The Climate Change Show uses stunning special effects to address the topic of global warming, and there is a humorous talking sheep as well.

10. Science North and the Ontario Science Centre in Toronto provide learning opportunities and entertainment for visitors of all ages.

Source: http://www.sciencenorth.on.ca

Exercise 2

1. The use of bar codes has a clear past but a future that is uncertain.

2. The bar-code scanner was first used on June 26, 1974, and the first product that it scanned was a pack of chewing gum.

3. That took place at one supermarket in Ohio, but since then the same company's bar-code business has grown to scan more than a billion items a day around the country.

4. The bar codes themselves had been used on products all the way back to the 1960s, but they were not used to add up a customer's bill at the checkout counter until that day in 1974.

5. Now the bar-code idea is spreading to other areas of item control.

6. Prisons track inmates, shipping companies scan railroad cars, hospitals verify blood samples, and even some cows are bar-coded by cattle ranchers to identify them.

7. Some people worry about the future use of bar codes and their possible misuse.

8. Several years ago, there was a rumour that governments might put bar codes on people's foreheads and then officials could keep track of these people for the rest of their lives.

9. Such a paranoid idea and one that is so far-fetched is usually not true.

10. But the possibilities of bar codes do make people wonder about how they will be used, where they will be used, and the reasons for their use in the years to come.

Sources: New York Times, June 27, 1999; *Wall Street Journal,* Apr. 19, 1999.

Exercise 3

1. I was washing my car two weeks ago, and that's when I noticed a few bees buzzing around the roof of my garage.

2. I didn't worry about it at the time, but it was something that I should have worried about.

3. As I drove into my driveway a week later, a whole swarm of bees flew up and down in front of my windshield.

4. The swarm wasn't that big, but the bees flying tightly together looked really frightening.

5. They flew in a pattern as if they were riding on a roller coaster or almost like waves.

6. I was glad that my wife and kids were away for the weekend.

7. There was nothing I could do but to wait in my car until they went away.

8. Finally, the bees flew straight up into the air and then disappeared.

9. Once inside my house, I opened the phone book and started to call a bee expert.

10. The bees had made a hive out of part of my garage roof, the expert said, but once I replace the lumber in that area, I should not be bothered with bees anymore.

Exercise 4

1. Leonard Cohen is a poet, novelist, and performer, and he has spent much of his career writing songs.

2. He published his first book of poetry in 1956, and was producing a large and respected body of work in subsequent years.

3. Visitors to the many websites devoted to Cohen and his work can read his poems, lyrics, and interviews and appreciate them.

4. Cohen has said that in order to write a novel, he needs a woman and children in his life, and that stability is essential, too.

5. Vocalist Jennifer Warnes was admiring Cohen's songs and produced a tribute album.

6. Cohen famously declined a Governor General's Award, earned a reputation as a ladies' man, and he has spent time in a Buddhist retreat.

7. One of his more recent artistic goals was to write, direct, and to score videos.

8. Cohen has collaborated on a rock opera movie, appeared on the TV show *Miami Vice,* has several Juno Awards, and travels extensively.

9. His most popular songs include "Suzanne," "Bird on a Wire," and many people also remember him for "Famous Blue Raincoat."

10. Many of Cohen's fans were surprised when he became a Zen Buddhist and was retiring to a California monastery.

Source: http://www.leonardcohen.com

Exercise 5

1. To cut down on fuel bills while cooking, consider the following energy-saving hints.

2. Avoid preheating your oven unless it is electric.

3. You should always cover pots when cooking.

4. Don't open the oven door to check on food.

5. You can use the oven light instead.

6. Many people use a flame that extends past the bottom of the pan, but don't do that; it's wasteful.

7. Follow the directions given in a recipe for the time of cooking and what temperature to cook at.

8. Prepare your whole meal in the oven or on top of the stove, not both.

9. It's very important to check all the burners and be sure they are off after use.

10. If you follow these suggestions, you will save money on your energy bills and you probably will also cook better meals.

PROOFREADING EXERCISE

Proofread the following paragraph about Canadian silent film star Mary Pickford and revise it to correct any errors in parallel structure.

Mary Pickford was born in Toronto in 1892, and in 1900 she joined the vaudeville circuit. In 1908, she went to Hollywood. There she worked with legendary filmmaker D.W. Griffith, and her specialty was "damsel in distress" roles. She became known to the public as "Little Mary," "America's Sweetheart," and she was also called "The Girl with Golden Hair." Among the films she starred in are *Rebecca of Sunnybrook Farm, Coquette,* and *The Little Darling* was one of her earliest. Her tremendous popularity gave her the clout she needed to dictate the terms of her contracts, develop her own production company, and she cofounded United Artists. In 1920, she married swashbuckling actor Douglas Fairbanks, who entertained movie audiences by swinging on ropes, jumping across high buildings, and sword play; they divorced in 1936. In her later years, Pickford donated many of her early films to the American Film Institute, received a lifetime achievement award from the Academy of Motion Picture Arts and Sciences, and she was active in promoting various charitable causes. She died of a stroke in 1979.

Source: Pickford: The Woman Who Made Hollywood (Macfarlane Walter & Ross, 1997).

SENTENCE WRITING

Write ten sentences that use parallel structure in a list or a pair of objects, actions, locations, or ideas. You may choose your own subject or describe a process that you carry out at your job.

Using Pronouns

Nouns name people, places, things, and ideas—such as *students, school, computers,* and *cyberspace*. Pronouns take the place of nouns to avoid repetition and to clarify meaning. Look at the following two sentences. Nouns are needlessly repeated in the first sentence, but the second uses pronouns.

> The boy's mother felt that the children at the party were too loud, so the boy's mother told the children that the party would have to end if the children didn't calm down.

> The boy's mother felt that the children at the party were too loud, so *she* told *them* that *it* would have to end if *they* didn't calm down.

In the second sentence, *she* replaces *mother,* *they* and *them* replace *children,* and *it* takes the place of *party*.

Of the many kinds of pronouns, the following cause the most difficulty because they include two ways of identifying the same person (or people), but only one form is correct in a given situation:

SUBJECT GROUP	OBJECT GROUP
I	me
he	him
she	her
we	us
they	them

Use a pronoun from the Subject Group in two instances:

1. Before a verb as a subject:

> *He* is my cousin. (*He* is the subject of the verb *is*.)

> *He* is taller than *I*. (The sentence is not written out in full. It means "*He* is taller than *I* am." *I* is the subject of the verb *am*.)

Whenever you see *than* or *as* in a sentence, ask yourself whether a verb is missing at the end of the sentence. Add the verb in both speaking and writing, and then you'll automatically use the correct pronoun. Instead of saying, "She's smarter than (I, me)," say, "She's smarter than I *am*." Also, instead of saying "She is as tall as (he, him)," say "She is as tall as he *is*."

2. After a linking verb (*is, am, are, was, were*) as a pronoun that renames the subject:

> The one who should apologize is *he.* (*He* is *the one who should apologize.* Therefore the pronoun from the Subject Group is used.)

> The winner of the lottery was *she.* (*She* was *the winner of the lottery.* Therefore the pronoun from the Subject Group is used.)

Modern usage allows some exceptions to this rule, however. For example, *It's me* and *It is her* (instead of the grammatically correct *It is I* and *It is she*) are common in spoken English.

Use pronouns from the Object Group for all other purposes. In the following sentence, *me* is not the subject, nor does it rename the subject. It follows a preposition; therefore, it comes from the Object Group.

> My boss went to lunch with Rachel and *me.*

A good way to tell whether to use a pronoun from the Subject Group or the Object Group is to leave out any extra name (and the word *and*). By leaving out *Rachel and,* you will say, *My boss went to lunch with me.* You would never say, *My boss went to lunch with I.*

> My father and *I* play chess on Sundays. (*I* play chess on Sundays.)

> *She* and her friends rented a video. (*She* rented a video.)

> We saw Joseph and *them* last night. (We saw *them* last night.)

> The teacher gave *us* students certificates. (Teacher gave *us* certificates.)

> The coach asked Raj and *me* to wash the benches. (Coach asked *me* to wash the benches.)

PRONOUN AGREEMENT

Just as subjects and verbs must agree, pronouns should agree with the words they refer to. If the word referred to is singular, the pronoun should be singular. If the noun referred to is plural, the pronoun should be plural.

> Each classroom has its own chalkboard.

The pronoun *its* refers to the singular noun *classroom* and therefore is singular.

> Both classrooms have their own chalkboards.

The pronoun *their* refers to the plural noun *classrooms* and therefore is plural.

The same rules that we use to maintain the agreement of subjects and verbs also apply to pronoun agreement. For instance, ignore any prepositional phrases that come between the word and the pronoun that takes its place.

The *box* of chocolates has lost *its* label.

Boxes of chocolates often lose *their* labels.

The *player* with the best concentration usually beats *her or his* opponent.

Players with the best concentration usually beat *their* opponents.

When a pronoun refers to more than one word joined by *and,* the pronoun is plural:

The *teacher* and the *tutors* eat *their* lunches at noon.

The *salt* and *pepper* were in *their* usual spots on the table.

However, when a pronoun refers to more than one word joined by *or,* the word closest to the pronoun determines its form:

Either the *teacher* or the *tutors* eat *their* lunches in the classroom.

Either the *tutors* or the teacher eats *her* lunch in the classroom.

Today many people try to avoid gender bias by writing sentences like the following:

If anyone wants help with the assignment, he or she can visit me in my office.

If anybody calls, tell him or her that I'll be back soon.

Somebody has left his or her pager in the classroom.

But those sentences are wordy and awkward. Therefore some people, especially in conversation, turn them into sentences that are not grammatically correct.

If anyone wants help with the assignment, they can visit me in my office.

If anybody calls, tell them that I'll be back soon.

Somebody has left their pager in the classroom.

Such ungrammatical sentences, however, are not necessary. It just takes a little thought to revise each sentence so that it avoids gender bias and is also grammatically correct:

Anyone who wants help with the assignment can visit me in my office.

Tell anybody who calls that I'll be back soon.

Somebody has left a pager in the classroom.

Probably the best way to avoid the awkward *he or she* and *him or her* is to make the words plural. Instead of writing, "Each actor was in his or her proper place on stage," write, "All the actors were in their proper places on stage," thus avoiding gender bias and still having a grammatically correct sentence.

Pronoun Reference

A pronoun replaces a noun to avoid repetition, but sometimes the pronoun sounds as if it refers to the wrong word in a sentence, causing confusion. Be aware that when you write a sentence, *you* know what it means, but your reader may not. What does this sentence mean?

The students tried to use the school's computers to access the Internet, but they were too slow, so they decided to go home.

Who or what was too slow, and who or what decided to go home? We don't know whether the two pronouns (both *they*) refer to the students or to the computers. One way to correct such a faulty reference is to use singular and plural nouns:

The students tried to use a school computer to access the Internet, but it was too slow, so they decided to go home.

Here's another sentence with a faulty reference:

Sylvie told her mother that she needed a haircut.

Who needed the haircut—Sylvie or her mother? One way to correct such a faulty reference is to use a direct quotation:

Sylvie told her mother, "You need a haircut."

Sylvie said, "Mom, I need a haircut."

Or you could always rephrase the sentence completely:

Sylvie noticed her mother's hair was sticking out in odd places, so she told her mother to get a haircut.

Another kind of faulty reference is a *which* clause that appears to refer to a specific word, but doesn't really.

I wasn't able to finish all the problems on the exam, which makes me worried.

The word *which* seems to replace exam, but it isn't the exam that is the cause of the worry. The sentence should read

I am worried that I wasn't able to finish all the problems on the exam.

The pronoun *it* causes its own reference problems. Look at this sentence, for example:

When replacing the ink cartridge in my printer, it broke, and I had to call the technician to come and fix it.

Did the printer or the cartridge break? Here is one possible correction:

The new ink cartridge broke when I was putting it in my printer, and I had to call the technician for help.

E X E R C I S E S

Exercise 1

Underline the correct pronoun. Remember the trick of leaving out the extra name to help you decide which pronoun to use. Use the correct grammatical form even though an alternative form may be acceptable in conversation.

1. My sister Maggie and (I, me) went shopping over the weekend.

2. I usually enjoy shopping more than (she, her).

3. This time, however, both (she and I, her and me) enjoyed ourselves.

4. Since Maggie is less style conscious than (I, me), she doesn't normally want to shop in certain stores.

5. Every time (she and I, her and me) have been shopping before, Maggie has just waited outside the trendy stores while I looked around.

6. But the one who was the most daring this weekend was (she, her).

7. Maggie may be more conservative than (I, me) most of the time, but she needed an impressive outfit for her upcoming high-school reunion.

8. Just between (you and me, you and I), I think she found it.

9. Maggie was thrilled when a salesperson came right up to (she and I, her and me) and said, "You're looking for the perfect outfit, aren't you?"

10. Instead of ignoring Maggie's clothing advice in the future, I will start listening to (she, her).

Exercises 2 and 3

Underline the pronoun that agrees with the word the pronoun replaces. If the correct answer is *his or her,* revise the sentence to eliminate the need for this awkward expression. Check your answers frequently as you go through these two exercises.

Exercise 2

1. I live a long way from the city centre and don't own a car, so I use public transportation and depend on (its, their) reliability.

2. Based on my experiences, I'd say the city's system of buses has (its, their) problems.

3. Each of the bus routes that I travel on my way to work falls behind (its, their) own schedule.

4. Many of the other passengers also transfer on (his or her, their) way to work.

5. One day last week, each of the passengers had to gather (his or her, their) belongings and leave the bus, even though it had not reached a scheduled stop.

6. Both the driver and the mechanic who came to fix the bus offered (his, their) apologies for making us late.

7. Once the bus was fixed, the passengers were allowed to bring (his or her, their) things back on board.

8. Everyone did (his or her, their) best to hide (his or her, their) annoyance from the driver because he had been so nice.

9. As every passenger stepped off the bus at the end of the line, the driver thanked (him or her, them) for (his or her, their) patience and understanding.

10. Sometimes it is the people within a system that makes (it, them) work after all.

Exercise 3

1. Last weekend's guided tour of several wineries was a treat for my friends and (I, me).

2. Each of the visitors who participated in the tour learned a great deal about (his or her, their) taste in wine.

3. Every member of the group had (his or her, their) opinion of the Cabernet Sauvignon, Pinot Noir, and Merlot wines.

4. My best friend and (I, me) definitely prefer dry wines to sweet ones.

5. When it comes to French wines, no one is more knowledgeable than (she, her).

6. Each of the wineries was very generous in (its, their) offerings.

7. All of the tour participants responded to (his or her, their) wine samples in different ways.

8. Many of the wineries that were part of the tour operate (its, their) own restaurant.

9. One owner gave my friends and (I, me) a few tips on how to select a good wine.

10. Wine from various producers in the Niagara Peninsula is often said to have (its, their) charm.

Exercise 4

Most—but not all—of the sentences in the next two sets aren't clear because we don't know what word the pronoun refers to. Revise such sentences, making the meaning clear. Since there are more ways than one to rewrite each sentence, yours may be as good as the ones at the back of the book. Just ask yourself whether the meaning is clear.

1. When guidance counsellors advise students, they help a lot.

2. Last year, our school counsellor had a meeting with Karima in her office.

3. Karima told her counsellor that she didn't know which college to apply to.

4. Karima's counsellor advised her to read a comprehensive guide to Canadian colleges.

5. Karima ordered the guide, and it arrived the next week.

6. Karima completed her college application, put the top back on her pen, and took it to the post office.

7. When the offer of admission to the college arrived in the mail, it delighted her.

8. Many students move into residences for their social life.

9. If you live in residence, it gives you an opportunity to meet more people.

10. Most colleges offer special services for people with disabilities, but they are not always adequate.

Exercise 5

1. George Chuvalo was a Canadian boxer who had many victories in the ring, which made him famous.

2. Muhammad Ali told him that he had a hard head.

3. Chuvalo was the first boxer to go fifteen rounds with Ali, and he was never knocked off his feet in his career.

4. Chuvalo was Canadian heavyweight boxing champion for twenty-one years, and it made him a legend.

5. Now sixty-five, Chuvalo is still fighting, but it doesn't take place in the ring.

6. He devoted his time to the fight against drugs after it claimed the lives of his wife and three of his sons.

7. Chuvalo saw firsthand how drug abuse affects people's health, and it sometimes never recovers.

8. When Chuvalo created his "Fight Against Drugs" website, it shed light on the problem of substance abuse.

9. Chuvalo speaks to students and parents in communities across North America, and they hear how drugs have affected his life.

10. In 1990, Chuvalo was inducted into the Canadian Sports Hall of Fame, which he says is less important than his fight against drugs.

Source: http://www.fightagainstdrugs.ca

PROOFREADING EXERCISE

The following paragraph contains errors in the use of pronouns. Find and correct the errors.

My friend Kevin and me went out the other day. We saw a movie at the new theatre complex down the block. After the cashier handed Kevin and I our tickets, we went into the lobby and were impressed with their decorations. Old movie posters lined the hallways to the theatres, and they were in really fancy gold frames. After the movie, I asked Kevin if he liked it. He said that it was the worst one he had ever been to. He told me that the parking was impossible, the screen was too small, and the seats were uncomfortable. He said that he would rather go to the place where we saw our last movie. At least it had a full-size screen and good sound, even if it wasn't as pretty as the new one.

SENTENCE WRITING

Write ten sentences about a conversation between you and someone else. Then check that your pronouns are grammatically correct, that they agree with the words they replace, and that references to specific nouns are clear.

Avoiding Shifts in Person

To understand what "person" means when using pronouns, imagine a conversation between two people about a third person. The first person speaks using "I, me, my . . ."; the second person would be called "you"; and when the two of them talked of a third person, they would say "he, she, they . . . ." You should never forget the idea of "person" if you remember it as a three-part conversation.

First person — *I, me, my, mine, we, us, our, ours*

Second person — *you, your, yours*

Third person — *he, him, his, she, her, hers, they, them, their, theirs, one, one's, anyone, anyone's*

> **NOTE:** All nouns (singular or plural) are third person.

You may use all three of these groups of pronouns in a paper, but don't shift from one group to another without good reason.

Wrong: Few people know how to manage *their* time. *One* need not be an efficiency expert to realize that *one* could get a lot more done if *he* budgeted *his* time. Nor do *you* need to work very hard to get more organized.

Better: *Everyone* should know how to manage *his or her* time. *One* need not be an efficiency expert to realize that *a person* could get a lot more done if *one* budgeted *one's* time. Nor does *one* need to work very hard to get more organized. (Too many *one*'s in a paragraph make it sound overly formal, and words such as *everyone* lead to the necessity of avoiding sexism by using *s/he* or *he or she*, etc. Sentences can be revised to avoid using either *you* or *one*.)

Best: Many of *us* don't know how to manage *our* time. *We* need not be efficiency experts to realize that *we* could get a lot more done if *we* budgeted *our* time. Nor do *we* need to work very hard to get more organized.

Often students write *you* in a paper when they don't really mean "you, the reader."

You wouldn't believe how many times I saw that movie.

Such sentences are always improved by getting rid of the *you*.

I saw that movie many times.

Use the second person only when you are actually referring to the reader.

You should try to find the main idea in each paragraph.

PROOFREADING EXERCISES

Which of the following student paragraphs shift *unnecessarily* between first-, second-, and third-person pronouns? In those that do, revise the sentences to eliminate such shifting, thus making the entire paragraph read smoothly. (First, read the paragraphs to determine whether unnecessary shifting takes place. One of the paragraphs is correct.)

1. I read an article about the first cloned sheep, whose name was Dolly. Dolly was cloned in 1996 from a six-year-old sheep, and scientists studied Dolly to see if she aged any differently than a "normal" sheep. Initially, they found that she seemed to be getting older faster than an uncloned animal, but the differences were visible only on a molecular level. From the outside, Dolly seemed perfectly average. Dolly, however, can no longer provide answers to the scientists' questions. She died on February 14, 2003, and left scientists wondering about the effects of cloning on animals. She had many babies of her own, but they reveal that nature may correct itself after cloning takes place. Some of Dolly's babies have her "older" molecules, and some have only brand new ones. Therefore, the future of cloning will be affected by continued studies of her offspring.

Source: *U.S. News & World Report,* June 7, 1999.

2. Communicating through e-mail has made people lose their manners. You used to get a letter with a polite salutation at the top, such as "Dear Sirs" or even "To whom it may concern," and with a signature or printed name at the bottom to tell us who sent it. And an old-fashioned letter had not only the sender's address but also your address on it too. Then there was the postmark to tell what town the letter was mailed from. Now, with different people using the same e-mail accounts and sending them from all over the world, you never know where your electronic mail comes from unless the person follows the old rules of correspondence. But many people writing e-mail don't include salutations or signatures. I miss the old days when people took more time on their correspondence.

3. Christopher Wolfe will always have a reason to be proud, and I bet you'll never guess what it is. When he was seven years old, Christopher discovered a new dinosaur, and scientists named it after him. They called it *Zuniceratops christopheri*. This unknown species of dinosaur had two horns, one over each eye. You might have heard of other discoveries of dinosaurs with horns, but the one whose bones Christopher found lived twenty million years earlier than any others. Christopher's father, Douglas Wolfe, was with him when he spotted the fossil in the Arizona/ New Mexico desert. Douglas, a paleontologist, knew right away that his son's find was genuine. However, the kids at school had a hard time believing Christopher when he came in the next school day and told his classmates that he had discovered a new dinosaur species.

Source: People, Nov. 2, 1998.

REVIEW OF SENTENCE STRUCTURE ERRORS

One sentence in each pair contains an error. Read both sentences carefully before you decide. Then write the letter of the incorrect sentence in the blank. Try to name the error and correct it if you can. You may find any of these errors:

awk	awkward phrasing
cliché	overused expression
dm	dangling modifier
frag	fragment
mm	misplaced modifier
pro	incorrect pronoun
pro agr	pronoun agreement error
pro ref	pronoun reference error
ro	run-on sentence
shift	shift in person
s/v agr	subject/verb agreement error
wordy	wordiness
//	not parallel

1. ___ **A.** I am sick and tired of news programs that report only gossip.

   B. We heard two different lectures on the death penalty.

2. ___ **A.** Each of the pieces of cake were the same size.

   B. The teacher gave Jane and me extra credit for the results of our Internet research.

3. ___ **A.** When the blizzard struck, all flights into the area were cancelled.

   B. After a quick phone call, the dog next door was quiet.

4. ___ **A.** For lunch, we ate tuna sandwiches and potato chips.

   B. One of my ankles was sore after playing tennis all afternoon.

5. ___ **A.** The customers filled out suggestion cards they contained some good ideas.

   B. I can't imagine Sigmund Freud at an amusement park.

6. ___ **A.** The thing is, I never really have been interested in politics.

   B. The weather should be perfect in March.

7. ___ **A.** I still have trouble knowing when to use commas and semicolons.

   B. Everyone at the party brought their swimsuits.

8. ___ **A.** I enjoy watching videos at home because you can stop the tape and eat a snack whenever you want.

   B. Shopping over the Internet is easier now than it ever was.

9. ___ **A.** The last one to get home that night was she.

   B. We stared at a tank of goldfish waiting for a table at the new restaurant.

10. ___ **A.** The combination to my art locker is a secret between the art department and me.

   B. I wouldn't take that class if it were the last class on earth.

11. ___ **A.** We applied for a scholarship, a loan, and to be accepted into the honours program.

   B. Few people know how to reduce stress.

12. ___ **A.** Many people wondering about what appears to be the shape of a face found on Mars.

   B. Many employees who use computers believe that their e-mail should be private.

13. ___ **A.** Two girls and a boy were playing at the sink when I began my observation.

   B. These studies of children's behaviour has to be done carefully.

14. ___ **A.** Trading collectible cards and toys is a new hobby for many young people.

   B. It is very difficult to know just what is and is not valuable, however.

15. ___ **A.** Either the students or the tutor is correct.

   B. Either the students or the tutor are correct.

PROOFREADING EXERCISE

Find and correct the sentence structure errors in the following essay.

Mother Tells All

The most memorable lessons I have learned about myself have come from my own children. A mother is always on display she has nowhere to hide. And children are like parrots. Whatever they hear her say will be repeated again. If I change my mind about anything, you can be sure they will repeat back every word I uttered out of my mouth.

For example, last summer I told my kids that I was going to go to an exercise class and lose about forty pounds. Well, I lost some of the weight, and I did go to that exercise class. But as soon as I lost weight, I felt empty like a balloon losing air. I felt that I did not want to lose any more weight or do exercise anymore. I thought that my children would accept what I had decided.

When I stopped, the first thing one of my sons said was, "Mom, you need to go back to exercise class." Then they all started telling me what to eat all the time and I felt horrible about it. I had given up these things because I wanted to, but my words were still being repeated to me like an alarm clock going off without stopping. Finally, my kids ran out of steam and got bored with the idea of my losing weight. Once in a while, one of them still make a joke about my "attempt" to lose weight it hurts me that they don't understand.

The lesson that I have learned from this experience is that, if I am not planning on finishing something, I won't tell my children about it. They will never let me forget.

Punctuation and Capital Letters

Period, Question Mark, Exclamation Point, Semicolon, Colon, Dash

Every mark of punctuation should help the reader. Here are the rules for six marks of punctuation. The first three you have known for a long time and probably have no trouble with. The one about semicolons you learned when you studied independent clauses (p. 74). The ones about the colon and the dash may be less familiar.

Put a period (.) at the end of a sentence and after most abbreviations.

> The students elected Ms. Daniels to represent the class.

> Tues.   etc.   Jan.   Ph.D.   Ave.

Put a question mark (?) after a direct question but not after an indirect one.

> Will the exam be an open-book or a closed-book test? (direct)

> I wonder if the exam will be an open-book or a closed-book test. (indirect)

Put an exclamation point (!) after an expression that shows strong emotion. Use it sparingly.

> I can't believe I did so well on my first exam!

Put a semicolon (;) between two independent clauses in a sentence *unless* they are joined by one of the connecting words *for, and, nor, but, or, yet, so*.

> My mother cosigned for a loan; now I have my own car.

Some careers go in and out of fashion; however, people will always need doctors.

To be sure that you are using a semicolon correctly, see if a period and capital letter can be used in its place. If they can, you are putting the semicolon in the right spot.

My mother cosigned for a loan. Now I have my own car.

Some careers go in and out of fashion. However, people will always need doctors.

Put a colon (:) after a complete statement that introduces something: one item, a list, a direct question, or a quotation.

The company announced its Employee-of-the-Month: Minh Tran. (The sentence before the colon introduces the name that follows.)

In London, we plan to visit the following famous sites: the Tower of London, Piccadilly Circus, and Madame Tussaud's Wax Museum. (Here *the following famous sites* ends a complete statement and introduces the list that follows, so a colon is used.)

In London, we plan to visit the Tower of London, Piccadilly Circus, and Madame Tussaud's Wax Museum. (Here *we plan to visit* does not end a complete statement, so no colon is used.)

All the kids in the class were wondering about the same thing: why is the sky blue? (Here *All the kids in the class were wondering about the same thing* is a complete statement that introduces a direct question, so a colon is used.)

All the kids in the class were wondering why the sky was blue. (Here *All the kids in the class were wondering* is not a complete statement, so a colon is not used.)

Thoreau had this to say about time: "Time is but the stream I go a-fishin in." (*Thoreau had this to say about time* is a complete statement. Therefore, a colon comes after it before adding the quotation.)

Thoreau said, "Time is but the stream I go a-fishin in." (*Thoreau said* is not a complete statement. Therefore, a colon does not come after it.)

Use a dash (—) to indicate an abrupt change of thought or to emphasize what follows. Use it sparingly.

I found out today—or was it yesterday?—that I have inherited a fortune.

We have exciting news for you—we're moving!

E X E R C I S E S

Add to these sentences the necessary punctuation (periods, question marks, exclamation points, semicolons, colons, and dashes). The commas used within the sentences are correct and do not need to be changed.

Exercise 1

1. Wasn't the weather beautiful today

2. I wonder when the autumn breezes will start to blow

3. It still felt like summer at least while the sun was shining

4. At sunset the white, wispy clouds turned pink then the blue sky behind them started to turn gold

5. It was breathtaking

6. The only hint of fall came after the sun went down the temperature dropped about ten degrees in an hour

7. I have always thought of summer as my favourite season however, today may have convinced me to switch to fall

8. I never noticed that the leaves are so beautiful even after they have dropped from the trees

9. I walked through the park and collected a bouquet of huge autumn leaves it was fun

10. I hope tomorrow will be as pretty as today

Exercise 2

1. Nancy Cartwright is a well-known actress on television however, we never see her when she is acting

2. Cartwright is famous for playing one part the voice of Bart Simpson

3. Besides her career as the most mischievous Simpson, Cartwright is married and has children of her own a boy and a girl

4. Wouldn't it be strange if your mother had Bart Simpson's voice

5. Cartwright admits that she made her own share of trouble in school

6. But the similarities between her and her famous character end there

7. Bart is perpetually ten years old Cartwright is in her forties

8. Bart is a boy Cartwright is obviously a woman

9. It's no surprise that Cartwright is very popular with her children's friends

10. When they yell for her to "Do Bart Do Bart" she declines with Bart's favourite saying "No way, man"

Source: People, Dec. 14, 1998.

Exercise 3

1. I have just discovered the fun of fondue

2. The story of the invention of fondue goes this way a farmer's wife accidentally dropped a chunk of cheese on the warming pan near the fire, and after mopping up the liquefied cheese with a piece of bread, she popped the morsel in her mouth and decided to make a meal of it

3. Since its discovery, fondue has always been a process rather than a product there are special pans to melt the cheese, fuel to keep it warm, and forks to hold the bread or meat to dip in it

4. I now understand why fondue was especially popular in the 1960s and 1970s

5. People then probably enjoyed the ritual of sitting down together and participating in a meal eaten from one pot

6. And the ingredients of bread and cheese couldn't be simpler, could they

7. There is also a rule that we might find distasteful now but thirty years ago must have seemed like fun according to the book *Fabulous Fondues,* the person who lost a piece of bread in the fondue pot had to pay a forfeit

8. The forfeits were listed as follows if a man lost the cube of bread, he owed the hostess a bottle of wine however, if a woman lost the cube of bread, she had to give one of the men at the table a kiss

9. Of course, other foods can be substituted for the traditional chunks of bread boiled potatoes, celery sticks, pretzels, crackers, mushrooms, and even nuts

10. I plan to have a fondue party as soon as I possibly can

Exercise 4

1. In the 1500s, early French settlers became friendly with the Huron they even joined forces with the Huron to fight the Iroquois

2. How many Canadians know that the North American phase of the Seven Years' War was called the French and Indian War

3. Passed in 1867, the British North America Act created the Dominion of Canada with the union of four provinces Ontario, Quebec, New Brunswick, and Nova Scotia

4. During World War II, Prime Minister William Lyon Mackenzie King introduced conscription it worsened relations between Anglophones and Francophones in Canada

5. Quebec's opposition to conscription was even stronger during World War I nevertheless, the Conservative government of Robert Borden passed the controversial Military Services Act in 1917

6. The introduction of conscription during World War I helped to re-elect the Borden government however, as a military measure, it was a failure

7. Pierre Berton's *The National Dream* and *The Last Spike* two books that were turned into a successful CBC drama-documentary series dealt with the building of the Canadian Pacific Railway

8. The subject allowed Berton to take full advantage of his greatest strength a formidable gift for storytelling

9. In an earlier book, Berton wrote about the Klondike gold rush of 1897–98 an event that temporarily boosted the population of the new town of Dawson

10. In 2003, the wildly prolific Berton published his forty-ninth book

Source: The Canadian Encyclopedia (McClelland & Stewart, 1999).

Exercise 5

1. Here are some facts you may or may not! know about Canada

2. Did you know, for example, that Canada's population is over thirty million

3. Canada has two official languages English and French

4. Its highest mountain is Mount Logan in the Yukon Territory some people wanted to rename it Mount Trudeau to commemorate the former prime minister, but the original name remains

5. Canada's longest bridge is Confederation Bridge it connects New Brunswick and Prince Edward Island

6. Canada's population except near its southern border with the United States is very sparse

7. Isn't Baffin Island the largest island in Canada

8. Canada's northernmost point is on Ellesmere Island its southernmost point is Middle Island in Lake Erie

9. According to a recent census, the majority of Canadians are Catholic and Protestant interestingly, 4 percent of Canadians are practising Hindus

10. Canada has only one bordering country the United States

PROOFREADING EXERCISE

Can you find the five errors in this student paragraph?

The ingredients you will need for a lemon meringue pie are: lemon juice, eggs, sugar, cornstarch, flour, butter, water, and salt. First you combine flour, salt, butter, and water for the crust and bake until lightly brown then you mix and cook the lemon juice, egg yolks, sugar, cornstarch, butter, and water for the filling. Once the filling is poured into the cooked crust; you whip the meringue. Meringue is made of egg whites and sugar! Pile the meringue on top of the lemon filling; place the pie in the hot oven for a few minutes, and you'll have the best lemon meringue pie you've ever tasted.

SENTENCE WRITING

Write ten sentences of your own that use periods, question marks, exclamation points, semicolons, colons, and dashes correctly. Imitate the examples used in the explanations if necessary. Write about an interesting assignment you have done for a class, or choose your own topic.

Comma Rules 1, 2, and 3

Commas and other pieces of punctuation guide the reader through sentence structures in the same way that signs guide drivers on the highway. Imagine what effects misplaced or incorrect road signs would have. Yet students often randomly place commas in their sentences. Try not to use a comma unless you know there is a need for it. Memorize this rhyme about comma use: *when in doubt, leave it out*.

Among all of the comma rules, six are most important. Learn these six rules, and your writing will be easier to read. You have already studied the first rule on page 75.

1. Put a comma before *for, and, nor, but, or, yet, so* (remember them as the *fanboys*) when they connect two independent clauses.

> The neighbours recently bought a minivan, and now they go everywhere together.

> We wrote our paragraphs in class today, but the teacher forgot to collect them.

> She was recently promoted, so she has moved to a better office.

If you use a comma alone between two independent clauses, the result is an error called a **comma splice.**

> The ice cream looked delicious, it tasted good too. (comma splice)

> The ice cream looked delicious, and it tasted good too. (correct)

Before using a comma, be sure that the *fanboys* word connects two independent clauses. The following sentence is merely one independent clause with one subject and two verbs. Therefore, no comma should be used.

> The ice cream looked delicious and tasted good too.

2. Use a comma to separate three or more items in a series.

> Students in the literature class are reading short stories, poems, and plays.

> On Saturday I did my laundry, washed my car, and cleaned my room.

Occasionally, writers leave out the comma before the *and* connecting the last two items of a series, but it is more common to use it to separate all the items equally.

Some words work together and don't need commas between them even though they do make up a kind of series.

> The team members wanted to wear their brand-new green uniforms.

> The bright white sunlight made the room glow.

To see whether a comma is needed between words in a series, ask yourself whether *and* could be used naturally between them. It would sound all right to say *short stories and poems and plays;* therefore, commas are used. But it would not sound right to say *brand and new and green uniforms* or *bright and white sunlight;* therefore, no commas are used.

If an address or date is used in a sentence, put a comma after every item, including the last.

> My father was born on August 19, 1941, in Saint John, New Brunswick, and grew up there.

> She lived in Vancouver, British Columbia, for two years.

When only the month and year are used in a date, no commas are needed.

> She graduated in May 1985 from McGill University.

3. Put a comma after an introductory expression (it may be a word, a phrase, or a dependent clause) or before a comment or question that is tacked on at the end.

> Finally, he was able to get through to his insurance company.

> During his last performance, the actor fell and broke his foot.

> Once I have finished my homework, I will call you.

> He said he needed to ruminate, whatever that means.

> The new chairs aren't very comfortable, are they?

E X E R C I S E S

Add commas to the following sentences according to the first three comma rules. Some sentences may not need any commas, and some may need more than one. Any other punctuation already in the sentences is correct. Check your answers after the first set.

Exercise 1

1. For the first time in my life I feel like an adult.

2. I am taking general education classes in college and I am getting good grades.

3. Even though I receive some financial aid I mostly support myself.

4. I have a job a car and an apartment of my own.

5. When I am ready I plan to transfer to a university.

6. After I complete the course work at community college my parents will be proud of me but they will be even prouder when I get my degree.

7. I know that my father wants me to major in business yet my mother wants me to be a teacher.

8. Eventually it will be my decision.

9. Although I don't see myself in front of a class full of students I have always loved the school environment.

10. And it's easier to see myself there than in front of a room full of salespeople.

Exercise 2

1. When people say they are interested in astrology they are often ridiculed.

2. Although they scoff at astrology skeptics invariably know what sign they were born under.

3. And most of them also know that there are twelve signs in the zodiac that there are four elements and that each sign lasts about thirty days.

4. Aries Leo and Sagittarius are known as the fire signs.

5. Even though many of us don't take astrology seriously every major newspaper carries a daily astrology column.

6. Superstitions are still widespread for we tend to hold onto childhood fears and wishes.

7. The belief that the time and place of one's birth can have a profound influence on one's destiny persists in both Western and Eastern cultures.

8. If you were born under a water sign like Cancer Scorpio or Pisces an astrologer might describe you as strong emotional and creative.

9. A person born under Sagittarius has the same zodiacal sign as Ludwig van Beethoven Winston Churchill and Jane Austen.

10. Most of us don't believe that our lives are influenced by the positions and movements of the stars and planets but the notion of fate entertains us all the same.

Exercise 3

1. If you have studied Canadian history you may know that Canada has had twenty-one prime ministers so far.

2. Lester Pearson is remembered most for serving as president of the UN General Assembly winning the Nobel Peace Prize and introducing the new Canadian flag.

3. R.B. Bennett's legacy is not as positive for he was in power during the Depression.

4. Among Canada's first three prime ministers—John A. Macdonald Alexander Mackenzie and Joseph Abbott—only Macdonald is well remembered today.

5. Interestingly Joseph Abbott was the first prime minister to be born in Canada.

6. Canada has had four French-Canadian prime ministers: Wilfrid Laurier Louis St. Laurent Pierre Trudeau and Jean Chrétien.

7. William Lyon Mackenzie King had an unconventional private life yet he dominated Canada's political landscape for almost three decades.

8. Even though she was in power for only a few months Kim Campbell had the distinction of being Canada's first woman prime minister.

9. Macdonald Laurier and Trudeau each served as prime minister for more than fifteen years.

10. In contrast Sir Charles Tupper and John Turner each served for just over two months.

Source: The Canadian Encyclopedia (McClelland & Stewart, 1999).

Exercise 4

1. People used to think that emeralds had magical powers.

2. They were supposed to cure disease lengthen life and protect innocence.

3. Part of their appeal was their rarity for emeralds are even rarer than diamonds.

4. Geologists have been mystified by emeralds because they are produced through a unique process—the blending of chromium vanadium and beryllium.

5. These are substances that almost never meet nor do they often combine—except in emeralds.

6. In South Africa Pakistan and Brazil emeralds were created by intrusions of granite millions to billions of years ago.

7. These areas are known for their beautiful gems but emeralds from Colombia are larger greener and more sparkling.

8. Scientists believe that the difference lies in the makeup of the sedimentary rock in Colombia.

9. Instead of the granite found in other emerald-rich countries the predominant substance in Colombia is black shale.

10. Even though these lustrous green gems can now be synthesized a real emerald always contains a trapped bubble of fluid and this minuscule natural imperfection is known in the gem business as a "garden."

Source: Discover, May 1999.

Exercise 5

1. During his lifetime Sir Frederick Grant Banting was voted most famous living Canadian in several polls.

2. Along with Charles Herbert Best Banting is best remembered for his discovery of insulin.

3. Banting and Best received support for their research from the University of Toronto and it was there that they made their famous discovery.

4. As a result of his discovery Banting received the Nobel Prize in medicine and he gave half his prize money to Best.

5. Banting wanted to develop a procedure to control diabetes in humans so he ran an experiment on a dog named Maggie.

6. First he tied off the dog's pancreatic ducts.

7. The dog went into a coma and Banting revived it with insulin taken from a cow.

8. After only twenty minutes the dog was walking again.

9. Although Banting received the Nobel Prize in 1923 he was not knighted until 1934.

10. For people with diabetes Banting's discovery amounts to a new lease on life.

Source: http://www.discoveryofinsulin.com

PROOFREADING EXERCISE

Apply the first three comma rules to the following paragraph.

When Niels Rattenborg studied the brains of mallard ducks he made an interesting discovery. Rattenborg wondered how ducks protected themselves as they slept. The ducks slept in rows and these rows were the secret to their defence. To his surprise Rattenborg found that the two ducks on the ends of the row did something special with the sides of their heads facing away from the row. Instinctively the ducks on the edge kept one eye open and one half of their brains awake as they slept. The rest of the ducks slept with both eyes closed and both sides of their brains inactive. The two guard ducks were able to frame the ducks in the middle watch for danger and sleep almost as soundly as their neighbours.

Source: Discover, May 1999.

SENTENCE WRITING

Combine the following sets of sentences in different ways using all of the first three comma rules. You may need to reorder the details and change the phrasing.

I am taking a yoga class.

It's more fun than I expected it to be.

I get home from school.

I do my homework.

I eat dinner.

I watch a little television.

I go to sleep.

Grant and Gretchen don't know what to do.

They are getting married.

Grant's last name is Ketchem.

Gretchen doesn't want to be known as Gretchen Ketchem.

She might keep her maiden name instead.

Comma Rules 4, 5, and 6

The next three comma rules all involve using a pair of commas to enclose information that is not needed in a sentence—information that could be taken out of the sentence without affecting its meaning. Two commas are used—one before and one after—to signal unnecessary words, phrases, and clauses.

4. Put commas around the name of a person spoken to.

> Did you know, Danielle, that you left your knapsack at the library?

> We regret to inform you, Mr. Chen, that your policy has been cancelled.

5. Put commas around expressions that interrupt the flow of the sentence (such as *however, moreover, therefore, of course, by the way, on the other hand, I believe, I think*).

> I know, of course, that I have missed the deadline.

> They will try, however, to use the rest of their time wisely.

> Today's exam, I think, is only a practice test.

Read the preceding sentences aloud, and you'll hear how those expressions interrupt the flow of the sentence. But sometimes such expressions flow smoothly into the sentence and don't need commas around them.

> Of course he checked to see if their plane had been delayed.

> We therefore decided to stay out of it.

> I think you made the right decision.

Remember that when one of the previous expressions (*however*, etc.) joins two independent clauses, that expression needs a semicolon before it. It may also have a comma after it, especially if there seems to be a pause before the rest of the sentence continues. (See p. 74.)

> The bus was late; *however,* we still made it to the museum before it closed.

> I am improving my study habits; *furthermore,* I am getting better grades.

> She was interested in journalism; *therefore,* she took a job at a local newspaper.

> I spent hours studying for the test; *finally,* I felt prepared.

Thus words like *however* or *therefore* may be used in three ways:

1. as an interrupter (commas around it)

2. as a word or expression that flows into the sentence (no commas needed)

3. as a connector between two independent clauses (semicolon before and often a comma after)

6. Put commas around additional information that is not needed in a sentence.

Such information may be interesting, but the subject and main idea of the sentence would be clear without it. In the following sentence

Maxine Taylor, who organized the fundraiser, will introduce the candidates.

the clause *who organized the fundraiser* is not needed in the sentence. Without it, we still know exactly who the sentence is about and what she is going to do: Maxine Taylor will introduce the candidates. Therefore, the additional information is set off from the rest of the sentence by commas to show that it could be left out. But in the following sentence

The woman who organized the fundraiser will introduce the candidates.

The clause *who organized the fundraiser* is needed in the sentence. Without it, the sentence would read: The woman will introduce the candidates. We would have no idea which woman. The clause *who organized the fundraiser* couldn't be left out because it tells us which woman. Therefore, commas are not used around it. In this sentence

Hamlet, Shakespeare's famous play, has been made into a movie many times.

the additional information *Shakespeare's famous play* could be left out, and we would still know the main meaning of the sentence: *Hamlet* has been made into a movie many times. Therefore, the commas surround the added material to show that it could be omitted. But in this sentence

Shakespeare's famous play *Hamlet* has been made into a movie many times.

the title of the play is necessary. Without it, the sentence would read: Shakespeare's famous play has been made into a movie many times. We would have no idea which of Shakespeare's famous plays was being discussed. Therefore, the title couldn't be left out, and commas are not used around it.

To determine whether to use commas with additional information in a sentence, simply ask yourself whether the sentence needs that information in order to make sense. If the sentence does *not* need the information, use commas.

EXERCISES

Add any necessary commas to these sentences according to Comma Rules 4, 5, and 6. Delete any commas that are unnecessary. Some sentences may be correct.

Exercise 1

1. This year's Thanksgiving dinner I think was better than last year's.

2. I think this year's Thanksgiving dinner was better than last year's.

3. It was, certainly, more entertaining this year.

4. Certainly it was more entertaining this year.

5. The guest, who brought the apple pie, sang karaoke with our mom after dinner.

6. My sister's new boyfriend who brought the apple pie sang karaoke with our mom after dinner.

7. Uncle Ken the person responsible for basting the turkey did a great job; it was moist and delicious.

8. The person who was responsible for basting the turkey did a great job; it was moist and delicious.

9. The gravy however was better last year.

10. However the gravy was better last year.

Exercise 2

1. We trust of course that people who get their driver's licences know how to drive.

2. Of course we trust that people, who get their driver's licences, know how to drive.

3. The people who test drivers for their licences make the streets safer for all of us.

4. Mr. Kraft who tests drivers for their licences makes the streets safer for all of us.

5. We may therefore understand when we fail the driving test ourselves.

6. Therefore we may understand when we fail the driving test ourselves.

7. The driver's seat we know is a place of tremendous responsibility.

8. We know that the driver's seat is a place of tremendous responsibility.

9. We believe, that no one should take that responsibility lightly.

10. No one we believe should take that responsibility lightly.

Exercise 3

1. The writing teacher Ms. Nakamura has published several of her own short stories.

2. The Ms. Gonzales who teaches writing is not the Ms. Gonzales who teaches history.

3. My daughter's friend Harry doesn't get along with her best friend Jenny.

4. My daughter's best friend Jenny doesn't get along with one of her other friends Harry.

5. The tiger which is a beautiful and powerful animal symbolizes freedom.

6. The tiger that was born in September is already on display at the zoo.

7. The students who helped set up the chairs were allowed to sit in the front row.

8. Kim and Teresa who helped set up the chairs were allowed to sit in the front row.

9. My car which had a tracking device was easy to find when it was stolen.

10. A car, that has a tracking device, is easier to find if it's stolen.

Exercise 4

1. Wayne Gretzky born in Brantford, Ontario has become one of the best-known figures in sports history.

2. "The Great One" as he is known by his many fans was the first NHL player to score more than two hundred points in one season.

3. Gretzky grew up idolizing Gordie Howe who has been called the finest athlete ever to play hockey.

4. An equally important role model was Gretzky's father Walter.

5. Gretzky played for the Los Angeles Kings, the St. Louis Blues, and the New York Rangers later in his career.

6. His greatest achievements of course came during his years with the Edmonton Oilers.

7. In 1988, Gretzky left the team that he had led to four Stanley Cup championships.

8. His marriage to actress Janet Jones which also took place in 1988 was described in the press as "Canada's Royal Wedding."

9. Gretzky and the late actor-comedian John Candy were co-owners of a Canadian football team the Toronto Argonauts.

10. "The Great One" who retired from professional hockey in 1999 was inducted into the Hockey Hall of Fame.

Source: http://www.geocities.com/yasmine7399/bio.html

Exercise 5

1. Zippo lighters the only domestic lighters that can still be refilled are highly useful tools and highly prized collectibles.

2. A Zippo that was made in 1933 and that has the "Patent Pending" mark on it could sell for as much as $10,000 even though it cost less than $2 when it was made.

3. The value of Zippo lighters is well known in Guthrie, Oklahoma home of the National Lighter Museum.

4. Zippos have always been special to soldiers who have often had to rely on the flame from their Zippo to warm food or light a fire.

5. There are even those who claim that a Zippo in their pocket saved their life by deflecting bullets aimed at them during battle.

6. There have been many special edition Zippos made to celebrate an event—the first moon landing for example.

7. Eric Clapton famed guitarist and songwriter used a clicking Zippo as an instrument in a song he wrote for the movie *Lethal Weapon 2*.

8. George G. Blaisdell the man responsible for distributing, naming, and refining the Zippo as we know it died in the late 1970s, but he cared about his customers.

9. All Zippo lighters come with a lifetime guarantee which covers the lighters' inner workings but not the outer finish.

10. The Zippo Repair Clinic which fixes around a thousand lighters a day refunds any money sent by the customer.

Source: Smithsonian, Dec. 1998.

PROOFREADING EXERCISE

Insert the necessary commas into this paragraph according to Comma Rules 4, 5, and 6.

Roberta Bondar who was born in Sault Ste. Marie, Ontario is best known as the first Canadian woman in space. She attended university with the goal of becoming a medical doctor specifically a neurologist. She was admitted to the Royal College of Physicians and Surgeons of Canada in 1981 and studied at Tufts-New England Medical Center located in Boston. Bondar was one of only six applicants chosen from a field of over four thousand to be accepted into the newly formed Canadian Astronaut Program in 1983. Her lifelong dream of exploring space became a reality in 1992 when she flew aboard the space shuttle *Discovery* which was the third shuttle added to the Kennedy Space Center fleet. Bondar wrote about her experiences in space in the book *Touching the Earth* published in 1994. She has received numerous honours during her career including the Order of Canada, the NASA Space Medal, and induction into the Canadian Medical Hall of Fame.

Source: http://www.robertabondar.ca

SENTENCE WRITING

Combine the following sets of sentences in different ways using Comma Rules 4, 5, and 6. Try to combine each set in a way that needs commas and in a way that doesn't need commas. You may reorder the details and change the phrasing. Compare your answers with those at the back of the book.

Las Vegas Nevada is a city famous for its casinos.

Las Vegas also has lots of little chapels.

Some people choose to get married there.

I think.

She has a black belt in karate.

My roommate received scholarship money.

Her name is Barbara.

She thought that she had to pay back the scholarship money.

REVIEW OF THE COMMA

SIX COMMA RULES

1. Put a comma before *for, and, nor, but, or, yet, so* when they connect two independent clauses.

2. Put a comma between three or more items in a series.

3. Put a comma after an introductory expression or before an afterthought.

4. Put commas around the name of a person spoken to.

5. Put commas around an interrupter, like *however* or *therefore*.

6. Put commas around unnecessary additional information.

REVIEW EXERCISE

Add the missing commas, and identify which one of the six comma rules applies in the brackets at the *end* of each sentence. Each of the six sentences illustrates a different rule.

I'm writing you this reminder Tracy to be sure that you don't forget our plans to visit the zoo this Saturday. [ ] I know we're good friends but lately you have let our plans slip your mind. [ ] When we were supposed to go to the flea market last week you forgot all about it. [ ] I'm taking this opportunity therefore to refresh your memory. [ ] I can't wait to see the polar bears the gorillas the giraffes and the elephants. [ ] And I have made special plans for a behind-the-scenes tour of several of the exhibits by Max Bronson the zoo's public relations officer. [ ] See you Saturday!

SENTENCE WRITING

Write at least one sentence of your own to demonstrate each of the six comma rules.

Quotation Marks and Italics/Underlining

Put quotation marks around a direct quotation (the exact words of a speaker) but not around an indirect quotation.

The officer said, "Please show me your driver's licence." (a direct quotation)

The officer asked to see my driver's licence. (an indirect quotation)

John Keats said, "Heard melodies are sweet, but those unheard are sweeter." (a direct quotation)

John Keats said that the melodies that can be heard are sweet, but those that cannot be heard are even sweeter. (an indirect quotation)

If the speaker says more than one sentence, quotation marks are used before and after the entire speech.

She said, "One of your brake lights is out. You need to take care of the problem right away."

If the quotation begins the sentence, the words telling who is speaking are set off with a comma unless a question mark or an exclamation point is needed.

"I didn't even know it was broken," I said.

"Do you have any questions?" she asked.

"You mean I can go!" I yelled.

"Yes, consider this just a warning," she said.

Each of the preceding quotations begins with a capital letter. But when a quotation is broken, the second part doesn't begin with a capital letter unless it's a new sentence.

"If you knew how much time I spent on the essay," the student said, "you would give me an A."

"A chef might work on a meal for days," the teacher replied. "That doesn't mean the results will taste good."

Put quotation marks around the titles of short stories, poems, songs, essays, TV program episodes, or other short works.

I couldn't sleep after I read "Friend of My Youth," a short story by Alice Munro.

My favourite Gordon Lightfoot song is "Early Morning Rain."

We had to read George Orwell's essay "A Hanging" for my English class.

Jerry Seinfeld's troubles in "The Puffy Shirt" episode are some of the funniest moments in TV history.

Italicize **titles of longer works such as books, newspapers, magazines, plays, record albums or CDs, movies, or TV or radio series.**

The Handmaid's Tale is a novel by Margaret Atwood.

I read about the latest discovery of dinosaur footprints in *Maclean's*.

Gone with the Wind was rereleased in movie theatres in 1998.

My mother watches *Canada AM* on TV every morning.

You may need to underline instead of italicizing if you are working on a typewriter or writing by hand. Just be sure to use the same method consistently throughout your paper.

The Handmaid's Tale is a novel by Margaret Atwood.

I read about the latest discovery of dinosaur footprints in Maclean's.

Gone with the Wind was rereleased in movie theatres in 1998.

My mother watches Canada AM on TV every morning.

E X E R C I S E S

Punctuate the quotations, and italicize or put quotation marks around each title.

Exercise 1

1. Robertson Davies' novels Fifth Business, The Manticore, and World of Wonders describe life in small-town Canada.

2. Is there such a thing as a Canadian identity my English teacher asked.

3. Even though I think the Canadian identity does exist a student replied I don't believe it's very easy to define.

4. Given the Canadian appetite for American courtroom dramas like Law and Order, it's not surprising that some of us think the Fifth Amendment is part of our own Constitution.

5. Our most popular reality show, Canadian Idol, is a spinoff of its U.S. counterpart, American Idol.

6. Many Canadians read Maclean's in waiting rooms but subscribe to Time or Newsweek.

7. Margaret Atwood said People put down Canadian literature and ask us why there isn't a Moby Dick. The reason there isn't a Moby Dick is that if a Canadian did a Moby Dick, it would be done from the point of view of the whale.

8. Atwood has explored the elusive Canadian identity in books like Survival and poems like Thoughts from Underground.

9. One of Gordon Lightfoot's best-known songs about the Canadian identity is Canadian Railroad Trilogy.

10. On the literary importance of identity, Northrop Frye said This story of the loss and regaining of identity is, I think, the framework of all literature.

Exercise 2

1. We were taken aback when our teacher announced Your PowerPoint presentations will be worth 30 percent of the final grade.

2. But our trepidation gave way to enthusiasm when she added The topic of the presentation is up to you.

3. We should include wild colours on some of the slides Suzanne suggested at the first meeting of our four-person team.

4. Charged with the responsibility of choosing a title for our short presentation, I came up with The Pleasures and Dangers of Extreme Sports.

5. Before this meeting breaks up Linda said we should set a date for the next one.

6. Can everyone be here next Tuesday at four o'clock Suzanne asked.

7. I can't make the next meeting George said but you can fill me in via e-mail.

8. At the team's second meeting, I proposed the following George loves blading and snowboarding, so I bet he'd be willing to create three slides on the pleasures of extreme sports.

9. I'll e-mail him about it, Suzanne said and also let him know I'll be preparing some slides on the dangers of extreme sports.

10. This is a real eye opener Linda said as she passed around copies of the article on extreme sports that she'd found in the National Post.

Exercise 3

1. Before his emergence as a singer-songwriter, Leonard Cohen was best known for novels like The Favourite Game and books of poetry like The Spice-Box of Earth and Flowers for Hitler.

2. In his second novel, Beautiful Losers, Cohen writes A saint is someone who has achieved a remote human possibility. It is impossible to say what that possibility is. I think it has something to do with the energy of love.

3. Cohen's first album, The Songs of Leonard Cohen, contains such hits as Suzanne and So Long, Marianne.

4. In 1969, The Globe and Mail named Cohen Entertainer of the Year.

5. Cohen has lived abroad for long periods but maintains a home in Canada because, as he has said it is my native land, my home, with all the feeling one has for his homeland.

6. Cohen's compositions can be heard on the soundtracks of movies such as McCabe and Mrs. Miller, Exotica, and Natural Born Killers.

7. On the 1988 album I'm Your Man, the gravel-voiced singer pokes fun at his vocal limitations I was born with the gift of a golden voice.

8. Cohen was the subject of a 1996 biography entitled Various Positions: A Life of Leonard Cohen.

9. Don't let the facts get in the way of truth Cohen once advised his biographer.

10. The last refuge of the insomniac Cohen famously said is a sense of superiority to the sleeping world.

Source: http://collections.ic.gc.ca/heirloom_series/volume6/206-207.htm

Exercise 4

1. John Diefenbaker, who was prime minister from 1957 to 1963, expressed his political views in a three-volume memoir, One Canada.

2. Diefenbaker wanted all Canadians to be, in his words unhyphenated Canadians.

3. As a letter printed in the Ottawa Citizen explained Dief the Chief just disliked the labelling that goes with hyphenation.

4. I am not anti-American Diefenbaker said in 1958 But I am strongly pro-Canadian.

5. During the 1965 election campaign, Diefenbaker was speaking off the record when he attacked a political ally turned foe The papers say Dalton Camp is revolting. I cannot disagree.

6. Of Pierre Trudeau, the prairie populist asked Have you ever seen him kiss a farmer?

7. The eroding value of the Canadian dollar in 1975 inspired this Diefenbaker quip I'm disturbed because the doctors tell me I'm as sound as a dollar.

8. In 1970, Diefenbaker told The Toronto Star I would never have been Prime Minister if the Gallup poll were right.

9. In his article The Last Best Dief, journalist Larry Zolf wrote about a Diefenbaker few Canadians knew about This was Dief the unifier, the pacifier, the holistic magician.

10. Diefenbaker, the deaf canine sidekick on the Canadian police drama Due South, was named after Canada's thirteenth prime minister.

Source: http://www.ggower.com/dief/quote.shtml

Exercise 5

1. P.L. Travers wrote the book Mary Poppins about a magical English nanny who defies the laws of physics and alters the lives of everyone she meets.

2. Asked about the character of Mary Poppins, Travers said I never for one moment believed that I invented her. Perhaps she invented me.

3. Travers believed A writer is only half a book—the reader is the other half.

4. Travers never felt comfortable in the spotlight following the success of Mary Poppins. I never talk about personal matters she said only ideas.

5. And Travers had firm ideas about the audience for her stories [T]hey were never in the first place written for children, but for everybody—or maybe to ease my own heart.

6. When Mary Poppins was made into a movie that differed in many ways from the book, Travers felt extremely uneasy.

7. The characters are entrusted to you Travers commented I don't want it ever to be possible that somebody could take [Mary Poppins] and write a story about her that wasn't mine.

8. Travers also found it difficult to convey to Mary Shepard, the illustrator of the original Mary Poppins books, just exactly how Mary Poppins should look.

9. Finally Travers explained I went out and found a little Dutch doll and showed it to her. But even then there were disagreements.

10. In an essay entitled Lively Oracles, which Travers wrote for the journal Parabola, she shared her thoughts about time Where the center holds and the end folds into the beginning there is no such word as farewell.

Source: The Horn Book Magazine, Sept./Oct. 1996.

PROOFREADING EXERCISE

Punctuate quotations, and underline or put quotation marks around titles used in the following paragraph.

I've been reading the book How Children Fail by John Holt. I checked it out to use in a research paper I'm doing on education in North America. Holt's book was published in the early 1960s, but his experiences and advice are still relevant today. In one of his chapters, Fear and Failure, Holt describes intelligent children this way Intelligent children act as if they thought the universe made some sense. They check their answers and their thoughts against common sense, while other children, not expecting answers to make sense, not knowing what is sense, see no point in checking, no way of checking. Holt and others stress the child's self-confidence as one key to success.

SENTENCE WRITING

Write ten sentences that list and discuss your favourite songs, TV shows, characters' expressions, movies, books, and so on. Be sure to punctuate titles and quotations correctly. Refer to the rules at the beginning of this section if necessary.

Capital Letters

1. Capitalize the first word of every sentence.

Peaches taste best when they are cold.

2. Capitalize the first word of a direct quotation.

She said, "My brother has never worked so hard before."

"He has finished most of his homework," she said, "but I still have a lot to do." (The *but* is not capitalized because it continues the same quotation and does not begin a new sentence.)

"My English class is fun," she said. "Maybe I'll change my program." (*Maybe* is capitalized because it begins a new sentence.)

3. Capitalize the first, last, and every important word in a title. Don't capitalize prepositions (such as *in, of, at, with*), short connecting words, the *to* in front of a verb, or *a, an,* or *the*.

I saw a copy of Darwin's *The Origin of Species* at a yard sale.

The class enjoyed the essay "How to Write a Rotten Poem with Almost No Effort."

Shakespeare in Love is a comedy based on Shakespeare's writing of the play *Romeo and Juliet.*

4. Capitalize specific names of people, places, languages, races, and nationalities.

Dr. Norman Bethune	China	Ashley MacIsaac
Ireland	Spanish	Japanese
Kofi Annan	Saskatoon	Robson Street

5. Capitalize the names of months, days of the week, and special days, but not the seasons.

March	Victoria Day	spring
Tuesday	Easter	winter
Valentine's Day	Labour Day	fall

6. Capitalize a title of relationship if it takes the place of the person's name. If *my* (or *your, her, his, our, their*) is in front of the word, a capital is not used.

I think Dad wrote to her.	*but*	I think my dad wrote to her.
She visited Aunt Sophia.	*but*	She visited her aunt.
We spoke with Grandpa.	*but*	We spoke with our grandpa.

7. Capitalize names of particular people or things, but not general terms.

I admire Professor Schwartz.	*but*	I admire my professor.
We saw the famous Welland Canal.	*but*	We saw the famous canal.
Are you from the West?	*but*	Is your house west of the mountains?

I will take Philosophy 120 and Sociology 100.	*but*	I will take philosophy and Sociology.
She graduated from Sutter Secondary School.	*but*	She graduated from secondary school.
They live at 119 Forest Street.	*but*	They live on a beautiful street.
We enjoyed the Royal Ontario Museum.	*but*	We enjoyed the museum.

E X E R C I S E S

Add all of the necessary capital letters to the sentences that follow.

Exercise 1

1. i have always wanted to learn another language besides english.

2. right now i am taking english 1204 in addition to my writing class.

3. the course title for english 1204 is basic grammar.

4. english 1204 is a one-unit, short-term class designed to help students with their verb forms, parts of speech, phrases, and clauses.

5. i hope that learning more about english grammar will help me understand the grammar of another language more easily.

6. now i must decide whether i want to take a spanish, french, italian, or american sign language course.

7. i guess i could even take a course in greek or russian.

8. when i was in high school, i did take french for two years, but my clearest memory is of the teacher, mlle. gauthier.

9. she was one of the best teachers that walkerton high school ever had.

10. unfortunately, i did not study hard enough and can't remember most of the french that she taught me.

Exercise 2

1. sir laurence olivier was one of the most famous british actors of the 20th century.

2. he was well known for playing the leading roles in shakespeare's plays.

3. he performed in london, on such stages as the old vic theatre and st. james's theatre, and for several years, he was director of the national theatre.

4. of course, olivier also played to audiences in cities around the world, such as montreal, los angeles, moscow, and berlin.

5. among olivier's most celebrated roles were henry V, othello, richard III, and king lear.

6. although we can no longer see him on stage, we can still watch the film versions of his classic performances.

7. olivier also directed many plays and some of his own films.

8. he directed the 1948 black-and-white film version of *hamlet* and received the academy award for best actor for his performance in the title role.

9. one of olivier's most treasured memories was of a single live performance of *hamlet* in elsinore, denmark; it was scheduled to have been played outside but had to be moved inside at the last minute, causing all the actors to be especially brilliant under pressure.

10. north american audiences might remember sir laurence olivier best for his portrayal of the tempestuous heathcliff in the movie *wuthering heights,* but he was a shakespearean actor at heart.

Source: Laurence Olivier on Acting (Simon & Schuster, 1986).

Exercise 3

1. my mom and dad love old movie musicals.

2. that makes it easy to shop for them at christmas and on other gift-giving occasions.

3. for mom's birthday last year, i gave her the video of gilbert and sullivan's comic opera *the pirates of penzance.*

4. it isn't even that old; it has kevin kline in it as the character called the pirate king.

5. i watched the movie with her, and i enjoyed the story of a band of pirates who are too nice for their own good.

6. actually, it is funnier than i thought it would be, and kevin kline sings and dances really well!

7. dad likes musicals, too, and i bought him tickets to see the revival of *chicago* on stage a few years ago.

8. he loved all those big production numbers and the bob fosse choreography.

9. there aren't many musicals made these days, but my folks did say that they would like a copy of the 1997 movie *evita*, starring madonna.

10. *evita* is the andrew lloyd webber musical about the former first lady of argentina, eva peron.

Exercise 4

1. keanu reeves was born in beirut, lebanon, on september 2, 1964.

2. his father, samuel, is of hawaiian and chinese descent.

3. growing up in toronto, ontario, keanu attended jesse ketchum public school and four high schools, including the toronto school for the performing arts, before dropping out at age seventeen.

4. after moving to hollywood, he considered changing his name to k.c. reeves.

5. keanu had his first starring role in the 1986 movie *river's edge*.

6. the actor has since appeared in such films as *something's gotta give, bill and ted's excellent adventure, my own private idaho,* and *sweet november* with south african actress charlize theron.

7. of course, keanu is best known for his role as neo in *the matrix* and its two sequels, *the matrix reloaded* and *the matrix revolutions*.

8. in the early 1990s, keanu was rejected by the stratford festival at an audition.

9. he captured the attention of the north american press in 1995 when he played the title role of hamlet at the manitoba theatre centre in winnipeg.

10. in addition to acting in films, keanu has done tv commercials for kellogg's corn flakes and played bass guitar in the bands dogstar and becky.

Sources: http://www.keanunet.com/bio.shtml; *The Canadian Encyclopedia* (McClelland & Stewart, 1999).

Exercise 5

1. in 1999, new york's american museum of natural history featured an extremely popular exhibit.

2. the title of the exhibit was "the *endurance:* shackleton's legendary antarctic expedition."

3. the *endurance* was a british ship that set sail for antarctica in 1914.

4. ernest shackleton was the ship's captain, and frank hurley was the photographer shackleton took along to document the expedition's success.

5. shackleton and his crew were attempting to be the first to cross antarctica on foot and to claim this accomplishment for britain.

6. having nearly reached its landing site, the *endurance* got stuck in the ice, and the crew lived on the icebound ship for nearly a year before it was crushed by the ice and sunk.

7. the crew escaped the sinking ship but were forced to live on the ice and eventually to travel to an uninhabited island.

8. realizing that they could not survive much longer on their supplies, shackleton took five men with him in a lifeboat named the *james caird* and covered 1300 kilometres before they reached another ship.

9. shackleton made it back to rescue the crew members he left behind, and all of them returned home safely.

10. the new york exhibit's displays, which included the *james caird* itself and frank hurley's pictures, brought the voyage of the *endurance* and the heroic efforts of shackleton and his crew to life for all of the visitors who saw them.

Source: U.S. News & World Report, May 31, 1999.

REVIEW OF PUNCTUATION AND CAPITAL LETTERS

Punctuate these sentences and add capital letters where needed. All the rules for punctuation and capitalization that you have learned are represented. Compare your answers carefully with those at the back of the book. Sentences may require several pieces of punctuation or capital letters.

1. the cross on mount royal is a famous landmark in the city of montreal

2. have you ever seen david cronenbergs early films such as rabid or they came from within

3. Theyve remodelled their house and now theyre ready to sell it

4. how much will the final exam affect our grades the nervous student asked

5. we have reviewed your policy mr martin and will be sending you a refund soon

6. the two students who earn the most points for their speeches will face each other in a debate

7. ms thomas the new english 1200 professor recently received a national poetry award

8. even though I enjoy my french class I believe I should have taken spanish first

9. you always remember valentines day and our anniversary but you forget my birthday

10. his favourite part in the original toy story movie is when buzz lightyear shouts to infinity and beyond

11. my sister subscribes to canadian geographic magazine and my whole family loves to look through it when shes finished reading it

12. finding low airfares takes time patience and luck

13. my friend is reading the novel thousand pieces of gold in her english class

14. I wonder how much my art history textbook will cost

15. bill gates founder of microsoft is one of the richest people in the world

Comprehensive Test

In these sentences you'll find all the errors that have been discussed in the entire text. Try to name the error in the blank before each sentence, and then correct the error if you can. You may find any of these errors:

awk	awkward phrasing
apos	apostrophe
c	comma needed
cap	capitalization
cliché	overused expression
cs	comma splice
dm	dangling modifier
frag	fragment
mm	misplaced modifier
p	punctuation
pro	incorrect pronoun
pro agr	pronoun agreement
pro ref	pronoun reference
ro	run-on sentence
shift	shift in time or person
sp	misspelled word
s/v agr	subject/verb agreement
wordy	wordiness
ww	wrong word
//	not parallel

A perfect—or almost perfect—score will mean you've mastered the first part of the text.

1. _____ She asked her sister if she could go to the store.

2. _____ Instructors break their classes up into groups when they wanted the students to learn on their own.

3. _____ I wonder if the real estate agent has called yet?

4. _____ A mans' overcoat lay in a corner of the bus shelter near my house until someone finally took it away.

5. _____ The teacher's lecture had an affect on all of us.

6. _____ We don't know which of the events occured first.

7. _____ There are several problems with the parking situation in the campus lots.

8. _____ My favourite high-school teacher moved to vancouver when she retired.

9. _____ The school awarded scholarships to my roommate and I, and we're both so happy.

10. _____ Cranberries can be harvested dry or another way is to gather them wet off the top of flooded bogs.

11. _____ The dishes need to be done and the trash needs to be taken out before you leave the cabin.

12. _____ Children can learn about dinosaurs going to museums.

13. _____ Since the room required a deposit but my cheque had not arrived.

14. _____ I haven't finished my term paper, the library has been closed for the long weekend.

15. _____ Each of the branches are covered with lights.

16. _____ After a long vacation, our house didn't seem as small as it did when we left.

17. _____ The hills were steeper than we thought none of us had worn the right shoes.

18. _____ From time to time, I get in the habit of eating too much junk food.

19. _____ I returned the book back to the library; it had been overdue for a long time.

20. _____ Everyone in town turned their porch lights on in support of the proposition.

P A R T 4

Writing

Aside from the basics of spelling, sentence structure, and punctuation, what else do you need to understand to write better? Just as sentences are built according to accepted patterns, so are other structures of English—paragraphs and essays, for example.

Think of writing as including levels of structure, beginning small with words connecting to form phrases, clauses, and sentences—and then sentences connecting to form paragraphs and essays. Each level has its own set of "blueprints." To communicate clearly in writing, words must be spelled correctly; a sentence needs a subject, a verb, and a complete thought; paragraphs are indented and contain a main idea and support; and essays explore a topic in several paragraphs, usually including an introduction, body, and conclusion. These consistent structures comfort beginning writers as patterns that they can learn to use themselves.

Not everyone approaches writing as structure, however. One can write better without thinking about structure at all. A good place to start might be to write what you care about and care about what you write. You can make an amazing amount of progress by simply being genuine, being who you are naturally. No one has to tell you to be yourself when you speak, but beginning writers often need encouragement to be themselves in their writing.

Writing is almost never done without a reason. The reason may come from an experience, such as fighting an unfair parking ticket, or from a requirement in a class. And when you are asked to write, you often receive guidance in the form of an assignment: tell a story to prove a point, paint a picture with your words, summarize an article, compare two subjects, share what you know about something, explain why you agree with or disagree with an idea.

Learning to write well is important, one of the most important things you will do in your education. Confidence is the key. The Writing sections will help you build confidence, whether you are expressing your own ideas or summarizing and responding to the ideas of others. Like the Sentence Structure sections, the Writing sections are best taken in order. However, each one discusses an aspect of writing that can be reviewed on its own at any time.

What Is the Least You Should Know about Writing?

"Unlike medicine or the other sciences," William Zinsser points out, "writing has no new discoveries to spring on us. We're in no danger of reading in our morning newspaper that a breakthrough has been made in how to write [clearly]. . . . We may be given new technologies like the word processor to ease the burdens of composition, but on the whole we know what we need to know."

One thing we know is that we learn to write by *writing*—not by reading long discussions about writing. Therefore the explanations and instructions in this section are as brief as they can be, followed by samples from student and professional writers.

Understanding the basic structures and learning the essential skills covered in this section will help you become a better writer.

BASIC STRUCTURES	**WRITING SKILLS**
I. The Paragraph	**III.** Writing in Your Own Voice
II. The Essay	**IV.** Finding a Topic
	V. Organizing Ideas
	VI. Supporting with Details
	VII. Revising Your Papers
	VIII. Presenting Your Work
	IX. Writing about What You Read

Basic Structures

I. THE PARAGRAPH

A paragraph is unlike any other structure in English. Visually, it has its own profile: the first line is usually indented about five spaces, and sentences continue to fill the space between both margins until the paragraph ends (which may be in the middle of the line).

_____

_____

_____

_____

_____

_____ .

Beginning writers often forget to indent their paragraphs, or they break off in the middle of a line within a paragraph, especially when writing in class. You must remember to indent whenever you begin a new paragraph and fill the space between the margins until it ends. (Note: In business writing, paragraphs are not indented but double-spaced in between.)

Defining a Paragraph

A typical paragraph centres on one idea, usually phrased in a topic sentence from which all the other sentences in the paragraph radiate. The topic sentence does not need to begin the paragraph, but it most often does, and the other sentences support it with specific details. (For more on topic sentences and organizing paragraphs, see p. 212.) Paragraphs usually contain several sentences, though no set number is required. A paragraph can stand alone, but more commonly paragraphs are part of a larger composition, such as an essay. There are different kinds of paragraphs, based on the jobs they are supposed to do.

Types of Paragraphs

Introductory paragraphs begin essays. They provide background information about the essay's topic and usually include the thesis statement or main idea of the essay. (See p. 210 for information on how to write a thesis statement.) Here is the introductory paragraph of a student essay entitled "Really Understanding":

> I was so excited when my parents told me that I could join them in Canada. Four years earlier, they left China to open a Chinese fast-food restaurant in Vancouver. After my parents asked me to help them in the restaurant, I started to worry about my English because I knew only a few words that I learned in China. They told me not to worry, that I would quickly grasp the language once I heard it every day. Soon after I joined them, I made a big mistake because of my lack of English skills and my conceit. From this experience, I learned the importance of really understanding.

In this opening paragraph, the student leads up to the main idea—"the importance of really understanding"—with background information about her family's restaurant and "a big mistake" that she made.

Body paragraphs are those in the middle of essays. Each body paragraph contains a topic sentence and presents detailed information about one subtopic or idea that relates directly to the essay's thesis. (See p. 212 for more information on organizing body paragraphs.) Here are the body paragraphs of the same essay:

> My mistake happened during my second week at the restaurant. Usually my mom and I stayed in front, dishing out the food and keeping the tables clean, and my father cooked in the kitchen. If I needed any help or if someone

asked a question in English, my mom took care of it. However, that day my mom was sick, so she stayed home. My father and I went to work. He went straight to the kitchen, and I wiped those six square tables. By noon, my father had put big steaming trays of food on the counter. There was orange chicken, chicken with mushrooms, sweet and sour pork, kong bao chicken, and B.B.Q. pork. People came in, ordering their favourite foods.

After I took care of the lunch rush, it was 2:00, but my favourite customer had not arrived. He was an old, kind, educated man who came in almost every day at 12:00. Why hadn't he come for the last two days? Was he sick? I looked at his favourite dish and started to worry about him. As I was wondering, he walked through the door. I smiled to see him. He ordered "the usual"—chicken with mushrooms and steamed rice—and sat down at the table in the left corner. I wanted to ask him why he came late to show that I cared about him, but more customers came in, and I had to serve them. They ordered all the chicken with mushrooms left in the tray, so I called to my father to cook more. The old man finished his food and walked toward me. He looked at that tray of newly cooked chicken with mushrooms for a second, and then he asked me something. I understood only the word *yesterday*. Since he had not been in yesterday, I guessed that he said "Were you open yesterday?" I quickly answered, "Oh, yes!" He looked at me, and I could see that he didn't believe my answer, so I said "Yes" again. He just turned and walked away.

I did not understand what had happened. Two days passed, and he did not return. I thought about what he could have asked me and stared at the chicken and mushrooms for a minute. Suddenly, I realized what must have happened. He had come in two hours later than usual, at 2:00 that day, but the dish had been cooked at 12:00. Fast food cooked two hours earlier would not taste as fresh as if it were just prepared. He must have asked me, "Was this *cooked* yesterday?" How could I have answered "Yes" not once but twice? He must have felt so bad about us. "He will never come back," I told myself.

Notice that each of the three body paragraphs discusses a single stage of the experience that taught her the value of really understanding.

Concluding paragraphs are the final paragraphs in essays. They bring the discussion to a close and share the writer's final thoughts on the subject. (See p. 225 for more about concluding paragraphs.) Here is the conclusion of the sample essay:

Four years have passed since then, and my favourite customer has not come back. It still bothers me. Why didn't I ask him to say the question again? If I had not been so conceited, I would have risked looking foolish for a moment. Now I am so repentant. I will never answer a question or do anything before I really understand what it means.

In this concluding paragraph, the student describes the effects of her experience—the regret and the lesson she learned.

SAMPLE OF A PARAGRAPH ALONE

Single-paragraph writing assignments may be given in class or as homework. They test the beginning writer's understanding of the unique structure of a paragraph. They may ask the writer to answer a single question, perhaps following a reading, or to provide details about a limited topic. Look at this student paragraph, the result of a homework assignment asking students to report on a technological development in the news:

> I just read that scientists are trying to breed or clone an extinct animal, just the way they did in the movie *Jurassic Park*. Only this is real. A group of Japanese biologists have the idea of bringing the woolly mammoth back to life. The woolly mammoth was an elephant-like beast with huge tusks and long hair. It stood about four metres high. Now thousands of years after the last mammoth walked the earth, reproductive science might allow frozen mammoth remains to be used to generate a new woolly mammoth. I think that if the scientists are doing it to be able to save current animals from becoming extinct, then it's worthwhile. But if they are just doing it to say they can, I think they should watch *Jurassic Park* again.

Source: Discover, Apr. 1999.

These shorter writing assignments help students practise presenting information within the limited structure of a paragraph.

The assignments in the upcoming Writing Skills section will sometimes ask you to write paragraphs. Remember that you may review the previous pages as often as you wish until you understand the unique structure of the paragraph.

II. THE ESSAY

Like the paragraph, an essay has its own profile, usually including a title and several paragraphs.

Title

_____

_____
_____
_____
_____ .

_____
_____
_____
_____ .

_____

_____

_____

_____

_____

_____ .

_____

_____

_____

_____

_____

_____ .

_____

_____

_____

_____ .

    While the paragraph is the single building block of text used in almost all forms of writing (letters, novels, newspaper stories, and so on), an essay is a more complex structure.

The Five-Paragraph Essay and Beyond

On pages 197–98, you read a five-paragraph student essay illustrating the different kinds of paragraphs within essays. Many people like to include five paragraphs in an essay: an introductory paragraph, three body paragraphs, and a concluding paragraph. Three is a comfortable number of body paragraphs—it is not two, which makes an essay seem like a comparison even when it isn't; and it is not four, which may be too many subtopics for the beginning writer to organize clearly.

    However, as writers become more comfortable with the flow of their ideas and gain confidence in their ability to express themselves, they are free to create essays of many different shapes and sizes. As in all things, learning about writing begins with structure and then expands to include all possibilities.

Defining an Essay

There is no such thing as a typical essay. Essays may be serious or humorous, but the best of them are thought-provoking and, of course, informative. Try looking up the word _essay_ in a dictionary right now. Some words used to define what an essay is might need to be explained themselves:

> An essay is _prose_ (meaning it is written in the ordinary language of sentences and paragraphs).

An essay is *nonfiction* (meaning it deals with real people, factual information, and actual opinions and events).

An essay is a *composition* (meaning it is created in parts that make up the whole, several paragraphs that explore a single topic).

An essay is *personal* (meaning it shares the writer's unique perspective, even if only in the choice of topic, method of analysis, and details).

An essay is *analytical* and *instructive* (meaning it examines the workings of a subject and shares the results with the reader).

A SAMPLE ESSAY

For an example of a piece of writing that fits the above definition, read the following biographical essay about the woman responsible for inventing the Melitta coffeemaker (from the book *Mothers of Invention,* by Ethlie Ann Vare and Greg Ptacek).

Drip Coffee

In 1908 a housewife in Dresden, Germany, became annoyed with the time-consuming method of brewing coffee by wrapping the loose grounds in a cloth bag and boiling water around it. Worse, coffee made that way (or by the shortcut of boiling coffee grounds right in the water) was bitter-tasting and grainy.

So Melitta Bentz ripped a sheet of blotting paper from her son's schoolbook, cut a circle of the porous paper, and stuck it in the bottom of a brass pot that she had poked full of holes. She reasoned that if she put the coffee grounds on top of this filter and poured the boiling water over it, she could get the taste of the coffee without the bad side effects.

Melitta Bentz was right about the coffee filtration system—so right, in fact, that she and her husband, Hugo, hired a tinsmith to produce the newfangled coffeepots for sale. In 1909 they brought their drip system to the Leipzig trade fair and sold more than 1200 "coffeemakers," as they called them. The Melitta company was born.

By 1912 Melitta was manufacturing its own line of coffee filters. Frau Bentz's company continued to grow, owned and operated by her children and her children's children. Her original disk-shaped filter was replaced by the familiar cone shape of today, and early metal pots were replaced by porcelain and plastic models. The Melitta coffeemaker is used today in 150 countries worldwide; a majority of coffee drinkers use the drip preparation method.

From a cottage in Dresden and a hausfrau with a taste for good coffee grew an international concern and a woman's first name that will forever remain synonymous with this omnipresent appliance.

Now that you have learned more about the basic structures of the paragraph and the essay, you are ready to practise the skills necessary to write them.

Writing Skills

III. WRITING IN YOUR OWN VOICE

All writing "speaks" on paper. And the person "listening" is the reader. Some beginning writers forget that writing and reading are two-way methods of communication, just like spoken conversations between two people. When you write, your reader listens; when you read, you also listen.

When speaking, you express a personality in your choice of phrases, your movements, your tone of voice. Family and friends probably recognize your voice messages on their answering machines without your having to identify yourself. Would they also be able to recognize your writing? They would if you extended your "voice" into your writing.

Writing should not sound like talking, necessarily, but it should have a "personality" that comes from the way you decide to approach a topic, to develop it with details, to say it your way.

The beginning of this book discusses the difference between spoken English (following looser patterns of speaking) and Standard Written English (following accepted patterns of writing). Don't think that the only way to add "voice" to your writing is to use the patterns of spoken English. Remember that Standard Written English does not have to be dull or sound "academic." Look at this example of Standard Written English that has a distinct voice, part of the book *You Can't Show Kids in Underwear and Other Little-Known Facts about Television,* by Barbara Seuling:

> When you think about it, it's kind of a miracle. You turn [it on], and within seconds you have another part of the world in your living room, talking, moving, and alive.
>
> This miracle-in-a-box, called television, happened about [seventy-five] years ago . . . and in that short time, it has grown into the most influential means of communication the world has ever known.
>
> Television has changed our behavior, saved lives, taught us, been companion to the lonely, and entertained and informed vast masses of people. It has shown us the moon, close up, and brought Olympic stadiums into our homes. It has made us witnesses to murder, and let us share rare moments

with the great people of the world. It has recorded the extraordinary happenings of our time as history has never been recorded before. The possibilities of the tube seem endless.

Seuling's excerpt illustrates Standard Written English at its best—from its solid sentence structures to its precise use of words. But more importantly, Seuling's clear voice speaks to us and involves us in her world, in her amazement at the power of television. Students can involve us in their writing too, when they let their own voices through. Writing does not need to be about something personal to have a voice. Here is an example of a student writing about computer hackers:

> Some mischievous hackers are only out to play a joke. One of the first examples was a group who created the famous "Cookie Monster" program at Massachusetts Institute of Technology. Several hackers programmed MIT's computer to display the word "cookie" all over the screens of its users. In order for users to clear this problem, they had to "feed" the Cookie Monster by entering the word "cookie" or lose all the data on their screens.

Notice that both the professional and the student writer tell stories (narration) and paint pictures (description) in the sample paragraphs. Narration and description require practice, but once you master them, you will gain a stronger voice and will be able to add interest and clarity to even the most challenging academic writing assignments.

Narration

Narrative writing tells the reader a story, and since most of us like to tell stories, it is a good place to begin writing in your own voice. An effective narration allows readers to experience an event with the writer. Since we all see the world differently and feel unique emotions, the purpose of narration is to take readers with us through an experience. As a result, the writer gains a better understanding of what happened, and readers get to live other lives momentarily. Listen to the "voice" of this student writer telling the story of a difficult lesson he learned in his childhood:

```
                        A Sticky Situation


     About thirty-two years ago when I was only six, my
sister Renee—who was older and wiser—gave me some advice.
She told me to chew gum all day and keep it in my mouth
```

all night. That way, she said, I would never have to brush my teeth again. Of course, I listened to her. From then on, day and night, I had a wad of gum in my mouth. Bubble gum was my favourite, and as the flavour of each piece faded, I unwrapped a fresh pink rectangle of Bazooka and added it to the chunk already in my mouth. Looking back, I should have noticed that Renee didn't follow her own advice, and I should have realized that she was tricking me.

A few days into my new round-the-clock gum routine, I awoke with a pain on my head, not in my head but *on* my head. I got out of bed and went to the mirror. Back in those days, we boys had either a Beatlemania hairdo or a big goofy Afro. I had the typical Beatlemania hairdo, with one added feature—a shapeless clump of Bazooka plastered to the front of it.

Discovering the clump was just the start of my troubles. Getting it out was worse. My mom pulled and yanked and tweezed at every piece of hair with gum on it. But I had a better idea. After my mom had given up, I went to the bathroom and got the scissors. I still remember my six-year-old face in the mirror looking up cross-eyed to get every last bit of gum stuck to my hair. When I was finished, it looked as if a beaver had taken a bite out of my bangs.

The reason that I remember an event that happened so long ago is that the next day was "Picture Day" at school. And for over thirty years my family has kept the results in a frame on the piano. It shows me, a smiling six-year-old, missing two front teeth and wearing a bowl-shaped haircut with a perfect square cut out of the front. The missing teeth and the missing hair matched up perfectly. It's always been Renee's favourite picture of me.

I can't say that I learned just one lesson from this experience; I think I learned two. One is never to listen to your older brother or sister, especially your sister. The other lesson was never, never cut your own hair.

Description

Descriptive writing paints word pictures with details that appeal to the reader's five senses—sight, sound, touch, taste, and smell. The writer of description often uses comparisons to help readers picture one thing by imagining something else, just as the writer of "A Sticky Situation" compares the shape of his missing hair to a beaver bite. In the short paragraph below, a student uses several comparisons to help describe a problem in her neighbourhood that she would like to have solved:

> A complaint I have about my community has to do with young children playing in the street. These are small, troll-like children between six and ten years old, scattered like a broken jar of jellybeans along the street. They chase each other carelessly through car gaps and vanish instantly like puffs of smoke.

Here is another example, from writer Michael Ondaatje's short story "The Bridge." As we read his description, we feel as though we are there with the men on the flatbed of the truck, travelling through the streets of Toronto at dawn.

> A truck carries fire at five A.M. through central Toronto, along Dundas Street and up Parliament Street, moving north. Aboard the flatbed, three men stare into passing darkness—their muscles relaxed in this last half-hour before work—as if they don't own the legs or the arms jostling against their bodies and the backboard of the Ford.
>
> Written in yellow over the green door is Dominion Bridge Company. But for now all that is visible is the fire on the flatbed burning over the three-foot by three-foot metal dish, cooking the tar in a cauldron, leaving this odour on the streets for anyone who would step out into the early morning and swallow the air.
>
> The truck rolls burly under the arching trees, pauses at certain intersections where more workers jump onto the flatbed, and soon there are eight men, the fire crackling, hot tar now and then spitting onto the back of a neck or an ear. Soon there are twenty, crowded and silent.
>
> The light begins to come out of the earth. They see their hands, the textures on a coat, the trees they had known were there. At the top of Parliament Street the truck turns east, passes the Rosedale fill, and moves towards the half-built viaduct.
>
> The men jump off. The unfinished road is full of ruts and the fire and the lights of the truck bounce, the suspension wheezing. The truck travels so slowly the men are walking faster, in the cold dawn air, even though it is summer.

Source: Michael Ondaatje, "The Bridge," from *In the Skin of a Lion* (Toronto: McClelland & Stewart, 1987). Reprinted by permission from the author.

You may have noticed that all of the examples in this section use both narration and description. In fact, most effective writing—even a good résumé or biology lab report—calls for clear storytelling and the creation of vivid word pictures for the reader.

Writing Assignments

The following two assignments will help you develop your voice as a writer. For now, don't worry about topic sentences or thesis statements or any of the things we'll consider later. Narration and description have their own logical structures. A story has a beginning, a middle, and an end. And we describe things from top to bottom, side to side, and so on.

Assignment 1
NARRATION: FAMOUS SAYINGS

The following is a list of well-known expressions. No doubt you have had an experience that proves at least one of these to be true. Write a short essay that tells a story from your own life that relates to one of these sayings. (See if you can tell which of the sayings fits the experience narrated in the student essay "A Sticky Situation" on p. 203.) You might want to identify the expression you have chosen in your introductory paragraph. Then tell the beginning, middle, and end of the story. Be sure to use vivid details to bring the story to life. Finish with a brief concluding paragraph in which you share your final thoughts on the experience.

The grass is always greener on the other side of the fence.

Absence makes the heart grow fonder.

We learn best from our mistakes.

A picture is worth a thousand words.

Success is the best revenge.

When you have your health, you have everything.

Assignment 2
DESCRIPTION: A VALUABLE OBJECT

Describe an object that means a lot to you. It could be a gift that you received, an object you purchased for yourself, an heirloom in your family, or a memento from your childhood. Your goal is to make the reader visualize the object. Try to use details and comparisons that appeal to the reader's senses in some way. Look back at the examples for inspiration. Be sure the reader knows—from your choice of details—what the object means to you.

IV. Finding a Topic

You will most often be given a topic to write about, perhaps based on a reading assignment. However, when the assignment of a paper calls for you to choose your own topic without any further assistance, try to go immediately to your interests.

Look to Your Interests

If the topic of your paper is something you know about and—more important—something you *care* about, then the whole process of writing will be smoother and more enjoyable for you. If you ski, if you are a musician, or even if you just enjoy watching a lot of television, bring that knowledge and enthusiasm into your papers.

Take a moment to think about and jot down a few of your interests now (no matter how unrelated to school they may seem), and then save the list for use later when deciding what to write about. One student's list of interests might look like this:

> surfing the Internet
>
> playing video games with friends
>
> skateboarding in summer
>
> collecting hockey cards

Another student's list might be very different:

> playing the violin
>
> going to concerts
>
> watching old musicals on video
>
> drawing caricatures of my friends

While still another student might list the following interests:

> going to the horse races
>
> reading for my book club
>
> travelling in the summer
>
> buying lottery tickets

These students have listed several worthy topics for papers. And because they are personal interests, the students have the details needed to support them.

Starting with a general topic, you can use several ways to gather the details needed to support it in a paragraph or an essay.

Focused Free Writing (or Brainstorming)

Free writing is a good way to begin. When you are assigned a paper, try writing for ten minutes, putting down all your thoughts on one subject—watching old movies on video, for example. Don't stop to think about organization, sentence structures, capitalization, or spelling—just let details flow onto the page. Free writing will help you see what material you have and will help you figure out what aspects of the subject to write about.

Here is an example:

> When I watch old movie musicals, I want to live back then. All the clothes were so fancy and it looks like people cared about each other more than they do now. I was watching a movie called guys and dolls the other night, and it was all about a bunch of gamblers in NYC who knew each other and one of them fell in love with a girl who worked for the salvation army. She hated gambling, and he hated her snooty attitude. But they fell in love anyway I guess opposites do attract after all. It had M. Brando, Frank Sinatra, and Jean somebody in it. I also saw the music man which was kind of similar. It was also about a criminal a con-man but in this one he was in a town full of backwards people and he fell for a woman a librarian so I guess she had a more open mind.

Now the result of this free-writing session is certainly not ready to be typed and turned in as a paragraph. But what did become clear in it was that the student could probably compare the two musicals to show how they told the same story—that opposites attract—in two different ways.

Clustering

Clustering is another way of thinking a topic through on paper before you begin to write. A cluster is more visual than free writing. You could cluster the topic of "going to the horse races," for instance, by putting it in a circle in the centre of a piece of paper and then drawing lines to new circles as ideas or details occur to you. The idea is to free your mind from the limits of sentences and paragraphs to generate pure details and ideas. When you are finished clustering, you can see where you want to go with a topic.

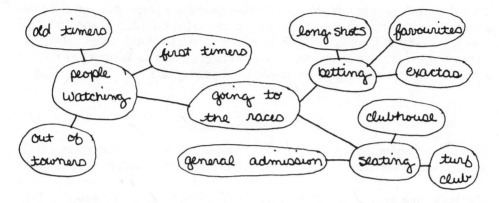

This cluster shows that the student has found three general aspects of attending the horse races: the variety of seating, types of bets, and groups of people to watch. This cluster might lead to another where the student chooses one aspect—groups of people to watch, for instance—and thinks of more details about it.

Talking with Other Students

It may help to talk to others when deciding on a topic. Many teachers break their classes up into groups at the beginning of an assignment. Talking with other students helps you realize that you see things just a little differently. Value the difference—it will help your written voice that we discussed earlier emerge.

Assignment 3
LIST YOUR INTERESTS

Make a list of four or five of your own interests. Be sure that they are as specific as the examples listed on page 207. Keep the list for later assignments.

Assignment 4
DO SOME FREE WRITING

Choose one of your interests, and do some focused free writing about it. Write for ten minutes with that topic in mind but without stopping. Don't worry about anything such as spelling or sentence structures while you are free writing. The results are meant to help you find out what you have to say about the topic *before* you start to write a paper about it. Save the results for a later assignment.

Assignment 5

TRY CLUSTERING IDEAS

Choose another of your interests. Put it in the centre of a piece of paper, and draw a cluster of details and ideas relating to it, following the sample on page 209. Take the cluster as far as it will go. Then choose one aspect to cluster again on its own. This way you will arrive at specific, interesting details and ideas—not just the first ones that come to mind. Save the results of all your efforts.

V. Organizing Ideas

The most important thing to keep in mind, no matter what you are writing, is the idea you want to get across to your reader. Whether you are writing a paragraph or an essay, you must have in mind a single idea that you want to express. In a paragraph, such an idea is called a topic sentence; in an essay, it's called a thesis statement, but they mean the same thing—an idea you want to get across. We will begin with a discussion of thesis statements.

Thesis Statements

Let's choose one of the students' interests listed on page 207 as a general topic. "Surfing the Internet" by itself doesn't make any point. What about it? What does it do for you? What point about surfing the Internet would you like to present to your reader? You might write

Surfing the Internet is a good way to discover new things.

But this is a vague statement, not worth developing. You might move into more specific territory and write

I have improved my reading and writing skills by surfing the Internet.

Now you have said something specific. *When you write in one sentence the point you want to present to your reader, you have written a thesis statement.*

All good writers either have a thesis in mind when they begin to write or develop the thesis as they write. Whether they are writing essays, novels, poems, or plays, they eventually have in mind an idea they want to present to the reader. They may develop it in various ways, but behind whatever they write is their ruling thought, their reason for writing, their thesis.

For any writing assignment, after you have done some free writing or clustering to explore your topic, the next step is to write a thesis statement. As you write your thesis statement, keep two things in mind:

1. A thesis statement must be a sentence *with a subject and a verb* (not merely a topic).

2. A thesis statement must be *an idea that you can explain or defend* (not simply a statement of fact).

Exercise 1
THESIS OR FACT?

Which of the following are merely topics or facts, and which are thesis statements that you could explain or defend? In front of each one that could be a thesis statement, write THESIS. In front of each one that is a fact, write FACT. Check your answers with those at the back of the book.

1. _____ The Great Lakes contain one-fifth of the world's drinkable water.

2. _____ Leaving home for the first time takes courage.

3. _____ The discovery of a single case of mad-cow disease in Alberta had serious financial consequences for the Canadian cattle industry.

4. _____ Some typists use the hunt-and-peck system.

5. _____ SARS poses a greater threat to Canadians than the mosquito-borne West Nile virus.

6. _____ There are twenty-six bones in the human foot.

7. _____ Students who use calculators in math class lose the ability to do calculations in their heads.

8. _____ Spam is a potential problem for anyone who uses e-mail.

9. _____ I can teach anyone to make a great omelette.

10. _____ Dolly, the world's first cloned sheep, was euthanized after being diagnosed with a lung infection.

Assignment 6
WRITE A THESIS STATEMENT

Use your free writing or clustering results from Assignments 4 and 5 (pp. 209–10) and write at least one thesis statement based on one of your interests. Be sure that the thesis you write is phrased as a complete thought that can be defended or explained in an essay.

Organizing an Essay

Once you have written a good thesis and explored your topic through discussion with others or by free writing and clustering, you are ready to organize your essay.

First you need an introductory paragraph. It should catch your reader's interest, provide necessary background information, and either include or suggest your thesis statement. (See p. 197 and p. 203 for two examples of student writers' introductory paragraphs.) In your introductory paragraph, you may also list supporting points, but a more effective way is to let them unfold paragraph by paragraph rather than to give them all away in the beginning of the essay. Even if your supporting points don't appear in your introduction, your reader will easily spot them later if your paper is clearly organized.

Your second paragraph will present your first supporting point—everything about it and nothing more.

Your next paragraph will be about your second supporting point—all about it and nothing more.

Each additional paragraph will develop another supporting point.

Finally, you'll need a concluding paragraph. In a short paper, it isn't necessary to restate all your points. Your conclusion may be brief; even a single sentence to round out the paper may do the job. Remember that the main purpose of a concluding paragraph is to bring the paper to a close by sharing your final thoughts on the subject. (See p. 198 and p. 204 for two examples of concluding paragraphs.)

Learning to write this kind of paper will teach you to distinguish between the parts of an essay. Then when you're ready to write a longer paper, you'll be able to organize it clearly and elaborate on its design and content.

Topic Sentences

A topic sentence does for a paragraph what a thesis statement does for an essay—it states the main idea. Like thesis statements, topic sentences must be phrased as complete thoughts to be proven or developed through the presentation of details. But the topic sentence introduces an idea or subtopic that is the right size to cover in a paragraph. The topic sentence doesn't have to be the first sentence in a paragraph. It may come at the end or even in the middle, but putting it first is most common.

Each body paragraph should contain only one main idea, and no detail or example should be allowed to creep into the paragraph if it doesn't support the topic sentence. (See pp. 197–98 and pp. 202–5 for more examples of body paragraphs within essays and of paragraphs alone.)

Organizing Body Paragraphs (or Single Paragraphs)

A single paragraph or a body paragraph within an essay is organized in the same way as an entire essay but on a smaller scale. Here's the way you learned to organize an essay:

Thesis: stated or suggested in introductory paragraph

First supporting paragraph

Second supporting paragraph

Additional supporting paragraphs

Concluding paragraph

And here's the way to organize a paragraph:

> Topic sentence
>
> First supporting detail or example
>
> Second supporting detail or example
>
> Additional supporting details or examples
>
> Concluding or transitional sentence

You should have several details to support each topic sentence. If you find that you have little to say after writing the topic sentence, ask yourself what details or examples will make your reader believe that the topic sentence is true for you.

Transitional Expressions

Transitional expressions within a paragraph and between paragraphs in an essay help the reader move from one detail or example to the next and from one supporting point to the next. When first learning to organize an essay, you might start each supporting paragraph in a paper with a transitional expression.

There are transitions to show addition:

> Also
>
> Furthermore
>
> Another (example, point, step, etc.)
>
> In addition

There are transitions to show sequence:

First	One reason	One example
Second	Another reason	Another example
Finally	Most important	In conclusion

There are transitions to show contrast:

However	On the other hand	In contrast

Exercise 2

ADDING TRANSITIONAL EXPRESSIONS

Place the transitional expressions from the following list into the blanks in the following paragraph to make it read smoothly. Check your answers with those in the back of the book.

Therefore	Finally	Next	First of all

When I moved into my own apartment for the first time last month, I discovered the many hidden expenses of entering "the real world." _____ , I had no idea that utility companies needed a security deposit from anyone who hasn't rented before. Each utility required a $30 to $50 deposit. _____ , my start-up costs just for gas, electricity, and phone used up all the money I had saved for furnishings. _____ , I found out how expensive it was to supply a kitchen with the basic staples of food and cleaning supplies. My initial trip to the grocery store cost $125, and I hadn't even bought my curtains at that point. _____ , I was able to budget my money and keep a little aside for any other unexpected expenses of living on my own.

Assignment 7
WOULD YOU LIKE TO BE CLONED?

New scientific methods are laying the groundwork for human cloning. Without considering the philosophical questions—in other words, *practically* speaking— would you like to be cloned? Why or why not? Write a long paragraph or a short essay in which you briefly answer this question. Your answer will be your main idea, and the reasons and details that support it should be your own opinions. Try free writing, clustering, or discussing the subject with others to find out how you feel about the topic before you begin to write.

VI. SUPPORTING WITH DETAILS

Now you're ready to support your main ideas with subtopics and specific details. That is, you'll think of ways to convince your reader that what you say in your thesis is true. How could you convince your reader that surfing the Internet has improved your reading and writing skills? You might write

> My reading and writing skills have improved since I began surfing the Internet. (because)

1. The computer won't respond to sloppy spelling and punctuation.

2. I read much more on screen than I ever did on paper, and much faster.

3. I write e-mail to friends and family, but I never wrote real letters to them before.

> **NOTE:** Sometimes if you imagine a *because* at the end of your thesis statement, it will help you write your reasons or subtopics clearly and in parallel form.

Types of Support

The subtopics developing a thesis and the details presented in a paragraph are not always reasons. Supporting points may take many forms based on the purpose of the essay or paragraph. They may be

> *examples* (in an illustration)
>
> *steps* (in a how-to or process paper)
>
> *types or kinds* (in a classification)
>
> *meanings* (in a definition)
>
> *similarities and/or differences* (in a comparison/contrast)
>
> *effects* (in a cause-and-effect analysis)

Whatever they are, supporting points should develop the main idea expressed in the thesis or topic sentence and prove it to be true.

Here is the final draft of a student essay on the problem of not being able to trust instincts. Notice how the body paragraphs present examples of the student's indecision. And all of the details within the body paragraphs support her topic sentences.

Indecision

As far back as I can remember, I've always been fickle-minded. At first, my mind would settle on one decision. Then suddenly, in a snap, I would change it. I have trouble with everything from choosing birthday presents for my friends to deciding what to eat for dinner every night. My problem of indecision is worst at school, where I have never trusted my instincts.

For instance, whenever I take multiple-choice tests, I get two points lower than an *A* because of last-minute changes. I get the right answer first, yet I frequently

---

hear this inner voice tell me to change it when I review my answers. It feels as though I'm being torn between my left hand urging me to erase my first answer and my right hand trying to stop the other one from doing it. Then this weird voice orders me to change the answer anyway.

The sad part comes after the test. I open my notes and scan for the right answer. Then I realize that once again I have wasted my energy, my eraser, and most of all the point or points on the test. Next is the indescribable feeling of a "lump" in my throat and pressure on my chest when the tests are given back. I usually get *B*'s just because of erasures. This has happened in my anatomy, history, and psychology classes. I guess something in me is afraid of getting *A*'s.

The same problem of indecision occurred last week outside of school. We were assigned to purchase a basal thermometer for an experiment in my anatomy class. So I went to the pharmacy near my house, and I found two — one just like the sample the teacher showed us in class and another brand with the same information on the label. Once more my hands fought with my brain. Incredibly, I chose the off brand. I came home and tried it. The mercury read my temperature, but the silver line didn't go down when I shook the thermometer afterward. Once again I should have trusted my instincts and bought the one the teacher showed us. The following day, I had to take an extra trip on the bus just to exchange it.

After this incident, I have resolved to value my first judgements. I know that if I trust my initial decisions, I will be trusting myself. I will still go through my test papers a second time, but I won't change a thing unless I know an answer is 100 percent wrong. With this plan, I may become an *A* student yet.

(Note: See pp. 218–19 for a rough draft of the above essay, before its final revisions.)

Learning to support your main ideas with vivid details is perhaps the most important thing you can accomplish in this course. Many writing problems are not really *writing* problems but *thinking* problems. Whether you're writing a term paper or merely an answer to a test question, if you take enough time to think, you'll be able to write a clear thesis statement and support it with paragraphs loaded with meaningful details.

Assignment 8
WRITE AN ESSAY ON ONE OF YOUR INTERESTS

Return to the thesis statement you wrote about one of your interests for Assignment 6 on page 211. Now write a short essay to support it. You can explain the allure of your interest, its drawbacks, or its benefits (such as the one about the Internet improving the student's reading and writing skills). Don't forget to use any free writing or clustering you may have done on the topic beforehand.

Assignment 9
A WEAKNESS

Like the student writer of "Indecision," we all have minor personality weaknesses. We may procrastinate (put things off until the last minute), hide our true feelings, or gossip about people we know. These weaknesses affect our lives, yet we are usually aware of them. Write an essay about one of your minor personality weaknesses, and give examples of the effects it has had on your life. You may want to include how you might solve the problem.

VII. Revising Your Papers

Great writers don't just sit down and write a final draft. They write and revise. You may have heard the expression, "Easy writing makes hard reading." True, it is *easier* to turn in a piece of writing the first time it lands on paper. But you and your reader will be disappointed by the results. Try to think of revision as an opportunity instead of a chore, as a necessity instead of a choice.

Whenever possible, write the paper several days before the first draft is due. Let it sit for a while. When you reread it, you'll see ways to improve the organization or to add more details to a weak paragraph. After revising the paper, put it away for another day, and try again to improve it. Save all of your drafts along the way to see the progress that you've made or possibly to return to an area left out in later drafts but which fits in again after revision.

Don't call any paper finished until you have worked it through several times. Revising is one of the best ways to improve your writing.

Take a look at an early draft of the student essay you read on page 215 on the problem of indecision. Notice that the student has revised her rough draft by crossing out some parts, correcting word forms, and adding new phrasing or reminders for later improvement.

Indecision

give more background

As far back as I can remember, I've always been fickle-minded. At first, my mind would settle on one decision. Then suddenly, in a snap, I would change it.* I have never trusted my instincts.

For instance, whenever I ~~have~~ take tests ~~like scantrons or~~ multiple-choice, I get two points lower than ~~the grade I~~ an "A" ~~want~~ because of last minute changes. I ~~always~~ get the right answer ~~on my~~ first ~~choice~~, yet I frequently hear this inner voice say to change it when I ~~go back and~~ review my answers. It ~~always~~ feels ~~like~~ as though I'm being torn between by left hand's urge to erase my first answer and my right ~~holding~~ hand trying to keep my left hand ~~to keep~~ from doing it. Then comes the ~~wierd~~ weird voice that orders me to ~~do erase it~~ change the answer anyway.

The sad part comes after the test. I open my notes and scan ~~for the the question and~~ once again the right answer. Then I realize that ~~I went through all that trouble only to find out~~ I wasted my energy, eraser, ~~temptation,~~ and most of all the point or points on the test. ~~Next comes~~ is Next the indescribable feeling of a "lump" ~~sensation~~ pressure on my throat and chest when the ~~papers~~ tests are given back. I usually get B's just because of erasures. This has happened in a ~~lot of my subjects, like~~ my classes. Anatomy, History, and Psychology. ~~and a lot more~~ of indecision. I guess something in me is afraid of getting A's.

The same problem occurred last week. We were assigned outside of school to purchase a basal thermometer for an experiment in my anatomy class. So I went to the pharmacy near my house, and I found two — one just like the ~~one~~ sample the teacher showed

us in class and another ~~one a little different but~~ brand with
the same information on the label. Once more my hands
fought with my brain. Incredibly I chose the ~~new one~~ off brand. I came home
and tried it. The mercury read my temperature, but it the silver line didn't go down when I shook ~~it~~ the thermometer afterwards. Again, I should have
trusted my instincts and ~~got~~ bought the one the teacher showed
us. The following day, I had to take an extra trip on the
bus just to exchange it.

   After this incident, I resolved to ~~trust~~ have a value my first
judgements. I know that if I trust my initial decisions, I
will be trusting myself. I will still go through my test
papers a second time, but I won't change a thing unless I
know an answer is one hundred percent wrong. With this
plan, I ~~hope things will turn out better~~. may become an A student yet.

Can you see why each change was made? Analyzing the reasons for the
changes will help you improve your own revision skills.

Assignment 10
AN INVENTION

You've read a lot about famous inventions in this text. If you could invent
something that would make some aspect of our lives easier, more fun, or more
productive, what would it be? You might choose to write about why you believe
your invention is necessary, who would benefit from your invention, or what kind
of help you would need to produce it.

   Write a rough draft of the paper and then set it aside. When you finish
writing about your invention (Assignment 10), reread your paper to see what
improvements you can make to your rough draft. Use the checklist on page 220
to help guide you through this or any other revision.

Exchanging Papers

This checklist could also be used when you exchange papers with another student
in your class. Since you both have written a response to the same assignment, you
will understand what the other writer went through and learn from the differences
between the two papers.

REVISION CHECKLIST

Here's a checklist of revision questions. If the answer to any of these questions is no, revise that part of your paper until you're satisfied that the answer is yes.

1. Does the introductory paragraph introduce the topic clearly and suggest or include a thesis statement that the paper will explain or defend?

2. Does each of the other paragraphs support the thesis statement?

3. Does each body paragraph contain a clear topic sentence and focus on only one supporting point?

4. Do the body paragraphs contain enough details, and are transitional expressions well used?

5. Do the final thoughts expressed in the concluding paragraph bring the paper to a smooth close?

6. Does your (the writer's) voice come through?

7. Do the sentences read smoothly and appear to be correct?

8. Are the spelling and punctuation consistent and correct?

Proofreading Aloud

Finally, read your finished paper *aloud*. If you read it silently, you will see what you *think* is there, but you are sure to miss some errors. Read your paper aloud slowly, pointing to each word as you read it to catch omissions and errors in spelling and punctuation. Reading a paper to yourself this way may take fifteen minutes to half an hour, but it will be time well spent. There are even word-processing programs that will "speak" your text in a computer's voice. Using your computer to read your paper to you can be fun as well as helpful. If you don't like the way something sounds, don't be afraid to change it! Make it a rule to read each of your papers *aloud* before handing it in.

Here are four additional writing assignments to help you practise the skills of writing and revising.

Assignment 11

WHAT'S IN A NAME?

Write about your name—any part or all of it. Are there any special stories behind your name? Do you know its meaning, if any? Are you named after anyone special?

How do you feel about your name—would you ever consider changing it? Organize your responses to these questions into the structure of a brief essay.

Assignment 12

PICK A NUMBER, ANY NUMBER

We are all identified at times by numbers—birthdates, social insurance numbers, phone numbers, PINs, credit card numbers, just to name a few. What do you think about all of the numbers in your life? Which ones are most important to you, and which would you gladly get rid of, if any? Write a thesis statement that you then support with detailed body paragraphs.

Assignment 13

A BOOK OR MOVIE THAT MADE AN IMPRESSION

Choose a book you have read or a movie or TV show you have seen that made a strong impression on you. Write a brief overview of the book or movie, and then describe your reactions to it. Think back over all the stages of your life to find one that really made an impact. Be sure to explain why it affected you.

Assignment 14

A QUOTATION

Look through the following quotations (or use a famous one that comes to mind). Does one of them apply to you? Could you profit from following one of them? Write a short paper in which you react to or offer an explanation of one of the quotations and then support your reaction or explanation with examples from your own experiences.

> We can learn from our enemies.
>
> *Ovid*

> We know what a person thinks not when he tells us what he thinks but by his actions.
>
> *Isaac Bashevis Singer*

> Ask yourself whether you are happy and you will cease to be so.
>
> *John Stuart Mill*

> The essence of humour is human kindliness.
>
> *Stephen Leacock*

VIII. Presenting Your Work

Part of the success of a paper could depend on how it looks. The same paper written sloppily or typed neatly might even receive different grades. It is human nature to respond positively when a paper has been presented with care. Here are some general guidelines to follow.

Paper Formats

Your paper should be written on a computer or typed, double-spaced, or copied neatly in ink on 8 ½-by-11 paper on one side only. A one-inch margin should be left around the text on all sides for your instructor's comments. The beginning of each paragraph should be indented five spaces.

Most instructors have a particular format for presenting your name and the course material on your papers. Always follow such instructions carefully.

Titles

Finally, spend some time thinking of a good title. Just as you're more likely to read a magazine article with an interesting title, so your readers will be more eager to read your paper if you give it a good title. Which of these titles from student papers would make you want to read further?

An Embarrassing Experience	Super Salad?
Falling into The Gap	Buying Clothes Can Be Depressing
Hunting: The Best Sport of All?	Got Elk?

Remember these three things about titles:

1. Only the first letter of the important words in a title should be capitalized.

A Night at the Races

2. Don't put quotation marks around your own titles unless they include a quotation or title of an article, short story, or poem within them.

"To Be or Not to Be" Is Not for Me

3. Don't *italicize* or underline your own titles unless they include the title of a book, play, movie, or magazine within them.

Still Stuck on *Titanic*

A wise person once said, "Haste is the assassin of elegance." Instead of rushing to finish a paper and turn it in, take the time to give your writing the polish it deserves.

IX. WRITING ABOUT WHAT YOU READ

Reading and writing are related skills. The more you read, the better you will write. When you are asked to prepare for a writing assignment by reading a newspaper story, a magazine article, a professional essay, or part of a book, there are many ways to respond in writing. Among them, you may be asked to write your reaction to a reading assignment or a summary of a reading assignment.

Writing a Reaction

Reading assignments become writing assignments when your teacher asks you to share your opinion about the subject matter or to relate the topic to your own experiences. In a paragraph, you would have enough space to offer only the most immediate impressions about the topic. However, in an essay you could share your personal reactions, as well as your opinions on the value of the writer's ideas and support. Of course, the first step is always to read the selection carefully, looking up unfamiliar words in a dictionary.

SAMPLE REACTION PARAGRAPH

Here is a sample paragraph-length response following several readings about controversial court cases in history; the question was "Choose any one of the cases we have read about and explain your reaction to it." This student chose the case of Sue Rodriguez, a victim of ALS (more commonly known as Lou Gehrig's disease). ALS causes the slow deterioration of the nervous system while leaving the mind intact. It is a painful condition and has no cure. Rodriguez challenged the Canadian courts on the right-to-choose-to-die issue. Her case led to a close examination of the Criminal Code and the Charter of Rights concerning suicide.

When I read Sue Rodriguez's case, I was moved, saddened, confused, and sometimes angry. She was a 41-year-old woman, with a teenage son, who loved life and was very physically active prior to the onset of the disease in 1992. She wanted, however, to end her life prematurely so that her son would not have to witness her slow deterioration. Rodriguez chose what she thought was best for her son and ultimately for herself—assisted suicide. The current Criminal Code states that anyone who counsels or assists in suicide faces a fourteen-year prison term. Section 7 of the Charter of Rights gives Canadians the right to life, liberty, and the security of person. Rodriguez argued that the right to life also included the right to a dignified death, and she wanted to achieve this with the help of her physician. In the end, the Supreme Court of Canada maintained that Sue Rodriguez did not have the right to end her own life, so she had to act in secret with the help of friends to achieve her wish. It's strange. I always thought the government created legislation that was supposed to be in the best interest of all Canadians. I guess I was wrong.

Sources: 1) http://www.newsworld.cbc.ca/flashback/1993/sue1.html
2) http://www.newsworld.cbc.ca/flashback/1993/sue2.html
3) http://www.newsworld.cbc.ca/flashback/1993/sue3.html
4) http://www.web.apc.org/dwd/canlaw/html/#SEC1F

If this had been an essay-length assignment, the student would have included more details about the case. Perhaps he would have compared it with another case to broaden the discussion, or he would have explored in depth the reasons why he believed the laws governing assisted suicide are wrong.

Assignment 15
WRITE A REACTION PARAGRAPH

The following is an article by Megan Rooney in which she describes the "spotlight effect." Write a paragraph in which you respond thoughtfully to Rooney's topic and to the details she uses to support it.

In the Spotlight

Ever feel that you're Truman Burbank, with every eye trained on your every action, especially your blunders and shortcomings? Psychologists call the familiar feeling that the whole world is watching you the "spotlight effect." Thankfully (to everyone except narcissists), that social searchlight is turning out not to be as large or as bright as we fear. "We think that people notice us much more than they do," says Kenneth Savitsky, Ph.D., associate professor of psychology at Williams College, who has studied the phenomenon extensively with researchers from Williams, Cornell, and Northwestern.

In one experiment, a student wearing a Barry Manilow T-shirt was sent into a room filled with peers. Though the student was convinced that the "embarrassing" clothing would be noticed by at least half of the people, follow-up interviews found that less than 50% of the group recalled the shirt. In another semester-long experiment, dubbed the "Bad Hair Day Study," students rated their classmates on whether they looked better or worse than usual. The results show that the raters were less aware of variations in appearance than were the students they scored. Most people just don't notice when we're not looking our best or worst.

Why not? Simple egocentrism, declares Savitsky. Since we're focused on ourselves, we assume that others pay close attention to us, too, but everyone else is concerned with their own problems. "The truth is," says Cornell graduate student Justin Kruger, "we're just not as interesting to other people as we are to ourselves."

Source: Psychology Today magazine, 1998.

Before starting your reaction paragraph, *read the selection again carefully.* Be sure to use a dictionary to look up any words you don't know. You can also use the free writing and clustering techniques explained on pages 207–9. Or your instructor may want you to discuss the reading in groups.

Coming to Your Own Conclusions

Often you will be asked to come to your own conclusions based on a reading that simply reports information. In other words, you have to think about and write about what it all means.

Read the following Royal Canadian Mounted Police report, reprinted from the book *Maritime UFO Files.* This is a real police report, written by RCMP Constable F.D. Chaisson, that documents a possible UFO sighting in Newfoundland.

On 10 October 1974 at approximately 10:45 P.M. [Atlantic Time], a report of a possible sighting of an Unidentified Flying Object in the Central Newfoundland area was made to the Gander Airport Detail Office . . . by John Breen [of] Gander, Newfoundland. Breen, a three-year veteran Air Traffic Controller now employed at the Gander Air Traffic Control Centre, was at the time of the sighting flying a Cessna Aircraft [Canadian Registration C-GLCF]. Breen was flying at an approximate altitude of 5,000 feet, experiencing clear skies with occasional cloudy periods and was returning to Gander from Deer Lake, Newfoundland. When about 40 miles [64 km] northwest of Gander, Breen, along with his only passenger, sighted the possible UFO. Janice Gould [also of] Gander, Breen's passenger and girlfriend, sighted the object just as they passed over the town of Grand Falls, Newfoundland, a small town about 60 miles [100 km] west of Gander.

The object was described by Breen as a solitary, greenish, luminous light. When first noticed by Breen, the object was directly below his aircraft at approximately 3,000 feet. Breen's first interpretation of this greenish light was that it was his right navigation light . . . reflecting on something below. He turned off all his navigation lights for a moment; nevertheless, the greenish light continued directly below the aircraft. Breen at this time, along with Gould, attempted to determine whether or not the greenish light was part of a bigger unlighted mass; however, this met with negative results as nothing but the greenish light could be noted.

Breen further stated that at this time the Cessna was travelling at a speed of about 134 miles per hour [216 km/h], and that the greenish light could and did at times speed up and remain some distance ahead of the aircraft, still at approximately 3,000 feet. This greenish light would then slow down and allow Breen to get directly above it. The light would continue to slow down, and as a result, lag some distance behind, and then go back to its original position below Breen's aircraft. Breen's observation period of this greenish light was about 25 minutes.

When approximately 5 to 6 miles [8 to 10 km] northwest of Gander, Breen contacted the Air Traffic Control Centre and advised them of what was taking place. The Controllers at ATC then attempted to pick up this object on their radar screen. One Robert Lawrence, the supervising Controller on duty at the time, advised that the object was picked up by their 6-mile [10-km] radar; however, the object remained on the screen for only two sweeps of the needle. The target did not show up on the screen as an aircraft. The target did, however, indicate while on screen that its course had changed from northwest to a westerly course, and the reason it could no longer be seen on radar was that it was now believed to be flying at treetop level. Continued attempts to regain contact with the target met with negative results. Breen, upon arriving over the Gander area, circled his aircraft in an attempt to further identify the object; however, upon circling, all traces of the greenish light were gone.

Continual attempts to further identify the greenish light in question by both the Air Traffic Controllers and Breen met with negative results. . . .

Upon the landing of Breen's aircraft at Gander International Airport, both Breen and Gould were immediately contacted. It was noted at this time that neither Breen nor Gould was under any sort of influence, from either alcohol or drugs. Their accounts of the incident are neither exaggerated nor dramatized, and both Breen and Gould appear to be of a mature and responsible nature.

Source: Don Ledger, *Maritime UFO Files* (Halifax: Nimbus Publishing, 1998), 102–3.

Assignment 16

WHAT ARE YOUR CONCLUSIONS?

Does the language used in the report suggest that the constable made any assumptions about the people (or objects) involved in this case? What kind of assumptions can you detect? Could the report be written any more objectively? What kind of conclusions might you arrive at about the witnesses, the reporting officer, and the whole incident?

Writing 100-Word Summaries

One of the best ways to learn to read carefully and to write concisely is to write 100-word summaries. Writing 100 words sounds easy, but actually it isn't. Writing 200- or 300- or 500-word summaries isn't too difficult, but condensing all the main ideas of an essay or article into 100 words is a time-consuming task—not to be undertaken in the last hour before class.

A summary presents only the main ideas of a reading, *without including any reactions to it*. A summary tests your ability to read, understand, and *rephrase* the ideas contained in an essay, article, or book.

If you work at writing summaries conscientiously, you'll improve both your reading and your writing. You'll improve your reading by learning to spot main ideas and your writing by learning to construct a concise, clear, smooth paragraph. Furthermore, your skills will carry over into your reading and writing for other courses.

SAMPLE 100-WORD SUMMARY

First, read the following excerpt from an article about the life of Godtfred Christiansen, creator of the Lego building block. It is followed by a student's 100-word summary.

Godtfred Christiansen: A Pioneer

Few of the children who play with Lego are likely to know that they are using a building method devised in ancient Greece. They will be unaware that the studs which enable the bricks to click together so satisfyingly are similar to those securing dry walls in Athens. Such happy ignorance is probably just as well. Godtfred Kirk Christiansen (1920–1995) developed Lego into one of the world's most popular toys without upsetting the boys and girls devoted to it by calling it "educational" or "improving." That message, though, is self-evident to the main buyers of Lego, the grown-ups who fondly watch their pride and joy absorbed for hours actually making things; so different from the junk toys which reflect passing fashion, designed merely as fodder for Christmas, here today, discarded tomorrow.

The simple facts of Mr. Christiansen's life are that he was born in Billund, in Jutland [Denmark], and at 12 went to work for his father who ran a small firm making wooden toys. In 1957, when he was 37, he took over the firm from his father and built it up to become the world's fifth largest toymaker, measured by sales. He was a generous supporter of charities. He was married and he and his wife, Edith, had a son who now runs the business. That said, there is not a lot to add about Mr. Christiansen's personal life. . . . He was perfectly amiable. Did you know, he would ask a visitor, that six Lego bricks of the same colour could be combined in more than 120 million ways? . . . His father, he said, was keen on quality and gave his wooden toys three coats of varnish. The name Lego is a contraction of leg godt, which translates as "play well." Interesting, but that did not really help to explain how the uneducated Christiansen Junior became, according to some guesswork, one of the 100 wealthiest people in the world. . . . Mr. Christiansen raised commonsense questions when a more sophisticated person might not risk displaying his ignorance.

Neither Mr. Christiansen nor his father invented interlocking plastic building bricks. They had to see off several rivals. It sounds obvious, but Lego seems simply to have made a better brick: better finished, better colour, neater fitting. . . . It now sells about 11 billion of these little plastic bricks a year in more than 100 countries. Many analysts have tried to explain its success. But . . . the secret of Lego's success [may lie] in its strategy of repeat-buying. The purchase of a first kit for, say, a 5-year-old, leads on to many more sales. There are ever more advanced kits to tempt children right up to the teens. Legoland, a theme park in Denmark full of Lego models, feeds the addiction. [There is now a Legoland just outside of London, England, and another opened in Carlsbad, California, in March 1999.]

Did Mr. Christiansen think up this clever marketing method? Probably not. Lego has recruited many talented managers whose education lasted beyond the age of 12. But Mr. Christiansen had an instinct for an opportunity to match the times, and the drive to carry it through. . . .

Here is a student's 100-word summary of the article:

Godtfred Christiansen was a simple man who succeeded partly because of other people's good ideas. He didn't have a lot of education, but he had the kind of mind that it takes to become rich. His father's toy-making business in Denmark allowed Godtfred to sell Legos to children around the world. He loved talking about Legos more than about himself, and he passed on his company to his family. Legos have sold so well because parents have to keep buying more sets as their children grow. Today, the Lego company continues to expand because of smart business practices and Legolands.

Assignment 17

WRITE A 100-WORD SUMMARY

Your aim in writing the summary should be to give someone who has not read the article a clear idea of it. First, read the following excerpt, and then follow the instructions provided after it.

Why Write?

This is going to come as a shock to you, but being able to write well makes you sexy. What's more shocking is the fact that NOT being able to write well decreases your attractiveness to prospective mates. Intrigued? Read on!

Good writing is a skill that is necessary if you want to achieve three vital life objectives: communicate effectively and memorably, obtain and hold satisfying employment, and attract worthy sex partners. Once you come to appreciate these facts and fully understand the immense influence writing well can have on your life, then you will see how easily mastered trivia like faultless grammar, sound sentence structure, and an appealing style can transform you from road-kill on the Road of Life to a turbocharged powerhouse.

While spoken communication is easy, natural and, for most of us, automatic (far too automatic for some) it doesn't have the lasting power of written language. Even e-mail, the most easily deleted, impermanent form of written language, can be reread, forwarded, and redirected, attaining a kind of permanence impossible for conversation. Who wants to be the author of a message remembered for its unintended but hilarious grammatical flaws or syntactical blunders ("Sisters reunite after 18 years at check-out counter!")?

In all business environments, good writing is a predictor of success. People who communicate well do well; this fact has been emphasized repeatedly in surveys of executives, panels of recruitment officers, and polls of employers. At one time there was an attitude among novices heading for a career on the corporate ladder that good writing was something that secretaries did and executives didn't need. In the current climate of instant and incessant electronic business communication and networked industries, very few people can rely on a subordinate to correct their grammar or polish their style before their colleagues or clients see their work.

Throughout evolutionary history, men and women have always sought mates who had the skills and attributes that suggested they could thrive in the environment of the times. Eons ago, female survival depended on choosing a man with a concrete cranium and huge biceps because he was most likely to repel predators and survive attacks. Prehistoric men selected women for their squat, sturdy bodies and thick fat layer because such females were more likely than their sinewy cousins to survive an ice-age winter and even provide some warmth. Skills such as spear-hurling and fire-tending are not much in demand these days. Now, men and women are biologically on the lookout for mates with updated thriving expertise. Your ability to communicate effectively is one of the skills that place you among the 21st-century elite, those who will rise to the top of the corporate food chain, claiming the most desirable mates as you ascend! Besides, being able to write melting love notes or clever, affectionate e-mail is a far more effective turn-on these days than being able to supply a slab of raw mastodon or an exquisitely crafted loincloth. Go ahead—flex those writing muscles, flaunt that perfect grammar!

Why write? Excellent communication skills are the single most important attribute you can bring to the table when you're negotiating for power, profession, prestige, or partner.

Source: Adapted from Sarah Norton and Nell Waldman, *Canadian Content,* 4th ed. (Toronto: Harcourt Brace & Company Canada), 305–7.

A good way to begin the summary of an article is to figure out the thesis statement, the main idea the author wants to get across to the reader. Write that idea down now *before reading further*. How honest are you with yourself? Did you write that thesis statement? If you didn't, *write it now before you read further*. You probably wrote something like this:

Writing well is a skill that makes people more attractive.

Using that main idea as your first sentence, summarize the article by choosing the most important points. *Be sure to put them in your own words.* Your rough draft may be 150 words or more.

Now cut it down by including only essential points and by getting rid of wordiness. Keep within the 100-word limit. You may have a few words less but not one word more. (And every word counts—even *a, and,* and *the.*) By forcing yourself to keep within the 100 words, you'll get to the kernel of the author's thought and understand the article better.

When you have written the best summary you can, then and only then compare it with the summary on page 304. If you look at the model sooner, you'll cheat yourself of the opportunity to learn to write summaries because, once you read the model, it will be almost impossible not to make yours similar. So do your own thinking and writing, and then compare.

SUMMARY CHECKLIST

Even though your summary is different from the model, it may be just as good. If you're not sure how yours compares, answer these questions:

1. Did you include the same main ideas?

2. Did you leave out all unnecessary words and examples?

3. Did you rephrase the writer's ideas, not just recopy them?

4. Does the summary read smoothly?

5. Would someone who had not read the article get a clear idea of it from your summary?

Assignment 18

WRITE A REACTION OR A 100-WORD SUMMARY

Respond to Chris Sasaki's article, "ET Phone Earth: The Search for Extraterrestrial Intelligence" in any of the three ways we've discussed—in a reaction paragraph, an essay, or a 100-word summary. If you plan to respond with an essay, briefly summarize Sasaki's main ideas about the search for extraterrestrials in your introductory paragraph—how the search is conducted and what is hoped for. Then write about your reactions to his ideas in your body paragraphs. Save your final thought for your concluding paragraph.

ET Phone Earth: The Search for Extraterrestrial Intelligence

Huge "blips" appear on radar screens around the world as identified objects approach Earth from deep space. Strange craft enter the atmosphere and hover silently over cities around the world. The spacecraft lands. Doors open and mysterious creatures emerge. The aliens have arrived.

Is this how humans and intelligent creatures from another planet will first make contact? Maybe in movies like *Independence Day* and *Close Encounters of the Third Kind*. But chances are the first contact between humans and intelligent extraterrestrials will be nothing more than the detection of a faint radio signal coming from space.

Just as humans around the world communicate electronically, we can attempt to communicate with extraterrestrials by sending and listening for radio signals. In fact, that's pretty much all we can do for now. The Milky Way galaxy—the spiral collection of billions of stars we call home—is just too big for us to explore by spaceship. Even if we could build a starship that travelled at the speed of light, it would still take us thousands of years to explore even a small corner of our galaxy.

So for the time being, we're limited to interstellar telecommunication instead of interstellar travel. In 1974, scientists transmitted a radio message toward a star cluster called M13. The message was a picture showing a "map" of the solar system, mathematical and chemical information, and a representation of a human body.

Have any aliens received the message and replied? Not yet. In fact, the targeted star cluster is over 20 000 light years away. That means the radio message travelling at the speed of light won't get there for 20 000 years. And even if extraterrestrials receive the message and reply, we won't hear their answer for another 20 000 years! Stay tuned!

There's actually much more listening than transmitting going on. Around the world, researchers are using large radio antennas called radio telescopes to listen for signals from space. They hope to detect a message coming from an alien civilization with technology like ours. Such programs are called SETI: The Search for Extraterrestrial Intelligence. A number of programs, such as the SETI Institute's Project Phoenix, are scanning the skies right now.

Have SETI scientists found anything? Not yet. Still, they're hopeful that someday ET will phone us. In fact, it seems more and more likely that we're not alone in the galaxy. Recently, astronomers found planets in orbit around other stars and after all, without planets you can't have life. Scientists have also discovered evidence that there may have been life on Mars billions of years ago. If there was life on Mars, maybe there's life on other planets.

Perhaps, one day, an electronic signal will be received from space, a signal more important than any ever sent or received before. Perhaps, one day, we will hear a message from an alien civilization on a planet circling a distant star in the Milky Way galaxy: "Greetings, inhabitants of Earth. We wish to communicate with you . . ."

Source: Chris Sasaki, "ET Phone Earth: The Search for Extraterrestrial Intelligence," *YES Magazine—Canada's Science Magazine for Kids*, Issue 3, Autumn 1996.

Answers

PART 1 SPELLING

WORDS OFTEN CONFUSED, SET 1 (PP. 8–13)

EXERCISE 1

1. effects
2. course, already
3. an
4. Its
5. Conscious, its, its

6. our, desserts, all ready
7. feel
8. accept, complement, break
9. chose
10. due, a

EXERCISE 2

1. hear, know
2. an, its
3. do
4. chose, its
5. conscious

6. affect
7. advice, fill
8. an, its
9. chose, accepted
10. compliment

EXERCISE 3

1. forth, fill
2. here, affects
3. are, an
4. knew, it's
5. already

6. except
7. complement, already, know
8. have
9. fill, desserts
10. have

EXERCISE 4

1. already, do
2. clothes, choose
3. its

4. course, dessert
5. Du
6. feel, conscious

7. advice

8. have, complimented

9. course, do

10. except

EXERCISE 5

1. an, choose

2. course, it's

3. advice

4. effect

5. its, due

6. cloths, no, coarse

7. break

8. all ready, feel, it's

9. compliments

10. clothes

PROOFREADING EXERCISE

I like all the classes I chose this semester ~~accept~~ *except* my computing class. ~~Its~~ *It's* not what you might think. The teacher is nice, my classmates have a good attitude, and I enjoy learning software too. ~~Its~~ *It's* just that I don't ~~no~~ *know* how to design a good web page. Everyone has given me ~~advise~~ *advice,* but I can't seem to make a web page that is attractive. I have learned HyperText Markup Language, or HTML, but I still have problems creating something easy to read. Now that everyone knows about my lack of talent, I ~~fill~~ *feel* very self-~~conscience~~ *conscious* whenever ~~its~~ *it's* part of the assignment to put something on the web. I guess I always ~~new~~ *knew* that I should ~~of~~ *have* dropped this course and taken something else instead.

WORDS OFTEN CONFUSED, SET 2 (PP. 17–22)

EXERCISE 1

1. whether, write

2. who's (who has), You're, your

3. right, through, quite

4. led, too, write, personal

5. past

6. Personnel

7. They're, past, than

8. woman, principal

9. where

10. lose, than, lose

EXERCISE 2

1. piece, through

2. their, principal, to, weather

3. than

4. their, personal

5. who's (who is), too, where

6. quite

7. Then, than

8. piece, through

9. through, their

10. were, lose

EXERCISE 3

1. lead, You're, your
2. personal, lose
3. past, too
4. quite, wear, loose
5. than, their

6. weather
7. Then, to
8. two, there
9. whether, they're
10. who's (who is)

EXERCISE 4

1. principle, your
2. than, to
3. past, quiet
4. there
5. write

6. woman
7. through
8. women, right
9. threw
10. Whether, lose

EXERCISE 5

1. right, past
2. where, principal
3. lose, to
4. through, quite, than
5. Led, their

6. personal, women
7. whose
8. than, through
9. Whether
10. peace, their

PROOFREADING EXERCISE

Now that the ~~whether~~ *weather* is nice, my husband and I have decided to repaint the outside of our house. We are going to paint it ourselves. But it isn't going to be an easy job since many of the boards have come ~~lose~~ *loose* over the years. Sometime in the ~~passed~~ *past,* the previous owners repainted the house but didn't scrape and sand it first; now the paint is peeling and big flakes have started falling onto the grass. We worry that ~~their~~ *there* is ~~led~~ *lead* in the old paint, but we can't decide ~~weather~~ *whether* to call in a professional. One of my husband's friends, a woman ~~who's~~ *whose* house was just remodelled, told him, "~~Your~~ *You're* going to regret doing it yourselves. After what I've been ~~threw~~ *through,* I would strongly recommend hiring a professional. That's the only way to guarantee your ~~piece~~ *peace* of mind."

CONTRACTIONS (PP. 25–29)

EXERCISE 1

1. We've

2. don't

3. isn't

4. she's, we've, it's

5. wasn't

6. There's, he's

7. she'd, couldn't

8. don't

9. can't

10. we've, weren't

EXERCISE 2

1. we'd

2. didn't, I'd

3. couldn't, hadn't

4. wasn't

5. didn't

6. weren't, they're

7. isn't, didn't, I'd

8. no contractions

9. we'd

10. we're, couldn't

EXERCISE 3

1. hasn't

2. he'd, might've

3. it's

4. wasn't

5. didn't, they're

6. hasn't, it's

7. wouldn't

8. they'd

9. What's, they've, hasn't

10. It's

EXERCISE 4

1. there's, I'm

2. I've

3. We've, haven't

4. We'll, can't

5. she's, we've

6. it's

7. aren't

8. we're, we'll

9. That's, I'll, it's

10. there's

EXERCISE 5

1. Who's

2. I've, he's, who've

3. mightn't, would've

4. it's

5. wasn't

6. that's

7. it's

8. Cronenberg's (Cronenberg has)

9. they've, that've

10. he's

PROOFREADING EXERCISE

I ~~cant~~ *can't* even think of a roller coaster anymore without being afraid. I used to look forward to the warm ~~whether~~ *weather* and frequent trips to our local amusement parks. I loved everything about the rides—the speed, the dips, the turns, the loops. Then I was in a minor car accident ~~wear~~ *where* I injured my knee after crashing into the rear end of another car. It ~~was'nt~~ *wasn't* ~~to~~ *too* bad, and only my knee was hurt. I thought that a sore knee would be the only negative ~~affect~~ *effect*. I was wrong. For some reason, since the accident, I've become really frightened of going fast. I found out the hard way, by going ~~threw~~ *through* the most terrifying minutes of my life on a coaster that ~~Id~~ *I'd* been on several times in the ~~passed~~ *past*. I guess ~~its~~ *it's* time for me to find new ways of having fun.

POSSESSIVES (PP. 33–35)

Exercise 4

1. Picasso's
2. no possessives needing apostrophes
3. masterpiece's
4. guard's, painting's
5. woman's
6. days'
7. museum's
8. authorities', Amsterdam's, man's
9. Picasso's
10. no possessives needing apostrophes

Exercise 5

1. industry's
2. Egoyan's
3. Egoyan's
4. movie's
5. Copps' (*or* Copps's)
6. Awards', Academy's
7. Etrog's
8. Etrog's, World's
9. Jutra's
10. Hollywood's, films'

Proofreading Exercise

You might not know of Marion ~~Donovans~~ *Donovan's* claim to fame. She invented something most parents use thousands of times. When her ~~babys'~~ *baby's* crib became wet each night, Donovan used a shower curtain to create the ~~worlds~~ *world's* first plastic diaper cover. After patenting her device and calling it the "Boater," ~~Donovans'~~ *Donovan's* business sense guided her to sell the idea, for which she received $1 million (U.S.) in 1951. The Boater design led to the birth of the disposable diaper, and ~~its'~~ *its* sales currently bring in nearly $5 billion (U.S.) a year.

REVIEW OF CONTRACTIONS AND POSSESSIVES (PP. 36–37)

1. Secord's, company's
2. Secord's
3. Secord's

4. Laura's, portrait's, she's

5. Britain's

6. Fitzgibbon's

7. wasn't

8. Laura's

9. Laura's

10. Laura's

Home Is Where Your Stomach Is

For Shania Twain, ~~its~~ *it's* dill pickle potato chips, but ~~weve~~ *we've* all got our weaknesses when it comes to junk food. The attraction of many such foods is that they remind us of our ~~parents~~ *parents'* traditions or our ~~provinces~~ *province's* special charm—especially when we're away, eating them makes us feel as though ~~were~~ *we're* at home.

Whether ~~its~~ *it's* ~~Newfoundlands~~ *Newfoundland's* scruncheons or B.C. ~~Ferries~~ *Ferries'* infamous Sunshine Breakfast or Northern Ontario's *poutine,* each regional "junk food" carries with it some powerful memories. That's why each regional specialty, from pickled pigs feet to the Nanaimo bar, is ~~our's~~ *ours* to crave. In fact, if our own ~~regions'~~ *region's* food is considered disgusting by large ~~groups'~~ *groups* in the rest of the country, ~~were~~ *we're* even more proud.

RULE FOR DOUBLING A FINAL LETTER (PP. 39–40)

EXERCISE 1

1. eating

2. cutting

3. slipping

4. talking

5. weeding

6. conferring

7. clapping

8. trimming

9. quizzing

10. mopping

EXERCISE 2

1. snapping

2. tearing

3. healing

4. flopping

5. suggesting

6. cancelling

7. preferring

8. dreaming

9. dripping

10. transmitting

EXERCISE 3

1. patting
2. spanning
3. feeding
4. alarming
5. occurring

6. brushing
7. gathering
8. knotting
9. offering
10. hogging

EXERCISE 4

1. digging
2. reviewing
3. dealing
4. clogging
5. clicking

6. unhooking
7. running
8. pushing
9. aiming
10. delivering

EXERCISE 5

1. mourning
2. dressing
3. passing
4. buttoning
5. sitting

6. wishing
7. cooking
8. constructing
9. polishing
10. leading

PROGRESS TEST (P. 41)

1. A. year's
2. B. (could) have
3. A. submitted
4. A. lose
5. B. compliment
6. A. where
7. A. already
8. A. effect
9. B. principal
10. B. a (unique material)

PART 2 SENTENCE STRUCTURE

FINDING SUBJECTS AND VERBS (PP. 51–54)

EXERCISE 1

1. Pleasant childhood memories are often quite vivid.

2. We remember special places, people, and things from our youth.

3. The image of our first house stays in our minds, for instance.

4. There are the neighbourhood children to recall.

5. Such memories include favourite furniture and decorative objects.

6. (You) Think back to your childhood now.

7. Most likely, it brings back a flood of memories.

8. Perhaps colours and smells seemed brighter and sweeter then.

9. Such sensations strike most of us at some point in our lives.

10. At these times, we cherish the past and look forward to the future.

EXERCISE 2

1. The sperm business has an unfortunate history of mistrust.

2. Until recently, the system denied patients any choice at all.

3. The sperm simply came from the nearest willing medical student.

4. There were many health problems as a result.

5. In the 1980s, donor semen infected several women with HIV.

6. Only a decade ago, a doctor from the state of Virginia, Cecil Jacobson, went to prison.

7. Without telling his patients, Jacobson fathered as many as seventy-five children using his own sperm.

8. An internal audit at a Hamilton, Ontario, clinic sparked a two-year government probe of Canada's sperm business.

9. New stringent semen regulations came into effect in 1996.

10. As a result, the Canadian government now keeps track of donor semen and ensures proper screening for sexually transmitted and infectious diseases.

EXERCISE 3

1. Amateur talent <u>shows</u> <u>celebrate</u> the performer or "ham" in all of us.

2. <u>Schools</u> and <u>charities</u> <u>organize</u> these events and <u>raise</u> funds for their organizations.

3. There <u>are</u> <u>singers</u>, <u>dancers</u>, <u>comics</u>, and <u>acrobats</u> in nearly every community.

4. <u>They</u> <u>are</u> not always good singers, dancers, comics, and acrobats, however.

5. In fact, <u>crowds</u> often <u>love</u> the worst performers in talent shows.

6. A <u>sense</u> of <u>humour</u> in the audience and the performers <u>helps</u> enormously.

7. Otherwise, <u>participants</u> <u>feel</u> embarrassment instead of encouragement.

8. <u>Laughing</u> with someone <u>is</u> not the same as laughing at someone. (*Laughing* is not a real verb in this sentence.)

9. Amateur <u>performers</u> <u>need</u> courage and support.

10. Every <u>celebrity</u> <u>started</u> somewhere, perhaps even in a talent show.

EXERCISE 4

1. The <u>word</u> *toast* <u>has</u> a couple of different meanings.

2. <u>We</u> <u>toast</u> pieces of bread and <u>eat</u> them with butter and jam.

3. <u>People</u> also <u>make</u> toasts to the bride and groom at weddings.

4. There <u>are</u> Old French and Latin word <u>roots</u> for *toast*.

5. Both *toster* (Old French) and *torrere* (Latin) <u>refer</u> to cooking and drying.

6. *Toast* as the word for cooked bread slices <u>arrived</u> in the 1400s.

7. The <u>story</u> of *toast's* other meaning <u>makes</u> sense from there.

8. In the 1600s, there <u>was</u> a <u>tradition</u> in taverns.

9. <u>Revellers</u> <u>placed</u> spicy croutons in their drinks for added flavour.

10. Then <u>they</u> <u>drank</u> to the health of various ladies and <u>invented</u> the other meaning of *toast*.

EXERCISE 5

1. Canada's <u>tourism industry</u> <u>suffered</u> during the SARS outbreak of 2003.

2. <u>Canoeing</u> on the French River in Northern Ontario <u>is</u> an exhilarating experience for tourists.

3. <u>Halifax</u> <u>hosts</u> an annual festival that celebrates the talents of more than eighty of the world's finest street performers.

4. Though memorably named, <u>Eyebrow</u>, Saskatchewan, <u>is</u> a little-known tourist destination.

5. <u>Fringe festivals</u> <u>are</u> a popular attraction in cities like Edmonton.

6. <u>Springbank Gardens</u> in London, Ontario, <u>is</u> a beloved destination for children.

7. Nanaimo's annual <u>bathtub races</u> <u>attract</u> international attention.

8. Bernard <u>Callebaut</u> <u>produces</u> high-quality chocolate products at its factory in downtown Calgary.

9. <u>Chefs</u> throughout Canada <u>admire</u> the work of Michael Smith, co-owner of the Inn at Bay Fortune in Prince Edward Island.

10. Newfoundland's <u>attractions</u> <u>include</u> Signal Hill, a site rich in historical connections.

PARAGRAPH EXERCISE

My <u>aunt</u> and <u>uncle</u> <u>have</u> an incredible cookie jar collection. At the moment, <u>they</u> <u>own</u> about eight hundred jars and <u>get</u> new ones every day. <u>Some</u> of their cookie jars <u>date</u> back to the late 19th century. But <u>others</u> <u>commemorate</u> more current cartoon or movie characters. Celebrity <u>cookie jars</u> <u>bring</u> my aunt special happiness and <u>add</u> to the glamour of the collection. There <u>are</u> Elvis, Marilyn Monroe, and James Dean <u>jars</u> and even <u>ones</u> depicting The Grateful Dead's bus and The Beatles' psychedelic car. I really <u>appreciate</u> my aunt and uncle's collection and <u>hope</u> for one of my own someday.

LOCATING PREPOSITIONAL PHRASES (PP. 56–59)

EXERCISE 1

1. My <u>family</u> and <u>I</u> <u>live</u> (in a house) (at the top) (of a hilly neighbourhood) (in Vancouver).

2. (On weekday mornings), nearly <u>everyone</u> <u>drives</u> (down the steep winding roads) (to their jobs) or (to school).

3. (In the evenings), <u>they</u> all <u>come</u> back (up the hill) to be (with their families).

4. (For the rest) (of the day), <u>we</u> <u>see</u> only an occasional delivery van or compact school bus.

5. But (on Saturdays and Sundays), there <u>is</u> a different <u>set</u> (of drivers) (on the road).

6. Then <u>tourists</u> (in minivans) and prospective <u>home buyers</u> (in convertibles) <u>cram</u> the narrow streets.

7. (On these weekend days), <u>most</u> (of the neighbourhood residents) <u>stay</u> (at home).

8. Frequently, <u>drivers</u> unfamiliar (with the twists and turns) (of the roads) (up here) <u>cause</u> accidents.

9. The <u>expression</u> "Sunday driver" really <u>means</u> something (to those) (of us) (on the hill).

10. And <u>we</u> <u>could add</u> "Saturday driver" (to the list), as well.

EXERCISE 2

1. (In England), <u>Bob Martin</u> <u>is</u> a man (with a very strange claim) (to fame).

2. The seventy-year-old <u>Martin</u> <u>lives</u> (in Eastleigh), a town approximately 160 kilometres south (of London).

3. (For ten years), <u>he</u> <u>travelled</u> (by train) (to London) hundreds (of times) (for one specific purpose).

4. (During these trips), <u>Martin</u> <u>attended</u> 625 performances (of *Cats*), the long-running musical (by Andrew Lloyd Webber).

5. <u>Martin</u> <u>became</u> interested (in the show) (upon listening) (to the original cast album).

6. This devoted *Cats* <u>fan</u> always <u>sat</u> (in the orchestra section), but not always (in the same seat).

7. <u>Many</u> (of the actors and crew members) (in the productions) <u>befriended</u> Bob Martin (over the years).

8. (In the eyes) (of his extended family), <u>Martin</u> <u>is</u> just a happy eccentric.

9. (Without a wife or children) to think about, <u>Martin</u> <u>indulged</u> his interest (in *Cats*).

10. (As a result), <u>he</u> <u>travelled</u> more than 160,000 kilometres (over the rails) and <u>spent</u> more than $20,000 (U.S.) (on tickets) to see the same play over and over again.

EXERCISE 3

1. Canadian <u>musicians</u> (of every kind) <u>are honoured</u> annually (at the Juno Awards).

2. One <u>glance</u> (at the Juno Awards website) <u>will convince</u> you (of the overwhelming variety) (of Canadian musicians).

3. <u>Fans</u> (of pop music) <u><u>will recognize</u></u> Avril Lavigne (as a newly risen star) (of Canadian music).

4. (Besides pop, rap, country, and rock), the <u>Juno Awards</u> <u><u>celebrate</u></u> works (of contemporary jazz), classical compositions, and alternative musical genres (such as aboriginal and gospel).

5. One distinctive <u>feature</u> (of the Juno Awards) <u>is</u> their dedication (to promoting both English and French vocalists).

6. Now a singer (of international stature), <u>Céline Dion</u> <u><u>was</u></u> once a relative unknown nominated (for Francophone Album) (of the Year).

7. <u>Performers</u> (like Shania Twain and Diana Krall) <u><u>have become</u></u> better known (around the world) (because of the promotional endeavours) (of the Juno Awards).

8. (In the last few decades), (with renowned singer-songwriters) (like Gordon Lightfoot and Joni Mitchell), <u>Canadians</u> <u><u>have come</u></u> to dominate pop music (to a fair extent).

9. (In an eclectic range) (of categories), the <u>Junos</u> <u><u>salute</u></u> everyone (from Alanis Morissette) (to Fred Penner).

10. (Regardless of your taste), there <u>is</u> <u><u>something</u></u> (in Canadian music) (for your CD collection).

EXERCISE 4

1. <u>Louis Riel</u>, a leader (of his people) (in their resistance) (against the Canadian government), <u>is</u> perhaps the most controversial figure (in Canadian history).

2. <u>Riel</u> <u><u>was born</u></u> (in the Red River Settlement) (in what is now Manitoba) (in 1844).

3. <u>He</u> <u><u>emerged</u></u> (as a leader) (among the Métis) (of the Red River).

4. His provisional <u>government</u> <u><u>negotiated</u></u> the Manitoba Act (with the Canadian government).

5. <u>Riel</u> <u><u>was</u></u> the leader (of the short-lived 1885 Rebellion).

6. Increasingly, <u>he</u> <u><u>believed</u></u> himself chosen to lead the Métis people.

7. <u>Riel</u> <u><u>was forced</u></u> to surrender (to Canadian forces) and to stand trial (for treason).

8. (At his trial), <u>he</u> <u><u>demonstrated</u></u> his gifts (as a speaker).

9. Judged sane, <u>he</u> <u><u>was sentenced</u></u> (to death) (in 1885).

10. <u>Riel</u> <u>was hanged</u> (in Regina) (on November 16, 1885), (despite Quebec's opposition) (to his sentencing).

EXERCISE 5

1. <u>Gorgons</u> <u>have been</u> extinct (for 250 million years).

2. These <u>creatures</u> <u>lived</u> and <u>died</u> millions (of years) (before dinosaurs).

3. <u>They</u> <u>perished</u> (along with almost all life) (on the planet) (in a huge cataclysmic event).

4. (In fact), <u>dinosaurs</u> <u>met</u> a similar fate (of their own).

5. <u>Gorgons</u> <u>were</u> beasts (with both lion-like and lizard-like qualities).

6. Recently, <u>scientists</u> <u>discovered</u> a full-size fossilized skeleton (of a gorgon) (in South Africa).

7. (At 2.1 metres long), the <u>fossil</u> <u>tells</u> a lot (about these animals).

8. <u>They</u> <u>had</u> eyes (in the sides) (of their nearly one-metre-long heads).

9. And <u>they</u> <u>hunted</u> successfully (with the help) (of their ten-centimetre-long teeth).

10. The gorgons' extreme physical <u>features</u> <u>reveal</u> the harshness (of their prehistoric surroundings).

PARAGRAPH EXERCISE

Do you know (about Lucy Maud Montgomery's phenomenal success) (in Japan)? (For some reason), the Japanese are enamoured (of her first novel), *Anne* (*of Green Gables*), (along with its seven sequels), and they travel thousands (of kilometres) to visit Cavendish Beach. Many (of the Japanese tourists) arrange to be married (in Prince Edward Island) or to honeymoon there. (As a consequence), many Japanese-language tours are organized (in the province) to accommodate these visitors. (Despite the immense popularity) (of Montgomery) (in Japan) and (in other countries), no one has yet, (to my knowledge), tried to analyze exactly why the books (in the Anne series) are so appealing (to people) (from a completely different culture).

UNDERSTANDING DEPENDENT CLAUSES (PP. 62–66)

EXERCISE 1

1. If <u>you</u> want to spend your vacation in Canada, there <u>are</u> many wonderful <u>places</u> to visit in the Atlantic provinces or Ontario.

2. If you crave adventure, you should visit Newfoundland's Signal Hill, where Marconi received the first transatlantic radio signal in 1901.

3. If you like tall ships, you should travel to Lunenburg, Nova Scotia.

4. Because they have a rich history, places like Lunenburg are often used as backdrops for Hollywood movies.

5. The Citadel is a military fort that stands on a high point of land overlooking Halifax Harbour.

6. The fort, which was built in 1856, today houses exhibits of early military life.

7. After a cannon is fired at noon each day, soldiers in military dress conduct precision drills.

8. If you have children, (you) be sure to take them to Santa's Village in Bracebridge, Ontario.

9. African Lion Safari, which is located in Rockton, Ontario, will appeal to children who like monkeys and other exotic wildlife.

10. As these tourist sites demonstrate, the Atlantic provinces and Ontario have much to offer Canadians who prefer to vacation in their own country.

EXERCISE 2

1. On June 8, 1924, two British men, George Mallory and Andrew Irvine, disappeared as they were climbing to the top of Mount Everest.

2. When a reporter earlier asked Mallory why he climbed Everest, his response became legendary.

3. "Because it is there," Mallory replied.

4. No living person knows whether the two men reached the summit of Everest before they died.

5. Nine years after Mallory and Irvine disappeared, English climbers found Irvine's ice ax.

6. But nothing else of Mallory's or Irvine's was found until a Chinese climber spotted their bodies in 1975.

7. He kept the news of his sighting secret for several years but finally decided to tell a fellow climber on the day before he died himself in an avalanche on Everest.

8. In May 1999, a team of mountaineers searched the area where the Chinese man had seen something, and they found George Mallory's frozen body still intact after seventy-five years.

9. After they took DNA samples for identification, the mountaineers buried the famous climber on the mountainside where he fell.

10. Mallory and Irvine were the first climbers to try to get to the top of Everest, and the question remains whether they were on their way up or on their way down when they met their fate.

EXERCISE 3

1. If you ever plan a trip to Bangkok, (you) be sure to visit the Royal Dragon restaurant.

2. Somchai T. Amornrat designed the Royal Dragon so that it would break the record for the largest restaurant in the world.

3. Since the previous record-holding restaurant was also in Bangkok, Amornrat did some research and made his restaurant even bigger.

4. The Royal Dragon covers 4.8 hectares and is so sprawling that servers must wear roller skates to get around.

5. As many as ten thousand people a day eat at the Royal Dragon or Mangkorn Luang, as it is called in Thai.

6. After customers enter the huge park-like complex, they dine at tables that encircle a large reflecting pool.

7. And once every evening, a waitress entertains the diners as she flies from the top of a Pagoda that is seven stories high to a stage in the middle of the pool.

8. Before the flying waitress takes off, speakers play the theme song from *Mission: Impossible.*

9. If guests want to make their own music, they can visit one of the Royal Dragon's fifty karaoke bars.

10. The one thousand people who cook and serve the food and who do the dishes afterward never worry about being late to work since most of them live in the restaurant complex.

EXERCISE 4

1. Roch Carrier, a French-Canadian author, is best known for his novel *La Guerre, Yes Sir!* and for a touching story called "The Hockey Sweater."

2. This story is about a Francophone mother in a Quebec village who tries to order her son a hockey sweater from Eaton's.

3. The order forms are in English, a language that proves difficult for her.

4. The child's hero is Maurice "Rocket" Richard, who played for the Montreal Canadiens.

5. Because the boy expects for a Montreal Canadiens sweater, he is bitterly disappointed when Eaton's mistakenly sends him a blue-and-white Toronto Maple Leafs sweater.

6. "The Hockey Sweater" illustrates the split between French and English Canada, though ironically the two solitudes are united by a common love of hockey.

7. Critics have suggested that the story is autobiographical.

8. Carrier's work provides insight into rural Quebec in the 1940s and 1950s.

9. As he relates in the story's first two lines, the lives of young children revolved around the church, the school, and the skating rink.

10. The proof of the story's relevance to Canadian nationalism is that the first two lines of "The Hockey Sweater" appear on the new Canadian five-dollar bill.

EXERCISE 5

1. The National Ballet of Canada was founded in 1951 by English dancer Celia Franca, who performed in *Les Sylphides* that year.

2. In 1964, the National Ballet moved to Toronto's O'Keefe (later Hummingbird) Centre, where it will remain until the opening of the Four Seasons Centre for the Performing Arts.

3. The National Ballet first toured Europe in 1972, when it showcased Rudolf Nureyev's production of *The Sleeping Beauty.*

4. The company's North American tour in 1973 culminated in a triumphant debut at the Metropolitan Opera House in New York.

5. After Alexander Grant became artistic director in 1976, many new works by British choreographer Frederick Ashton were added to the repertoire.

6. In 1979, the National Ballet made its debut at the Royal Opera House, Covent Garden, in London.

7. After Erik Bruhn took over as artistic director in 1983, the company expanded its repertoire to include more works from modern dance.

8. Perhaps Canada's best-known ballerina is Karen Kain, who retired in 1997 after twenty-eight years with the National Ballet.

9. Since he became artistic director in 1996, James Kudelka has premiered many of his own and other choreographers' works.

10. In 2001, the National Ballet celebrated its fiftieth anniversary as an integral part of Canadian culture.

PARAGRAPH EXERCISE

If the <u>moon</u> is full and the night <u>skies</u> are alive with the calls of bird migrants, then the <u>way</u> is open for [an] adventure with your child, if <u>he</u> [or she] is old enough to use a telescope or a good pair of binoculars. The <u>sport</u> of watching migrating birds pass across the face of the moon <u>has become</u> popular and even scientifically important in recent years, and <u>it is</u> as good a way as <u>I know</u> to give an older child a sense of the mystery of migration.

(<u>You</u>) Seat yourself comfortably and <u>focus</u> your glass on the moon. <u>You must</u> learn patience, for unless <u>you are</u> on a well-travelled highway of migration <u>you may have</u> to wait many minutes before <u>you are</u> rewarded. In the waiting periods <u>you can study</u> the topography of the moon, for even a <u>glass</u> of moderate power <u>reveals</u> enough detail to fascinate a space-conscious child. But sooner or later <u>you should begin</u> to see the birds, lonely travellers in space glimpsed as <u>they pass</u> from darkness into darkness.

CORRECTING FRAGMENTS (PP. 69–73)

EXERCISE 1
Answers may vary, but here are some possible revisions.

1. Nellie McClung achieved fame as an advocate of women's rights in Canada.

2. Her birth name ~~being~~ *was* Helen Mooney.

3. She wrote popular novels about rural life in pre–World War I Canada.

4. Her novels ~~recording~~ *recorded* the realities of prairie experience and the struggles of farming families.

5. But today she is remembered as a political activist and essayist.

6. ~~Who~~ *She* became a reformer in the suffrage movement.

7. As a reformer, ~~protesting~~ *she protested* the harsh conditions of women's labour.

8. ~~Advancing~~ *She advanced* the feminist cause by touring on behalf of the Political Equality League.

9. In the courts and in Parliament, McClung ~~arguing~~ *argued* for women's right to be declared persons under the law.

10. Due to her efforts, women in Manitoba ~~getting~~ *got* the vote.

EXERCISE 2

Answers may vary, but here are some possible revisions.

1. In the 19th century, sculling *was* a popular sporting event.
2. Edward Hanlan *was* regarded by some as the best sculler of all time.
3. Born in Toronto, he sculled across Toronto Harbour every day to attend school.
4. Hanlan *was* competing in local regattas by age sixteen.
5. *Hanlan achieved* ~~achieving~~ a new world's record for sculling in 1878.
6. Hanlan *was* known for his eccentric style and flamboyant behaviour on the water.
7. He won both the American and English titles—the latter by eleven lengths.
8. Hanlan won the world professional championship in 1880 and went on to defend the title six times.
9. A monument on the grounds of Toronto's Canadian National Exhibition ~~honouring~~ *honours* him as "the most renowned oarsman of any age."
10. Part of one of the Toronto Islands *is* named Hanlan's Point.

EXERCISE 3

Answers may vary, but here are some possible revisions.

1. Finding a parking space on the first day of classes seems impossible. *I drive* endlessly around campus looking for an empty spot.
2. With hope that the situation will improve, I always spend the $200 for a parking permit.
3. My old car's engine doesn't like the long periods of idling. *It stalls* a lot and *won't start* up again easily.
4. In order to get a space close to my first class, I always follow anyone walking through the parking lot closest to the science building.
5. I am usually disappointed by this method, however. Most people *are* just walking through the parking lot to get to farther lots or to the bus stop.
6. I was really lucky on the first day of classes two semesters ago. *I drove* right into a spot vacated by a student from an earlier class.
7. Every morning, I see these early birds in their cars with their seats back. *They sleep* there for hours before class but in a great spot.
8. Maybe I should get up before dawn myself, *for that's* a foolproof way to secure a perfect parking place.
9. I don't think I can solve the problem this way. *I find* it hard to get out of bed in the dark.
10. Due to the increase in college enrolment, campus parking problems will most likely only get worse.

EXERCISE 4
Answers may vary, but here are some possible revisions.

1. We were writing in our journals when suddenly the fire alarm rang.

2. Everyone in the class looked at each other first and then at the teacher. *He* told us to gather up our things and follow him outside.

3. The series of short bells continued as we left the room and noisily walked out into the parking lot beside the main building.

4. The sunlight was very warm and bright compared to the classroom's fluorescent lights, which make everything look more clinical than natural.

5. As we stood in a large group with students and teachers from other classes, we wondered about the reason for the alarm.

6. I have never taken part in a fire alarm that was anything but a planned drill.

7. Without the danger of injury, a party atmosphere quickly develops since we all get a break from our responsibilities.

8. I've noticed that the teachers seem the most at ease because they don't have to be in control during these situations.

9. After we students and the teachers chatted for ten minutes or so, the final bell rang to signal the end of the drill.

10. When we sat down at our desks again, the teacher asked us to continue writing in our journals until the end of the hour.

EXERCISE 5
Answers may vary, but here are some possible revisions. (Added independent clauses are in italics.)

1. *I am surprised* that you know so much about the Canadian health-care system.

2. While the jury deliberated, *everyone else waited*.

3. But that story sounds unbelievable.

4. Be sure to send me a postcard.

5. Harry Houdini promised to visit his wife after his death.

6. Taking artistic photographs requires skill and patience.

7. *We returned* to the restaurant where we first met.

8. Until he noticed the price tag hanging from the side of the couch, *he liked it*.

9. *She was* a woman who travelled extensively during her childhood.

10. When the blizzard stops, *the game will go on*.

PROOFREADING EXERCISE
Answers may vary, but here are some possible revisions.

Although Barbara Ann Scott won the Olympic gold medal in women's figure skating in 1948, no other Canadian woman has managed to follow in her footsteps, a fact that demonstrates her extraordinary talent. She won many titles in her brief career, including North American and European championships and two world championships. Scott was known for her ability to overcome adverse conditions, an ability all the more remarkable because of her youth. She retired from competition at the tender age of twenty-five.

CORRECTING RUN-ON SENTENCES (PP. 76–80)

EXERCISE 1
Your answers may differ depending on how you chose to separate the two clauses.

1. Billy Bishop is a well-known Canadian war hero, for he once fought the infamous Red Baron.

2. Bishop wrote his wartime memoirs in 1918. He was the most famous of all the Allied aces.

3. The sentence is correct.

4. The sentence is correct.

5. That encounter took place in 1917; it ended in a draw.

6. The sentence is correct.

7. The Red Baron was buried in France with full military honours, but his remains were later exhumed and returned to Germany.

8. The sentence is correct.

9. Bishop was the most decorated Canadian in World War I, but many of his combat reports cannot be confirmed.

10. The Billy Bishop Heritage Museum in Owen Sound, Ontario, is dedicated to preserving artifacts of Canadian aviation history; more specifically, it displays materials documenting Bishop's achievements.

EXERCISE 2
Your answers may differ depending on how you chose to separate the two clauses.

1. Last week I decided to adopt a pet from an animal shelter, so I visited the SPCA near my house.

2. There were lots of great potential pets there. At first I couldn't choose between the dogs or the cats.

3. The sentence is correct.

4. My house doesn't have a fenced yard, so a dog would need to be walked in the mornings and evenings.

5. The sentence is correct.

6. But I am at work for most of the day; it might bark and disturb the neighbours.

7. The sentence is correct.

8. Cats are also independent; therefore, a cat wouldn't miss me during the day.

9. By coincidence, the shelter had just received a litter of gray and white kittens. I was lucky enough to have first choice and picked the best one.

10. I named her Dizzy, for she loves to chase the white tip of her tail around.

EXERCISE 3

Your answers may differ since various words can be used to begin dependent clauses.

1. Now that I've been learning about sleep in my psychology class, I know a lot more about it.

2. Sleep has five stages, which we usually go through many times during the night.

3. As the first stage of sleep begins, our muscles relax and mental activity slows down.

4. The sentence is correct.

5. Because stage two takes us deeper than stage one, we are no longer aware of our surroundings.

6. The sentence is correct.

7. Next is stage three, in which we become more and more relaxed and are very hard to awaken.

8. Stage four is so deep that we don't even hear loud noises.

9. The fifth stage of sleep is called REM (rapid-eye-movement) sleep because our eyes move back and forth quickly behind our eyelids.

10. Although REM sleep is only about as deep as stage two, we do all our dreaming during the REM stage.

EXERCISE 4

Your answers may differ since various words can be used to begin dependent clauses.

1. Lionel Conacher is not as well known as he should be, although his accomplishments are truly amazing.

2. He was an outstanding all-round athlete who was voted Canada's Athlete of the Half Century by the Canadian Press in 1950.

3. The sentence is correct.

4. As Canada's light-heavyweight boxing champion, he fought Jack Dempsey, who was the world heavyweight champion.

5. Even though he was one of the National Hockey League's leaders in penalty minutes, Conacher is widely regarded as one of the best defencemen in hockey.

6. Although he did not learn to skate until age sixteen, he won two Stanley Cups.

7. He practically won the 1921 Grey Cup by himself when he scored fifteen points during the Toronto Argonauts' 23–0 victory over the Edmonton Eskimos.

8. After he retired from sports, he became a member of Parliament.

9. The sentence is correct.

10. Conacher, who was nicknamed "The Big Train," was inducted into the Canadian Football Hall of Fame in 1963.

EXERCISE 5
Your answers may differ depending on how you chose to separate the clauses.

1. In 1999, the BBC released its documentary series called *The Life of Birds*. Sir David Attenborough was the host.

2. The series took nearly three years to complete as the crew filmed in more than forty countries and shot over three hundred kilometres of film.

3. The BBC spent $15 million (U.S.) making *The Life of Birds,* a cost that included Attenborough's travelling the equivalent of ten times around the world.

4. The BBC takes such shows very seriously; this one about birds comes after the BBC's amazing documentary called *The Private Life of Plants*.

5. For the plant series, BBC filmmakers even invented new ways to film plants and record the sounds they make, and a lot of the filming had to take place under artificial conditions. However, for the bird series, the BBC wanted a more realistic feeling.

6. All of the filming was done in the birds' own habitats so that it showed their natural behaviour, some of which had never been seen or filmed before.

7. To capture these rare moments, filmmakers had to live with birds in the wild, but it was not a very safe environment at times.

8. A tree full of BBC filmmakers was struck by lightning in an Amazon rain forest; they were covered with insects in Jamaica, and Attenborough had to speak to the camera in total darkness in a cave in Venezuela.

9. Makers of the series were especially proud of their bird of paradise footage, which they shot in New Guinea.

10. It turned out to be one of their biggest disappointments because the priceless film was erased by an especially powerful X-ray machine at the airport.

REVIEW OF FRAGMENTS AND RUN-ON SENTENCES (P. 81)

PROOFREADING EXERCISE
Your revisions may differ depending on how you chose to correct the errors.

Most people would not recognize the name Joseph Ignace Guillotin, but they probably have heard of the machine named after him, the guillotine. It's the device used when many a king or queen said, "Off with his—or her—head!" The guillotine consists of a slanted blade that falls down a window-frame-shaped tower and can be reset after it does its job. Guillotin was a doctor in France during the French Revolution. Even though he was not the inventor of the machine, he did suggest that it be used to behead people quickly and easily. Guillotin's name was first associated with the device in 1793. Now doctors everywhere also use the word *guillotine* to describe cutting procedures that they perform during tonsillectomies and other surgeries.

IDENTIFYING VERB PHRASES (PP. 83–87)

EXERCISE 1
1. I have always wondered how an Etch-A-Sketch works.

2. This flat TV-shaped toy has been popular since it first came out (in the 1960s).

3. Now I have discovered a website that answers questions (like the following): "How does an Etch-A-Sketch work?"

4. An Etch-A-Sketch is filled (with a combination) (of metal powder and tiny plastic particles).

5. This mixture clings (to the inside) (of the Etch-A-Sketch screen).

6. When the pointer that is connected (to the two knobs) moves, the tip (of it) "draws" lines (in the powder) (on the back) (of the screen).

7. The powder (at the bottom) (of the Etch-A-Sketch) does not fill in these lines because it is too far away.

8. But if the Etch-A-Sketch is turned upside down, the powder clings (to the whole underside surface) (of the screen) and "erases" the image again.

9. Although the basic Etch-A-Sketch has not changed since I was a kid, it now comes (in several different sizes).

10. Best (of all), these great drawing devices have never needed batteries, and I hope that they never will [need batteries].

EXERCISE 2

1. (In 1994), Toronto businessman Jack Rabinovitch founded the Giller Prize (for Canadian fiction) because he wanted to honour his late wife, Doris Giller.

2. The first winner (of the Giller Prize) was M.G. Vassanji, who has written extensively (about issues of race and identity).

3. Vassanji became a two-time winner when he was awarded the 2003 Giller Prize (for *The In-Between World of Vikram Lall*).

4. Other nominees (for the 2003 prize) included Ann-Marie MacDonald (for *The Way the Crow Flies*) and Margaret Atwood (for *Oryx and Crake*).

5. Already popular (in Canada), MacDonald became well known (to American readers) when her first novel, *Fall on Your Knees,* was chosen (for Oprah's Book Club).

6. Atwood's ninth novel, *Alias Grace,* won the Giller (in 1996).

7. Less well-known nominees (in 2003) included John Bemrose, who has published a play, two poetry collections, and an earlier novel.

8. Also (in the running) was John Gould (for *Kilter*), a collection (of fifty-five very short stories) that have been described as quirky gems.

9. Previous Giller winners have included Austin Clarke, Bonnie Burnard, Alice Munro, and Mordecai Richler.

10. The Giller Prize has helped to raise the profile (of both established and emerging Canadian writers).

EXERCISE 3

1. When we think (of ancient structures), Stonehenge (in England) and the Great Pyramids (of Egypt) come (to mind).

2. Fairly recently, Fred Wendorf discovered an arrangement (of stones) possibly a thousand years older (than Stonehenge).

3. Wendorf uncovered the stone structures (of Nabta Playa) while he was researching nomadic people (in Egypt).

4. Wendorf dug down (to the level) where eight huge stone tablets formed a circle.

5. He and other anthropologists believe that nomads must have created the site (for astronomical purposes).

6. The slabs and their arrangement date back seven thousand years.

7. They were placed (in groups) (of two) and were aligned (with different points) (of the compass).

8. (Near the circle) (of stones) was a tomb that had not been found before.

9. It had been used not (for a dead king) but (for the nomads' cattle).

10. These nomadic people may have been the first citizens (of the Nile Valley) so many thousands (of years) ago.

EXERCISE 4

1. (During the last semester) (of high school), my English teacher assigned a special paper.

2. He said that he was becoming depressed (by all the bad news) (out there), so each (of us) was assigned to find a piece (of good news) and write a short research paper (about it).

3. I must admit that I had no idea how hard that assignment would be.

4. Finally, I found an article while I was reading my favourite magazine.

5. The title (of the article) was a pun; it was called "Grin Reaper."

6. I knew instantly that it must be just the kind (of news) my teacher was searching for.

7. The article explained that one woman, Pam Johnson, had started a club that she named The Secret Society (of Happy People).

8. She had even chosen August 8 (as "(You) Admit You're Happy Day") and had already convinced more than fifteen governors (in the United States) to recognize the holiday.

9. The club and the holiday were created to support people who are happy so that the unhappy, negative people (around them) will not bring the happy people down.

10. As I was writing my essay, I visited the Happy People website and, (for extra credit), signed my teacher up (for their newsletter).

EXERCISE 5

1. Last night I took my daughter (to a performance) (by her favourite group).

2. The tickets were not too expensive, and I remembered how much fun I had had at concerts (in my younger days).

3. I had not been (to an open-air event) (for several years), however, and I was expecting the same kind (of experience).

4. I should have considered the changes that have occurred (since then).

5. The first difference was that, when we arrived, people were waiting (in a long line) (in the hot sunshine) to get (into the stadium) even though everyone had assigned seats.

6. I asked a staff member why they weren't spending time (in their cars) or (in the cool shade).

7. He told me that they were hoping to get in first so that they could buy the best souvenirs.

8. Once we were (inside the place), I saw what he meant; T-shirts (with $50 price tags) and every other kind (of object) (with the group's name or picture) (on it) were being bought (by frantic fans).

9. I understood then why the tickets had been so inexpensive; as long as they brought the customers (to the merchandise), they had done their job.

10. (After three opening acts), my daughter's favourite group finally arrived (on stage), overwhelmed the crowd (with special effects), and left everyone (with lots) (of souvenirs) (as memories).

REVIEW EXERCISE

Avril Lavigne is a Canadian singer who became a star (at the age) (of seventeen). Originally (from Napanee, Ontario), where she was born (on September 27, 1984), Lavigne has been adjusting (to life) (in the big city). (At sixteen), she was discovered (by Arista Records) and moved (to Manhattan) where she began work (on her debut album), *Let Go.* She later relocated (to Los Angeles).

Not long after Lavigne released *Let Go* (in 2002), fans responded (with enthusiasm) (to her dynamic spirit and fierce individuality). The Napanee native, who plays the guitar, explores her personal experiences (of love) and (of life) (in songs) (like "Losing Grip"). Although Lavigne was shut out (of the Grammy Awards), she triumphed (at the Junos) where she won single (of the year) (for the hit song)

"Complicated," album (of the year) and best pop album (for *Let Go),* and best new
artist.

(In recent years), <u>singers</u> (like Avril Lavigne and pop-country superstar Shania Twain) <u>have demonstrated</u> the growing prominence (of Canada) (in pop culture).

USING STANDARD ENGLISH VERBS (PP. 90–93)

EXERCISE 1
1. prepares, prepared   **6.** needs, needed
2. help, helped   **7.** has, had
3. are, were   **8.** is, was
4. have, had   **9.** works, worked
5. does, did   **10.** am, was

EXERCISE 2
1. are, were   **6.** counts, counted
2. does, did   **7.** are, were
3. has, had   **8.** do, did
4. opens, opened   **9.** look, looked
5. have, had   **10.** is, was

EXERCISE 3
1. changed, want   **6.** observed, had
2. had   **7.** watched, helped
3. signed, turned   **8.** had
4. was, were   **9.** imagined, had
5. did, were, does   **10.** needs, are, am

EXERCISE 4
1. watch   **6.** wager
2. watches, watch   **7.** add, calls, is
3. am, is   **8.** love, have
4. are   **9.** plan
5. decides   **10.** likes

EXERCISE 5

1. Yesterday my English teacher *assigned* a research paper.

2. The sentence is correct.

3. The sentence is correct.

4. They *were* about holiday traditions in different families.

5. In one paper, the writer *explained* the tradition of Thanksgiving at her house.

6. I *liked* the part about making pies for the adults and candy for the kids.

7. The second paper *outlined* the steps another family goes through to prepare for Chinese New Year.

8. That one *had* even more details about food and gifts for the children.

9. The sentence is correct.

10. I *started* my rough draft last night; it's about my dad's obsession with Halloween.

PROOFREADING EXERCISE

I have a new piano teacher, Mr. Stevenson, who *talks* very softly and *plays* the piano beautifully. When he wants to teach me a new song, he *starts* by showing me the sheet music. Then he *asks* me to look it over. I am always nervous if it *shows* a new hand position or a new dynamic sign. But then he *calms* me down with his soothing voice and patient manner. Once I figure the piece out by looking at it, I *play* it through slowly. Mr. Stevenson *doesn't* do any of the annoying things my other piano teachers did. I like him a lot.

USING REGULAR AND IRREGULAR VERBS (PP. 98–102)

EXERCISE 1

1. practise

2. practised

3. practising

4. practise

5. practised

6. practises

7. practise

8. practising

9. practising

10. practise

EXERCISE 2

1. try, tries

2. bought, buys

3. was, am

4. thought, think

5. grown, grown

6. leave, left

7. watches, watching

8. hears, hear

9. speaks, spoken

10. was, is

EXERCISE 3

1. took, supposed
2. did, earned
3. called, told, feel
4. thought, was
5. leaving, drove, saw

6. felt, knew, tell
7. tried, went
8. been, undo
9. wishes, take
10. used, called, does

EXERCISE 4

1. use, puts
2. does, do
3. transfers, spend
4. is, like, choose
5. does, wants

6. trusts, is
7. imagine, made
8. talking, asked, worries
9. looked, said, understand
10. trust, been

EXERCISE 5

1. lying, fell
2. was, done
3. wearing, shielded
4. lain, woke, realized, happened

5. felt, started

6. passed, turned, began
7. describe, experienced
8. was, felt, saw
9. looked, taped, was, protected, wearing

10. had, felt

PROGRESS TEST (PP. 102–3)

1. A. fragment (*I took* a nap for several hours in the afternoon.)
2. B. incorrect verb form (Last semester we *enrolled* in the same math class.)
3. B. fragment (Attach the dependent clause to the previous sentence.)
4. A. incorrect verb form (Karen *used* to take the bus . . .)
5. B. missing comma to prevent misreading (Because Tim was driving, his mother . . .)
6. B. unnecessary comma (I will write in my journal every day and will turn . . .)
7. A. incorrect verb form (were *supposed*)
8. A. incorrect verb form (had already *finished*)
9. B. incorrect verb form (were *lying*)
10. B. fragment (*Packing is especially difficult when the weather is uncertain.*)

MAINTAINING SUBJECT/VERB AGREEMENT (PP. 106–9)

EXERCISE 1

1. have
2. were
3. makes
4. includes
5. gives

6. are
7. use
8. is, has
9. fear
10. are

EXERCISE 2

1. are, involve
2. suffer
3. are
4. come, lead
5. start, works, plays

6. starts
7. are
8. cause
9. is
10. warn

EXERCISE 3

1. were
2. administers, has
3. takes
4. receive
5. is

6. sponsors, has
7. were
8. are
9. is
10. is

EXERCISE 4

1. is
2. has
3. starts
4. puts, wants
5. likes

6. have, looks
7. let, wants
8. have
9. helps, turn
10. am, is

EXERCISE 5

1. pictures, does
2. are, travel
3. expect
4. creates
5. have

6. Do
7. were
8. was, were
9. has
10. are

PROOFREADING EXERCISE

All of the students in my drama club *have* chosen the play *Cyrano de Bergerac* for our next production. There *are* actually two famous Cyrano de Bergeracs. One of them is the title character of the play, and the other is the real person who had that name. Both of these men *are* famous for their large noses and for their writing. But only the fictional Cyrano loves Roxane. The tragic story of Cyrano and Roxane *was* written by Edmond Rostand. In it, Cyrano *believes* that Roxane could never love an ugly man. She thinks that she *loves* Christian, Cyrano's fellow soldier, who is extremely handsome. But she really *loves* Cyrano, who writes all of the love letters that Christian gives Roxane. In those letters *is* the soul that Roxane *admires,* but she finds out too late. It's a very sad and dramatic story, and I hope that either my friend Lisa or I *get* the part of Roxane.

AVOIDING SHIFTS IN TIME (PP. 111–12)

PROOFREADING EXERCISES

1. Adrienne Clarkson was born in Hong Kong in 1939. She *came* to Canada as a refugee with her parents during the war. She attended schools in Ottawa and *went* on to obtain degrees in English literature from the University of Toronto. For almost twenty years, she worked as a host, writer, and producer for several influential CBC programs. Her career path *took* a striking turn when she served as a diplomat in Paris and subsequently *became* president and publisher of McClelland & Stewart. She returned to broadcasting in 1988 and, a little more than a decade later, *was* sworn in as Governor General of Canada.

2. The paragraph is correct.

3. I really enjoyed my summer vacation this year. It *wasn't* long enough, of course, but I made the most of the time I *had.* My geology club took a trip to Baja, California. We didn't pack enough to eat, but the beautiful scenery *took* my breath away. Once I *was* back home, I *played* a lot of tennis with my roommates. One night we stayed at the tennis court until after it *closed.* We *were* just hitting volleys in the dark with only the moon for lighting. It was an unplanned thing, and we could barely see the ball. It *was* fun to goof off with my friends on a summer evening. Overall, the trip to Baja and the after-hours tennis match *were* the highlights of my summer vacation.

RECOGNIZING VERBAL PHRASES (PP. 114–17)

EXERCISE 1

1. [Sending children to summer hockey camp] <u>is</u> an increasingly common practice in Canada.

2. Many parents <u>have decided</u> [to enrol their children in hockey camps] instead of [sending them to traditional camps].

3. Some families <u>spend</u> several months [investigating hockey camps for their sons or daughters].

4. A good camp <u>will help</u> children [to improve and broaden their hockey-playing skills].

5. [Preparing children for junior hockey] <u>is</u> the mandate of several hockey camps.

6. Most young hockey players <u>want</u> [to have the opportunity] [to join a top team].

7. One camp in Manitoba <u>has adopted</u> a coeducational curriculum, [allowing both boys and girls to attend].

8. [Taking an advanced hockey course] <u>will benefit</u> some players.

9. [Concerned about education], a player <u>may prefer</u> to play college or university hockey.

10. [Striking a healthy balance between school and sports] <u>is</u> a difficult task.

EXERCISE 2

1. A Japanese company [called Matsushita] <u>expects</u> [to offer fully interactive houses] [operated by computer network] in the near future.

2. [Getting ready for work in the morning] <u>will be</u> very different.

3. The electronic toilet-of-the-future <u>is designed</u> [to take care of everything]— [weighing you], [checking your health through various tests], and even [sending the data to your doctor if necessary].

4. [Talking into your television's remote control] <u>will turn</u> on the space-age TV screens of the future [positioned in almost every room of the house].

5. [Using a cell phone with its own video screen from your desk at work], you'll <u>be able</u> [to check the contents of your refrigerator] before [shopping for groceries].

6. And once you <u>return</u> home with the food, you <u>can update</u> the fridge's contents [using voice commands].

7. [Glancing at monitors] [set up in key areas], you <u>can check</u> the status of your laundry room, [living] room, and kitchen simultaneously.

8. The rooms themselves <u>will respond</u> to your movements through the use of infrared sensors—[lighting up], [cooling off], or [heating up] as necessary.

9. A security system <u>will be used</u> [to take the picture] of anyone [approaching the front door] and [to store the snapshot for twelve months].

10. Needless [to say], the fully [wired] Japanese house of the 21st century will be expensive, [costing nearly 5 percent more than an ordinary, [old-fashioned] one].

EXERCISE 3

1. The Fathers of Confederation, [attending their first conference on the possibility of a Maritime union], met in Charlottetown in 1864.

2. [Hearing of the planned conference], representatives proposed a larger union—that of British North America.

3. [Adjourned on September 9], the meeting continued among delegates in Saint John, Fredericton, and Halifax.

4. An [observing] delegation from the Maritime provinces went to the second conference.

5. John A. Macdonald was a [dominating] presence at the conference, though Étienne-Paschal Taché was the official chair.

6. [Following the second conference], a text [called the Quebec Resolutions] became the basis for the third conference.

7. [To avoid] [angering the United States], representatives decided [to call the new union a "dominion" instead of a "kingdom"].

8. [Lasting approximately four months], the last conference resulted in the British North America Act.

9. [To be precise], Canada officially became a country on July 1, 1867.

10. Its new prime minister was John A. Macdonald, a [practising] lawyer [born in Scotland].

EXERCISE 4

1. Canada East (also [known as Quebec]), Canada West (or Ontario), New Brunswick, and Nova Scotia joined Confederation in 1867.

2. Manitoba decided [to become part of the union in 1870].

3. [Separated from most of Canada], the land between British Columbia and the East was known as the Territories.

4. The sixth province [to enter Confederation] was British Columbia in 1871.

5. Prince Edward Island joined in 1873, [bringing the total to seven].

6. Alberta and Saskatchewan came on board in 1905, [frustrating Manitoba's plans] [to expand its borders west].

7. Newfoundland <u>entered</u> Confederation in 1949, [becoming the last province to join].

8. Canada <u>has</u> three territories [belonging to the union but not considered provinces].

9. [Created in 1870 and 1898 respectively], the Northwest Territories and Yukon Territory <u>have undergone</u> a complicated evolution.

10. The Inuit <u>advocated</u> the establishment of a new political entity, [resulting in the creation of Nunavut in 1999].

EXERCISE 5

1. Canadian places <u>are</u> often <u>given</u> unusual names, [derived from a variety of languages].

2. [Sighted by Leif Ericson], Baffin Island <u>was named</u> Helluland, [meaning "Land of Flat Stones"].

3. Jacques Cartier <u>assigned</u> the name Mont Royal to the city [known as Hochelaga] and [destined] [to become Montreal].

4. [Thinking them barriers to his path to China], Cartier <u>named</u> the Lachine Rapids.

5. Kanata, [meaning "our village"], <u>became</u> the name of the country [explored]: Canada.

6. A less [accepted] view is that the name Kanata <u>is derived</u> from the words *acada nada*, [meaning "nothing here"], [written on a map by Portuguese explorers].

7. [Located on the north shore of the St. Lawrence River], Quebec City <u>was</u> originally the site of an Indian village [called Stadacona].

8. Originally [named Bytown], Ottawa <u>gets</u> its name from the Algonquin word for "trade."

9. In December 1984, residents of Frobisher Bay <u>voted</u> [to rename the place Iqaluit], [meaning "place of fish"].

10. Regina, [named in honour of Queen Victoria], <u>was</u> originally <u>called</u> Pile of Bones.

PARAGRAPH EXERCISE

Margaret Atwood, the author of more than thirty books of poetry, fiction, and nonfiction, <u>was born</u> in Ottawa in 1939 and <u>grew up</u> in northern Quebec and Ontario, as well as Toronto. [Considered one of Canada's major contemporary writers], she <u>has</u>

managed [to achieve both popular and critical success], [topping bestseller lists] and [garnering numerous awards], [including the Booker Prize]. [Acclaimed internationally], her books have been published in over thirty-five countries and translated into more than thirty languages. Her novel *The Handmaid's Tale,* [published in 1985], was made into a feature film [starring Natasha Richardson and Robert Duvall]. *Survival,* her groundbreaking study of Canadian literature, continues [to shape the way Canadians look at themselves]. [Known for her keen interest in human rights], Atwood has been active in Amnesty International and International PEN, [serving as president of the latter organization's Anglo-Canadian branch from 1984 to 1986]. [Adding to her many achievements], she was inducted into Canada's Walk of Fame in 2001.

SENTENCE WRITING

Your sentences may vary, but make sure that your verbals are not actually the main verbs of your clauses. You should be able to double underline your real verbs, as was done here.

1. I enjoy [speaking French].

2. [Typing on a small keyboard] hurts my wrists.

3. [Driving to Regina from here] takes about three hours.

4. I spent the day [reading the final chapters of my book].

5. I love [to eat breakfast outside in the summer].

6. We were invited [to go out to dinner].

7. I would like [to chat with you], but I am late for a meeting.

8. [To cook like a real gourmet] takes practice.

9. [Impressed by my grades], my parents bought me a new car.

10. [Taken in small doses], aspirin helps prevent heart attacks.

CORRECTING MISPLACED OR DANGLING MODIFIERS (PP. 119–22)

EXERCISE 1

Your answers may differ slightly.

1. After checking out the online catalogue, *I found* my desire to spend grew.

2. I found many items *while* surfing the Internet this afternoon.

3. The sentence is correct.

4. Finding daily bargains on eBay, *I believe* online shopping comes naturally to me.

5. I bid on a notebook computer with a wireless mouse, but I'll *never make a bid like that* again.

6. My friends *e-mail* me advertisements from big box stores.

7. The sentence is correct.

8. After opening my presents, *I pleased* my parents with my reaction.

9. The sentence is correct.

10. When surfing the Internet, *people may find that* impulse buying *is* a problem.

Exercise 2

1. Getting ready for the fall, *we turned* our clocks back one hour.

2. The sentence is correct.

3. Forgetting to reset his clock, *my friend found* the adjustment more difficult.

4. *After the clocks are set* ahead one hour in the spring, traffic accidents increase for about a week.

5. The sentence is correct.

6. In the fall, I eat my bacon and eggs *while* waiting for the sun to come up.

7. Feeling like a coal miner, *I am depressed by* the return home from work in the dark.

8. Ignoring the time changes, my cat *habitually wakens* me at first light.

9. The sentence is correct.

10. *For those* living near the equator, time changes are almost unknown.

Exercise 3

1. Born in Newmarket, Ontario, Norm *Foster has written plays that* are popular with audiences across Canada.

2. Often compared to Neil Simon, *Foster writes plays that* are noted for their light comic touch.

3. *When Foster was fifty-two, he* and his wife toured as actors in his play *Here on the Flight Path.*

4. The sentence is correct.

5. Once a disc jockey in New Brunswick, *Foster now writes plays that* are produced across Canada and in the United States.

6. The sentence is correct.

7. *The Last Resort* is a funny and touching musical comedy *that Foster created while* working with Leslie Arden, a Canadian musician who studied with Stephen Sondheim.

8. The sentence is correct.

9. Thinking that it is easy, *people do not give comedy* the respect it deserves.

10. The sentence is correct.

EXERCISE 4

1. Margaret Atwood established her poetic reputation *by* winning a Governor General's Award for *The Circle Game.*

2. The sentence is correct.

3. *Before deciding to become a writer,* Atwood completed a master's degree in English literature at the University of Toronto.

4. I read the review of her eleventh novel, *Oryx and Crake, that appeared in The Globe and Mail.*

5. Atwood explored the death of a parent in a book of poetry entitled *Morning in the Burned House, which was* nominated for a Governor General's Award.

6. Critics *at home and abroad* routinely praise Atwood for her writing.

7. *In Alias Grace, which won the Giller Prize,* she fictionalized the life and times of a 19th-century domestic servant convicted of murder.

8. Indifferently reviewed in Canada, *The Blind Assassin won the 2000 Booker Prize.*

9. The sentence is correct.

10. Atwood explores themes of women's alienation in *The Edible Woman, published in 1969.*

EXERCISE 5

1. The sentence is correct.

2. Before writing the Wingfield plays, *Needles wrote a column for Harrowsmith magazine in which he recounted* the adventures of a big-city fellow turned farmer in Persephone Township.

3. The sentence is correct.

4. A talented raconteur, *Needles has performed* stories and songs dealing with life in rural Ontario.

5. *Rod Beattie is* a veteran of the Stratford Festival; *his* name has become synonymous with the character of Walt Wingfield.

6. Walt is a retired stockbroker turned farmer who recounts his adventures *on the farm* in a series of letters to the editor.

7. The sentence is correct.

8. Using a multitude of techniques, *Beattie cleverly portrays the seventeen entertaining characters that are featured in the Wingfield plays.*

9. Winner of a Dora Mavor Moore Award for his performances in the first three Wingfield plays, Beattie *did an Ontario tour of Love Letters with his wife, actress Martha Henry.*

10. The sentence is correct.

PROOFREADING EXERCISE

Corrections are italicized. Yours may differ slightly.

Hoping to become famous and wealthy, a man in Edinburgh, Scotland, has invented a device. *Located just above the trunk and visible from behind,* the device is a variation on the centre-mounted brake light used in the design of many new cars. Instead of just a solid red brake light, however, this invention displays to other drivers *words* written in bold, red-lighted letters.

With simplicity in mind, *the inventor limited the machine's vocabulary to* three words: "Sorry," "Thanks," and "Help." After making an aggressive lane change, *we could use the machine to* apologize. Or after being allowed to go ahead of someone, *we could thank* the considerate person responsible. Of course, *with the use* of the "Help" display, we could summon fellow citizens for assistance.

And there is no need to worry about operating the device while driving. With three easy-to-reach buttons, *we could activate the messages* without taking our eyes off the road.

FOLLOWING SENTENCE PATTERNS (PP. 126–29)

EXERCISE 1

       S   LV DESC.
1. My sister Belinda is allergic (to many things).

     S AV OBJ.
2. She gets hives (from mould and pollen).

               S   AV   OBJ.
3. (Of course), milk upsets her stomach.

         S   S   LV   DESC.
4. Strawberries and raspberries are many people's favourite fruits.

        S AV   OBJ.
5. But they give Belinda a rash (on her face and arms).

                    S   **AV**   **OBJ.**
6. The <u>doctor</u> <u>has made</u> a list (of Belinda's allergies).

                         S   **AV**   **OBJ.**
7. Soon <u>she'll</u> <u>be receiving</u> allergy shots.

                       S   **AV**   **OBJ.**
8. The <u>shots</u> <u>should reduce</u> Belinda's sensitivity (to these substances).

                  S   **AV**
9. <u>Everyone</u> (in my family) <u>is hoping</u> (for the best).

                             S   **LV**   **DESC.**
10. (With luck), <u>Belinda</u> <u>will feel</u> better soon.

EXERCISE 2
                 S   **AV**
1. <u>Scientists</u> (around the world) <u>are working</u> (on a new technology).

        S LV   **DESC.**
2. <u>It</u> <u>is</u> a special computer.

          S   **AV**   **OBJ.**
3. <u>It</u> <u>will translate</u> one language (into another) instantly.

           S   **AV**   **OBJ.**
4. <u>People</u> <u>will carry</u> the device (with them) (in their travels).

           S   **AV**   **OBJ.**   **S**   **AV**   **OBJ.**
5. <u>They</u> <u>will ask</u> a question (in English), and the <u>device</u> <u>will repeat</u> the question
    (in French, Spanish, German, or Japanese).

               S   **AV**   **OBJ.**
6. The <u>traveller</u> <u>will hear</u> the translation (over a pair) (of headphones).

                 S   **AV**   **OBJ.**
7. But <u>computers</u> still <u>have</u> some trouble (in recognizing people's speech).

                     S   **AV**   **OBJ.**
8. Ordinary <u>ramblings</u> usually <u>include</u> numerous interruptions, (such as "um,"
    "er," and "eh?").

            S   **AV**   **OBJ.**
9. <u>Nobody</u> <u>has programmed</u> totally accurate translating software yet.

     S **LV**   **DESC.**

10. But researchers are now closer than ever (to using computers) (as translators).

EXERCISE 3

        S   **AV**   **OBJ.**

 1. (In 2003), a gala live performance commemorated the Queen's fiftieth year (on the throne).

      S   **S** **AV**   **OBJ.**

 2. Sir Andrew Davis, who conducted the BBC Symphony Orchestra and Chorus,

   LV **DESC.**

   was among the performers.

       S   **AV**

 3. Dame Kiri Te Kanawa, a soprano originally from New Zealand, also gave a

   OBJ.   **S** **AV**

   performance, just as she did (at Charles and Diana's wedding) (in St. Paul's Cathedral) (in 1981).

      S   **LV** **DESC.**

 4. "The Party at the Palace" was a popular event (at the gala).

           S

 5. (At that event), pop singers (like Sir Paul McCartney and Sir Elton John)

   AV

   performed.

      S   **LV**   **DESC.**

 6. American bands (like the Beach Boys) were just as well received (as British pop stars) (like Rod Stewart and Cliff Richard).

     S   **AV** **OBJ.**

 7. Dame Edna, (also known as Barry Humphries), introduced the Queen (as "the

         S   **AV**

   birthday girl") when Her Majesty arrived part way (through the event).

     S   **AV**   **S**   **AV** **OBJ.**

 8. Many people remember that Prince Charles called his mother "mummy" (at the gala).

              S   **LV**

 9. (Despite some turbulent years), Queen Elizabeth II has become a much-

   DESC.

   respected figure (during her reign).

　　　S　　　　　　　　　　　　　　　　　　　　**AV**　　　　　**OBJ.**
10. <u>Millions</u> (of people) (around the world) <u>watched</u> the parades, processions, and performances staged (in her honour).

EXERCISE 4

　　　　　　　　　S　　**AV**　　**OBJ.**
1. (In Canada), <u>we</u> <u>love</u> our pets.

　　　　S　　**AV**　　　**OBJ.**
2. <u>We</u> <u>own</u> millions (of them).

　　　　　　　　S　　　　　　　　　**AV**
3. Most <u>people</u> (in Canada) <u>live</u> (with pets).

　　　　　　　　　　　　S　　　　**AV**　　　**OBJ.**
4. (Of these pet owners), <u>most</u> <u>have chosen</u> dogs (as their favourites).

　　　　　　　　　S　　　　　　　**AV OBJ.**
5. Many <u>people</u>, (of course), <u>prefer</u> cats.

　　　　　　　　　　　　S　　　　　　　　　　　**AV**
6. Pet food and supply <u>companies</u> (in Canada) <u>are prospering</u> (at the moment).

　　　S　　　　　　　**AV**　　　　　**OBJ.**
7. <u>Canadians</u> are even <u>buying</u> health insurance (for their pets).

　　　　　　　　　　　　　　　　　S
8. (In recent years), the average <u>cost</u> (of pet medical treatment) <u>has soared</u>.

　　　　　　　　S　　　**AV**　　　　　**OBJ.**
9. Now <u>people</u> <u>will spend</u> thousands (for pet-care measures).

　　　　　　　　　　　　　S　　　**AV**　　　　　**OBJ.**
10. The Canadian pet-care <u>industry</u> <u>makes</u> a great deal (of money) every year.

EXERCISE 5

　　　　　　　S　　　　　　　　　　　**AV**　　　　**OBJ.**
1. One <u>pet owner</u> (in my hometown) <u>tells</u> a fascinating story (about her dog).

　　　　S　**AV**　　　**OBJ.**
2. <u>She</u> <u>had</u> a Chihuahua named Peppy.

　　　　S　　**AV**　　**OBJ.**　　　　**S**　　　**AV**　　　**S**　　**AV**
3. <u>Peppy</u> <u>hated</u> mail carriers, and <u>he</u> even <u>knew</u> when <u>they</u> <u>were coming</u>.

S   AV
4. Every day (during the week), Peppy would bark (at the window) just before

S   AV
the mail carrier appeared.

S   LV   DESC.   S   LV   DESC.
5. Peppy was never wrong, even though the mail carrier was sometimes a bit late.

S   AV
6. (For some reason), the dog never barked (on weekends).

S   AV   S   AV   OBJ.
7. We all wondered how (on earth) he knew the mail carrier's time (of arrival).

S   AV   OBJ.
8. Every weekday, Peppy's owner watched a soap opera.

S   AV   OBJ.   S   AV
9. Then the network changed the scheduling (of the program), so that it aired an

hour earlier every day.

S   AV   OBJ.   S   LV
10. The music (of the soap opera) had warned Peppy when the mail carrier was

DESC.   S   AV   OBJ.
about to arrive, so the change (in the program's schedule) baffled him.

PARAGRAPH EXERCISE
Capital Cities

S   AV   S   LV   DESC.   S   AV
Most Canadians know that Ottawa is Canada's capital city. But they forget that the

S   LV   DESC.   S   AV   S
capital (of British Columbia) is beautiful Victoria. Some people assume that Vancouver,

LV   DESC.
the larger city, is the provincial capital. (Unlike many world capitals), however,

S   LV   DESC.   S   AV   OBJ.
provincial capitals are not always big cities; Charlottetown, for instance, has a population

S   LV   DESC.
(of only about 35,000). Some Canadians are more knowledgeable (about capital

cities) (in other countries), (such as the United States), than (about their own capitals).

S   AV   S   AV   OBJ.
Quiz shows (like *Jeopardy*) demonstrate that Americans have limited knowledge

(of Canada) (in general).

AVOIDING CLICHÉS, AWKWARD PHRASING, AND WORDINESS (PP. 133–37)

Your answers may differ from these possible revisions.

EXERCISE 4

1. I should practise my piano, but I can't.

2. I've been studying it for about two years.

3. At first, I wanted to learn the notes and hand positions, but now they seem old-fashioned.

4. Keyboards today play music themselves.

5. Sentence 5 may be omitted if combined with Sentence 6.

6. I bought a keyboard because I couldn't afford a piano.

7. My upright digital keyboard feels and sounds like a real piano.

8. But my music teacher doesn't know that, instead of practising for hours, I listen to the demo songs.

9. I just push a button to hear the theme from *Star Wars*.

10. I'll probably never learn to play the piano.

EXERCISE 2

1. My family reunited recently to celebrate my grandmother's birthday.

2. We wanted to surprise Grandma and see her happy face when she found us all there.

3. Each of us had to travel to reach the reunion since we live in different parts of the country.

4. Luckily, we all arrived before Grandma.

5. We had chosen my cousin Jeff to distract Grandma before the reunion.

6. He asked her to help him buy a new coat at the mall.

7. She was flattered and agreed to help.

8. While at the mall, Jeff pretended to remember a date with a friend, and he drove Grandma to the campground.

9. When they arrived, we hid behind trees and tables, then jumped out and yelled "Surprise!"

10. We sat Grandma down in a big chair and treated her like a queen.

EXERCISE 3

1. An article in *Discover* (Sept. 1999) explains that ancient Egyptians used makeup in many different ways.

2. First, they painted their faces to make themselves attractive.

3. Egyptians seemed to be as vain as we are.

4. Surprisingly, Egyptian men also wore makeup.

5. French scientists and beauty experts have studied the contents of vessels found inside the tombs of kings and queens of the Nile from as early as 2700 B.C.

6. From these remains, scientists have identified the ingredients that Egyptians used in their makeup.

7. The ingredients include goose fat, lettuce, animal blood, crushed beetles, cinnamon, and a few artificial ingredients.

8. Like us, the Egyptians knew enough about chemistry to create these artificial substances.

9. Finally, the Egyptians may have used makeup as medicine.

10. Two of their makeup's artificial ingredients, laurionite and phosgenite, may have helped cure eye infections commonly contracted from bacteria in the water when the Nile flooded the valley.

EXERCISE 4

1. This year I'll get an $800 tax return.

2. I used to do my own taxes.

3. I would wait for my T4 forms, fill out the short form, and receive a small refund.

4. Then my mom convinced me to be serious about my taxes.

5. Sentence 5 may be omitted if combined with Sentence 4.

6. I asked my friends at work for any recommendations, and Jason gave me a phone number.

7. I called Helen, Jason's tax preparer.

8. Helen explained that I could control the amount of taxes withheld from my paycheque.

9. Before speaking with Helen, I was ignorant about taxes.

10. And there may be more that I don't understand.

EXERCISE 5

1. Many Canadians order pizza at least once a week.

2. Sentence 2 may be omitted if combined with Sentence 1.

3. The fast-food industry wants to know what Canadians like to eat.

4. Tim Hortons and Wendy's have dominated the fast-food industry for many years.

5. Tim Hortons and Wendy's merged in order to strengthen their market position.

6. To increase sales, Tim Hortons opened new stores across Canada.

7. Despite the ambitious expansion, the company continues to establish more outlets.

8. Tim Hortons and Starbucks are the two main competitors in the coffee wars.

9. A company's ability to survive depends on consumer demand.

10. Employees in the highly competitive fast-food industry are kept busy.

PROOFREADING EXERCISE

Nobody in my family is "normal." The oddest of all is my Uncle Crank. His real name is Frank, but ever since I was young, Uncle Frank has been called Uncle "Crank" because his arm doesn't bend the right way at the elbow. It turns like the crank of an old car in silent films. My uncle is proud of his unique arm, but I wish the doctors had fixed it so that Uncle "Crank" could have just been normal Uncle Frank.

CORRECTING FOR PARALLEL STRUCTURE (PP. 139–43)

EXERCISE 1

1. I was in Sudbury, Ontario, last fall and paid a visit to Science North.

2. The educational features and children's activities that the museum offers draw many visitors.

3. The late F. Jean MacLeod was the daughter of one of Sudbury's earliest pioneers, and she established a trust that was used to fund Science North's butterfly gallery.

4. MacLeod's father worked as a geologist, assayer, prospector, and mining engineer.

5. The sentence is correct.

6. Visitors to Science North find the exhibits informative and entertaining.

7. Science North is famous for its visitor-friendly approach and interactive exhibits.

8. The museum is especially proud of its most popular attractions, such as the Climate Change Show, the 200-seat IMAX theatre, and the Virtual Voyages Adventure Ride.

9. The Climate Change Show uses stunning special effects and a humorous talking sheep to address the topic of global warming.

10. The sentence is correct.

EXERCISE 2

1. The use of bar codes has a clear past but an uncertain future.

2. The bar-code scanner was first used on June 26, 1974, and the product first scanned was a pack of chewing gum.

3. The sentence is correct.

4. Labelling products with bar codes dates back to the 1960s, but using bar codes at the checkout counter did not happen until 1974.

5. The sentence is correct.

6. Prisons track inmates, shipping companies scan railroad cars, hospitals verify blood samples, and cattle ranchers identify cows.

7. Some people worry about the future use and possible misuse of bar codes.

8. Several years ago, there was a rumour that governments might bar-code people and keep track of them for the rest of their lives.

9. Such paranoid and far-fetched ideas are usually not true.

10. But the possibilities of bar codes do make people wonder about how, where, and why they will be used in the years to come.

EXERCISE 3

1. I was washing my car two weeks ago and noticed a few bees buzzing around the roof of my garage.

2. I didn't worry about it at the time, but I should have.

3. The sentence is correct.

4. The sentence is correct.

5. They flew in a pattern as if they were riding on a roller coaster or over waves.

6. The sentence is correct.

7. There was nothing I could do but wait in my car until they went away.

8. Finally, the bees flew straight up into the air and disappeared.

9. Once inside my house, I opened the phone book and called a bee expert.

10. The sentence is correct.

EXERCISE 4

1. Leonard Cohen is a poet, novelist, performer, and songwriter.

2. He published his first book of poetry in 1956 and produced a large and respected body of work in subsequent years.

3. Visitors to the many websites devoted to Cohen and his work can read and appreciate his poems, lyrics, and interviews.

4. Cohen has said that in order to write a novel, he needs a woman, children, and stability in his life.

5. Vocalist Jennifer Warnes admired Cohen's songs and produced a tribute album.

6. Cohen famously declined a Governor General's Award, earned a reputation as a ladies' man, and lived in a Buddhist retreat.

7. One of his more recent artistic goals was to write, direct, and score videos.

8. Cohen has collaborated on a rock opera movie, appeared on the TV show *Miami Vice,* received several Juno Awards, and travelled extensively.

9. His most popular songs include "Suzanne," "Bird on a Wire," and "Famous Blue Raincoat."

10. Many of Cohen's fans were surprised when he became a Zen Buddhist and retired to a California monastery.

EXERCISE 5

1. To cut down on fuel bills while cooking, consider the following energy-saving hints.

2. Avoid preheating your oven unless it is electric.

3. Cover all pots when cooking.

4. Don't open the oven door to check on food.

5. Use the oven light instead.

6. Don't use a flame that extends past the bottom of the pan.

7. Follow the time and temperature directions given in a recipe.

8. Prepare your whole meal in the oven or on top of the stove, not both.

9. Check all the burners and be sure they are off after use.

10. If you follow these suggestions, you will save money on your energy bills and cook better meals.

PROOFREADING EXERCISE

Mary Pickford was born in Toronto in 1892 and joined the vaudeville circuit in 1900. In 1908, she went to Hollywood. There she worked with legendary filmmaker D.W. Griffith and specialized in "damsel in distress" roles. She became known to the public as "Little Mary," "America's Sweetheart," and "The Girl with Golden Hair." Among the films she starred in are *Rebecca of Sunnybrook Farm, Coquette,* and *The Little Darling.* Her tremendous popularity gave her the clout she needed to dictate the terms of her contracts, develop her own production company, and cofound United Artists. In 1920, she married swashbuckling actor Douglas Fairbanks, who entertained movie audiences by swinging on ropes, jumping across high buildings, and engaging in sword play; they divorced in 1936. In her later years, Pickford donated many of her early films to the American Film Institute, received a lifetime achievement award from the Academy of Motion Picture Arts and Sciences, and promoted various charitable causes. She died of a stroke in 1979.

USING PRONOUNS (PP. 148–52)

EXERCISE 1

1. I
2. she
3. she and I
4. I
5. she and I

6. she
7. I
8. you and me
9. her and me
10. her

EXERCISE 2

1. its
2. its
3. its
4. their
5. One day last week, *the passengers* had to gather *their* belongings and leave the bus, even though it had not reached a scheduled stop.
6. their
7. their
8. *The passengers* did *their* best to hide *their* annoyance from the driver because he had been so nice.
9. As the passengers stepped off the bus at the end of the line, the driver thanked *them* for *their* patience and understanding.
10. it

EXERCISE 3

1. me
2. *The visitors* who participated in the tour learned a great deal about *their* taste in wine.
3. Every member of the group had *an* opinion of the Cabernet Sauvignon, Pinot Noir, and Merlot wines.
4. I
5. she

6. its

7. their

8. their

9. me

10. its

EXERCISE 4

1. *Guidance counsellors help students* a lot.

2. Last year, our school counsellor had a meeting with Karima in *the counsellor's* office.

3. Karima told her counsellor, *"I don't know which college to apply to."*

4. Karima's counsellor advised *Karima* to read a comprehensive guide to Canadian colleges.

5. The sentence is correct.

6. Karima completed her college application, put the top back on her pen, and took *the application* to the post office.

7. *She was delighted* when the offer of admission to the college arrived in the mail.

8. Many students move into residences *because they want to improve* their social life.

9. *Living in residence* gives you an opportunity to meet more people.

10. Most colleges offer special services for people with disabilities, but *the services* are not always adequate.

EXERCISE 5

1. George Chuvalo was a Canadian boxer who *was famous for* his many victories in the ring.

2. Muhammad Ali told *Chuvalo, "You have a hard head."*

3. Chuvalo was the first boxer to go fifteen rounds with Ali *and was* never knocked off his feet in his career.

4. *As* Canadian heavyweight boxing champion for twenty-one years, *Chuvalo was* a legend.

5. Now sixty-five, Chuvalo is still fighting, *but not in the ring.*

6. He devoted his time to the fight against drugs after *substance abuse* claimed the lives of his wife and three of his sons.

7. Chuvalo saw firsthand how *some people never recover from the effects of drug abuse.*

8. *Chuvalo's* "Fight Against Drugs" *website sheds light* on the problem of substance abuse.

9. *In communities across North America, Chuvalo tells students and parents* how drugs have affected his life.

10. In 1990, Chuvalo was inducted into the Canadian Sports Hall of Fame, *an honour* that he says is less important than his fight against drugs.

PROOFREADING EXERCISE
Corrections are italicized.

My friend Kevin and *I* went out the other day. We saw a movie at the new theatre complex down the block. After the cashier handed Kevin and *me* our tickets, we went into the lobby and were impressed with *its* decorations. Old movie posters *in really fancy gold frames* lined the hallways to the theatres. After the movie, I asked Kevin if he liked *the new theatre complex.* He said that it was the worst one he had ever been to. He told me that the parking was impossible, the screen was too small, and the seats were uncomfortable. He said that he would rather go to the place where we saw our last movie. At least *that theatre* had a full-size screen and good sound, even if *the theatre itself* wasn't as pretty as the new one.

AVOIDING SHIFTS IN PERSON (PP. 154–55)

PROOFREADING EXERCISES
Your revisions may differ depending on whether you choose to begin in first, second, or third person.

1. The paragraph is correct.

2. Communicating through e-mail has made people lose their manners. A letter used to begin with a polite salutation at the top, such as "Dear Sirs" or even "To whom it may concern," and end with a signature or printed name at the bottom to identify who sent it. And an old-fashioned letter had not only the sender's address but also the receiver's address on it too. Then there was the postmark to tell what town the letter was mailed from. Now, with different people using the same e-mail accounts and sending them from all over the world, it is never clear where electronic mail comes from unless the person follows the old rules of correspondence. But many people writing e-mail don't include salutations or signatures. In the old days, people took more time on their correspondence.

3. Christopher Wolfe will always have a reason to be proud. When he was seven years old, Christopher discovered a new dinosaur, and scientists named it after him. They called it *Zuniceratops christopheri*. This unknown species of dino-saur had two horns, one over each eye. There have been other discoveries of dinosaurs with horns, but the one whose bones Christopher found lived twenty million years earlier than any others. Christopher's father, Douglas Wolfe, was with him when he spotted the fossil in the Arizona/New Mexico desert. Douglas, a paleontologist, knew right away that his son's find was genuine. However, the kids at school had a hard time believing Christopher when he came in the next school day and told his classmates that he had discovered a new dinosaur species.

REVIEW OF SENTENCE STRUCTURE ERRORS (PP. 155–58)

Your corrections may differ.

1. A. cliché (I *dislike* news programs that report only gossip.)

2. A. subject/verb agreement error (Each . . . *was* the same size.)

3. B. dangling modifier (After *I made* a quick phone call, the dog next door was quiet.)

4. B. dangling modifier (One of my ankles was sore after *I played* tennis all afternoon.)

5. A. run-on sentence (The customers filled out suggestion cards; they contained some good ideas.)

6. A. cliché (I never have been interested in politics.)

7. B. pronoun agreement error (Everyone at the party brought *a* swimsuit.)

8. A. shift in person (I enjoy watching videos . . . because *I* can stop . . . whenever *I* want.)

9. B. misplaced modifier (*Waiting for a table at the new restaurant,* we stared at a tank of goldfish.)

10. B. cliché (I *will never take that class*).

11. A. not parallel (We applied for *a scholarship, a loan, and the honours program.*)

12. A. fragment and wordiness (Many people *wonder* about the shape of a face found on Mars.)

13. B. subject/verb agreement error (These studies of children's behaviour *have* to be done carefully.)

14. B. wordiness (Knowing what is valuable is difficult, however.)

15. B. subject/verb agreement error (Either the *tutor or the students* are correct.)

PROOFREADING EXERCISE
Here are some possible solutions. Yours may differ.

Mother Tells All

I have learned the most memorable lessons about myself from my children. A mother is always on display; she has nowhere to hide. And children are like parrots; they repeat whatever they hear. If I change my mind about something, they will remind me of every word I said.

For example, last summer I told my kids that I planned to take an exercise class and lose about forty pounds. I did lose some weight, and I attended an exercise class. But I started to feel like a balloon losing air. I decided that I did not want to lose any more weight or exercise anymore. I expected my children to accept my decision.

When I stopped, one of my sons said, "Mom, you need to go back to exercise class." Then they all started telling me what to eat, and I felt horrible. I had given up these things because I wanted to, but my words were still being repeated like a nonstop alarm clock. Finally, my kids got bored with the idea of my losing weight. Sometimes, when one of them makes a joke about my "attempt" to lose weight, it hurts me that they don't understand.

From this experience, I have learned not to tell my children about a plan unless I am going to finish it. Otherwise, they will never let me forget.

PART 3 PUNCTUATION AND CAPITAL LETTERS

PERIOD, QUESTION MARK, EXCLAMATION POINT, SEMICOLON, COLON, DASH (PP. 161–64)

EXERCISE 1

1. Wasn't the weather beautiful today?

2. I wonder when the autumn breezes will start to blow.

3. It still felt like summer—at least while the sun was shining.

4. At sunset the white, wispy clouds turned pink; then the blue sky behind them started to turn gold.

5. It was breathtaking!

6. The only hint of fall came after the sun went down: (or ;) the temperature dropped about ten degrees in an hour.

7. I have always thought of summer as my favourite season; however, today may have convinced me to switch to fall.

8. I never noticed that the leaves are so beautiful even after they have dropped from the trees.

9. I walked through the park and collected a bouquet of huge autumn leaves; it was fun. (or !)

10. I hope tomorrow will be as pretty as today.

EXERCISE 2

1. Nancy Cartwright is a well-known actress on television; however, we never see her when she is acting.

2. Cartwright is famous for playing one part: the voice of Bart Simpson.

3. Besides her career as the most mischievous Simpson, Cartwright is married and has children of her own—a boy and a girl.

4. Wouldn't it be strange if your mother had Bart Simpson's voice?

5. Cartwright admits that she made her own share of trouble in school.

6. But the similarities between her and her famous character end there.

7. Bart is perpetually ten years old; Cartwright is in her forties.

8. Bart is a boy; Cartwright is obviously a woman.

9. It's no surprise that Cartwright is very popular with her children's friends.

10. When they yell for her to "Do Bart! Do Bart!" she declines with Bart's favourite saying: "No way, man!"

EXERCISE 3

1. I have just discovered the fun of fondue!

2. The story of the invention of fondue goes this way: a farmer's wife accidentally dropped a chunk of cheese on the warming pan near the fire, and after mopping up the liquefied cheese with a piece of bread, she popped the morsel in her mouth and decided to make a meal of it.

3. Since its discovery, fondue has always been a process rather than a product; there are special pans to melt the cheese, fuel to keep it warm, and forks to hold the bread or meat to dip in it.

4. I now understand why fondue was especially popular in the 1960s and 1970s.

5. People then probably enjoyed the ritual of sitting down together and participating in a meal eaten from one pot.

6. And the ingredients of bread and cheese couldn't be simpler, could they?

7. There is also a rule that we might find distasteful now but thirty years ago must have seemed like fun; according to the book *Fabulous Fondues,* the person who lost a piece of bread in the fondue pot had to pay a forfeit.

8. The forfeits were listed as follows: if a man lost the cube of bread, he owed the hostess a bottle of wine; however, if a woman lost the cube of bread, she had to give one of the men at the table a kiss.

9. Of course, other foods can be substituted for the traditional chunks of bread: boiled potatoes, celery sticks, pretzels, crackers, mushrooms, and even nuts.

10. I plan to have a fondue party as soon as I possibly can!

EXERCISE 4

1. In the 1500s, early French settlers became friendly with the Huron; they even joined forces with the Huron to fight the Iroquois.

2. How many Canadians know that the North American phase of the Seven Years' War was called the French and Indian War?

3. Passed in 1867, the British North America Act created the Dominion of Canada with the union of four provinces: Ontario, Quebec, New Brunswick, and Nova Scotia.

4. During World War II, Prime Minister William Lyon Mackenzie King introduced conscription; it worsened relations between Anglophones and Francophones in Canada.

5. Quebec's opposition to conscription was even stronger during World War I; nevertheless, the Conservative government of Robert Borden passed the controversial Military Services Act in 1917.

6. The introduction of conscription during World War I helped to re-elect the Borden government; however, as a military measure, it was a failure.

7. Pierre Berton's *The National Dream* and *The Last Spike*—two books that were turned into a successful CBC drama-documentary series—dealt with the building of the Canadian Pacific Railway.

8. The subject allowed Berton to take full advantage of his greatest strength: a formidable gift for storytelling.

9. In an earlier book, Berton wrote about the Klondike gold rush of 1897–98—an event that temporarily boosted the population of the new town of Dawson.

10. In 2003, the wildly prolific Berton published his forty-ninth book!

EXERCISE 5

1. Here are some facts you may—or may not!—know about Canada.

2. Did you know, for example, that Canada's population is over thirty million?

3. Canada has two official languages: English and French.

4. Its highest mountain is Mount Logan in the Yukon Territory; some people wanted to rename it Mount Trudeau to commemorate the former prime minister, but the original name remains.

5. Canada's longest bridge is Confederation Bridge; it connects New Brunswick and Prince Edward Island.

6. Canada's population—except near its southern border with the United States—is very sparse.

7. Isn't Baffin Island the largest island in Canada?

8. Canada's northernmost point is on Ellesmere Island; its southernmost point is Middle Island in Lake Erie.

9. According to a recent census, the majority of Canadians are Catholic and Protestant; interestingly, 4 percent of Canadians are practising Hindus.

10. Canada has only one bordering country: the United States.

PROOFREADING EXERCISE

The ingredients you will need for a lemon meringue pie are lemon juice, eggs, sugar, cornstarch, flour, butter, water, and salt. First you combine flour, salt, butter, and water for the crust and bake until lightly brown; then you mix and cook the lemon juice, egg yolks, sugar, cornstarch, butter, and water for the filling. Once the filling is poured into the cooked crust, you whip the meringue. Meringue is made of egg whites and sugar. Pile the meringue on top of the lemon filling; place the pie in the hot oven for a few minutes, and you'll have the best lemon meringue pie you've ever tasted!

COMMA RULES 1, 2, AND 3 (PP. 166–71)

EXERCISE 1

1. For the first time in my life, I feel like an adult.

2. I am taking general education classes in college, and I am getting good grades.

3. Even though I receive some financial aid, I mostly support myself.

4. I have a job, a car, and an apartment of my own.

5. When I am ready, I plan to transfer to a university.

6. After I complete the course work at community college, my parents will be proud of me, but they will be even prouder when I get my degree.

7. I know that my father wants me to major in business, yet my mother wants me to be a teacher.

8. Eventually, it will be my decision.

9. Although I don't see myself in front of a class full of students, I have always loved the school environment.

10. The sentence is correct.

EXERCISE 2

1. When people say they are interested in astrology, they are often ridiculed.

2. Although they scoff at astrology, skeptics invariably know what sign they were born under.

3. And most of them also know that there are twelve signs in the zodiac, that there are four elements, and that each sign lasts about thirty days.

4. Aries, Leo, and Sagittarius are known as the fire signs.

5. Even though many of us don't take astrology seriously, every major newspaper carries a daily astrology column.

6. Superstitions are still widespread, for we tend to hold onto childhood fears and wishes.

7. The sentence is correct.

8. If you were born under a water sign like Cancer, Scorpio, or Pisces, an astrologer might describe you as strong, emotional, and creative.

9. A person born under Sagittarius has the same zodiacal sign as Ludwig van Beethoven, Winston Churchill, and Jane Austen.

10. Most of us don't believe that our lives are influenced by the positions and movements of the stars and planets, but the notion of fate entertains us all the same.

EXERCISE 3

1. If you have studied Canadian history, you may know that Canada has had twenty-one prime ministers so far.

2. Lester Pearson is remembered most for serving as president of the UN General Assembly, winning the Nobel Peace Prize, and introducing the new Canadian flag.

3. R.B. Bennett's legacy is not as positive, for he was in power during the Depression.

4. Among Canada's first three prime ministers—John A. Macdonald, Alexander Mackenzie, and Joseph Abbott—only Macdonald is well remembered today.

5. Interestingly, Joseph Abbott was the first prime minister to be born in Canada.

6. Canada has had four French-Canadian prime ministers: Wilfrid Laurier, Louis St. Laurent, Pierre Trudeau, and Jean Chrétien.

7. William Lyon Mackenzie King had an unconventional private life, yet he dominated Canada's political landscape for almost three decades.

8. Even though she was in power for only a few months, Kim Campbell had the distinction of being Canada's first woman prime minister.

9. Macdonald, Laurier, and Trudeau each served as prime minister for more than fifteen years.

10. In contrast, Sir Charles Tupper and John Turner each served for just over two months.

EXERCISE 4

1. The sentence is correct.

2. They were supposed to cure disease, lengthen life, and protect innocence.

3. Part of their appeal was their rarity, for emeralds are even rarer than diamonds.

4. Geologists have been mystified by emeralds because they are produced through a unique process—the blending of chromium, vanadium, and beryllium.

5. These are substances that almost never meet, nor do they often combine—except in emeralds.

6. In South Africa, Pakistan, and Brazil, emeralds were created by intrusions of granite millions to billions of years ago.

7. These areas are known for their beautiful gems, but emeralds from Colombia are larger, greener, and more sparkling.

8. The sentence is correct.

9. Instead of the granite found in other emerald-rich countries, the predominant substance in Colombia is black shale.

10. Even though these lustrous green gems can now be synthesized, a real emerald always contains a trapped bubble of fluid, and this minuscule natural imperfection is known in the gem business as a "garden."

EXERCISE 5

1. During his lifetime, Sir Frederick Grant Banting was voted most famous living Canadian in several polls.

2. Along with Charles Herbert Best, Banting is best remembered for his discovery of insulin.

3. Banting and Best received support for their research from the University of Toronto, and it was there that they made their famous discovery.

4. As a result of his famous discovery, Banting received the Nobel Prize in medicine, and he gave half his prize money to Best.

5. Banting wanted to develop a procedure to control diabetes in humans, so he ran an experiment on a dog named Maggie.

6. First, he tied off the dog's pancreatic ducts.

7. The dog went into a coma, and Banting revived it with insulin taken from a cow.

8. After only twenty minutes, the dog was walking again.

9. Although Banting received the Nobel Prize in 1923, he was not knighted until 1934.

10. For people with diabetes, Banting's discovery amounts to a new lease on life.

PROOFREADING EXERCISE

When Niels Rattenborg studied the brains of mallard ducks, he made an interesting discovery. Rattenborg wondered how ducks protected themselves as they slept. The ducks slept in rows, and these rows were the secret to their defence. To his surprise, Rattenborg found that the two ducks on the ends of the row did something special with the sides of their heads facing away from the row. Instinctively, the ducks on the edge kept one eye open and one half of their brains awake as they slept. The rest of the ducks slept with both eyes closed and both sides of their brains inactive. The two guard ducks were able to frame the ducks in the middle, watch for danger, and sleep almost as soundly as their neighbours.

SENTENCE WRITING

Here are some possible combinations. Yours may differ.

I am taking a yoga class, and it's more fun than I expected it to be.

When I get home from school, I do my homework, eat dinner, watch a little television, and go to sleep.

Grant and Gretchen don't know what to do now that they are getting married, for Grant's last name is Ketchem, and Gretchen doesn't want to be known as Gretchen Ketchem, so she might keep her maiden name instead.

COMMA RULES 4, 5, AND 6 (PP. 174–79)

EXERCISE 1

1. This year's Thanksgiving dinner, I think, was better than last year's.

2. The sentence is correct.

3. It was certainly more entertaining this year.

4. Certainly, it was more entertaining this year.

5. The guest who brought the apple pie sang karaoke with our mom after dinner.

6. My sister's new boyfriend, who brought the apple pie, sang karaoke with our mom after dinner.

7. Uncle Ken, the person responsible for basting the turkey, did a great job; it was moist and delicious.

8. The sentence is correct.

9. We believe that no one should take that responsibility lightly.

10. You may leave the sentence alone, or you may use a comma after *However*.

EXERCISE 2

1. We trust, of course, that people who get their driver's licences know how to drive.

2. Of course we trust that people who get their driver's licences know how to drive.

3. The sentence is correct.

4. Mr. Kraft, who tests drivers for their licences, makes the streets safer for all of us.

5. The sentence is correct.

6. Therefore, we may understand when we fail the driving test ourselves.

7. The driver's seat, we know, is a place of tremendous responsibility.

8. The sentence is correct.

9. We believe that no one should take that responsibility lightly.

10. No one, we believe, should take that responsibility lightly.

EXERCISE 3

1. The writing teacher, Ms. Nakamura, has published several of her own short stories.

2. The sentence is correct.

3. My daughter's friend Harry doesn't get along with her best friend, Jenny.

4. My daughter's best friend, Jenny, doesn't get along with one of her other friends, Harry.

5. The tiger, which is a beautiful and powerful animal, symbolizes freedom.

6. The sentence is correct.

7. The sentence is correct.

8. Kim and Teresa, who helped set up the chairs, were allowed to sit in the front row.

9. My car, which had a tracking device, was easy to find when it was stolen.

10. A car that has a tracking device is easier to find if it's stolen.

EXERCISE 4

1. Wayne Gretzky, born in Brantford, Ontario, has become one of the best-known figures in sports history.

2. "The Great One," as he is known by his many fans, was the first NHL player to score more than two hundred points in one season.

3. Gretzky grew up idolizing Gordie Howe, who has been called the finest athlete ever to play hockey.

4. An equally important role model was Gretzky's father, Walter.

5. The sentence is correct.

6. His greatest achievements, of course, came during his years with the Edmonton Oilers.

7. The sentence is correct.

8. His marriage to actress Janet Jones, which also took place in 1988, was described in the press as "Canada's Royal Wedding."

9. Gretzky and the late actor-comedian John Candy were co-owners of a Canadian football team, the Toronto Argonauts.

10. "The Great One," who retired from professional hockey in 1999, was inducted into the Hockey Hall of Fame.

EXERCISE 5

1. Zippo lighters, the only domestic lighters that can still be refilled, are highly useful tools and highly prized collectibles.

2. The sentence is correct.

3. The value of Zippo lighters is well known in Guthrie, Oklahoma, home of the National Lighter Museum.

4. Zippos have always been special to soldiers, who have often had to rely on the flame from their Zippo to warm food or light a fire.

5. The sentence is correct.

6. There have been many special edition Zippos made to celebrate an event—the first moon landing, for example.

7. Eric Clapton, famed guitarist and songwriter, used a clicking Zippo as an instrument in a song he wrote for the movie *Lethal Weapon 2*.

8. George G. Blaisdell, the man responsible for distributing, naming, and refining the Zippo as we know it, died in the late 1970s, but he cared about his customers.

9. All Zippo lighters come with a lifetime guarantee, which covers the lighters' inner workings but not the outer finish.

10. The Zippo Repair Clinic, which fixes around a thousand lighters a day, refunds any money sent by the customer.

PROOFREADING EXERCISE

Roberta Bondar, who was born in Sault Ste. Marie, Ontario, is best known as the first Canadian woman in space. She attended university with the goal of becoming a medical doctor, specifically a neurologist. She was admitted to the Royal College of Physicians and Surgeons of Canada in 1981 and studied at Tufts-New England Medical Center, located in Boston. Bondar was one of only six applicants, chosen from a field of over four thousand, to be accepted into the newly formed Canadian Astronaut Program in 1983. Her lifelong dream of exploring space became a reality in 1992 when she flew aboard the space shuttle *Discovery,* which was the third shuttle added to the Kennedy Space Center fleet. Bondar wrote about her experiences in space in the book *Touching the Earth,* published in 1994. She has received numerous honours during her career, including the Order of Canada, the NASA Space Medal, and induction into the Canadian Medical Hall of Fame.

SENTENCE WRITING

Here are some possible combinations. Yours may differ.

Las Vegas, a city famous for its casinos, also has lots of little chapels, where some people choose to get married.

I think she has a black belt in karate. (or) She has a black belt in karate, I think.

Barbara, my roommate, received scholarship money, which she thought she had to pay back.

REVIEW EXERCISE

I'm writing you this reminder, Tracy, to be sure that you don't forget our plans to visit the zoo this Saturday. [4] I know we're good friends, but lately you have let our plans slip your mind. [1] When we were supposed to go to the flea market last week, you forgot all about it. [3] I'm taking this opportunity, therefore, to refresh your memory. [5] I can't wait to see the polar bears, the gorillas, the giraffes, and the elephants. [2] And I have made special plans for a behind-the-scenes tour of several of the exhibits by Max Bronson, the zoo's public relations officer. [6] See you Saturday!

QUOTATION MARKS AND ITALICS/UNDERLINING (PP. 181–86)

EXERCISE 1

1. Robertson Davies' novels *Fifth Business, The Manticore,* and *World of Wonders* describe life in small-town Canada.

2. "Is there such a thing as a Canadian identity?" my English teacher asked.

3. "Even though I think the Canadian identity does exist," a student replied, "I don't believe it's very easy to define."

4. Given the Canadian appetite for American courtroom dramas like *Law and Order,* it's not surprising that some of us think the Fifth Amendment is part of our own Constitution.

5. Our most popular reality show, *Canadian Idol,* is a spinoff of its U.S. counterpart, *American Idol.*

6. Many Canadians read *Maclean's* in waiting rooms but subscribe to *Time* or *Newsweek.*

7. Margaret Atwood said, "People put down Canadian literature and ask us why there isn't a *Moby Dick.* The reason there isn't a *Moby Dick* is that if a Canadian did a *Moby Dick,* it would be done from the point of view of the whale."

8. Atwood has explored the elusive Canadian identity in books like *Survival* and poems like "Thoughts from Underground."

9. One of Gordon Lightfoot's best-known songs about the Canadian identity is "Canadian Railroad Trilogy."

10. On the literary importance of identity, Northrop Frye said, "This story of the loss and regaining of identity is, I think, the framework of all literature."

EXERCISE 2

1. We were taken aback when our teacher announced, "Your PowerPoint presentations will be worth 30 percent of the final grade."

2. But our trepidation gave way to enthusiasm when she added, "The topic of the presentation is up to you."

3. "We should include wild colours on some of the slides," Suzanne suggested at the first meeting of our four-person team.

4. Charged with the responsibility of choosing a title for our short presentation, I came up with "The Pleasures and Dangers of Extreme Sports."

5. "Before this meeting breaks up," Linda said, "we should set a date for the next one."

6. "Can everyone be here next Tuesday at four o'clock?" Suzanne asked.

7. "I can't make the next meeting," George said, "but you can fill me in via e-mail."

8. At the team's second meeting, I proposed the following: "George loves blading and snowboarding, so I bet he'd be willing to create three slides on the pleasures of extreme sports."

9. "I'll e-mail him about it," Suzanne said, "and also let him know I'll be preparing some slides on the dangers of extreme sports."

10. "This is a real eye opener," Linda said as she passed around copies of the article on extreme sports that she'd found in the *National Post*.

EXERCISE 3

1. Before his emergence as a singer-songwriter, Leonard Cohen was best known for novels like *The Favourite Game* and books of poetry like *The Spice-Box of Earth* and *Flowers for Hitler*.

2. In his second novel, *Beautiful Losers,* Cohen writes, "A saint is someone who has achieved a remote human possibility. It is impossible to say what that possibility is. I think it has something to do with the energy of love."

3. Cohen's first album, *The Songs of Leonard Cohen,* contains such hits as "Suzanne" and "So Long, Marianne."

4. In 1969, *The Globe and Mail* named Cohen Entertainer of the Year.

5. Cohen has lived abroad for long periods but maintains a home in Canada because, as he has said, "it is my native land, my home, with all the feeling one has for his homeland."

6. Cohen's compositions can be heard on the soundtracks of movies such as *McCabe and Mrs. Miller, Exotica,* and *Natural Born Killers.*

7. On the 1988 album *I'm Your Man,* the gravel-voiced singer pokes fun at his vocal limitations: "I was born with the gift of a golden voice."

8. Cohen was the subject of a 1996 biography entitled *Various Positions: A Life of Leonard Cohen.*

9. "Don't let the facts get in the way of truth," Cohen once advised his biographer.

10. "The last refuge of the insomniac," Cohen famously said, "is a sense of superiority to the sleeping world."

EXERCISE 4

1. John Diefenbaker, who was prime minister from 1957 to 1963, expressed his political views in a three-volume memoir, *One Canada.*

2. Diefenbaker wanted all Canadians to be, in his words, "unhyphenated Canadians."

3. As a letter printed in the *Ottawa Citizen* explained, "Dief the Chief just disliked the labelling that goes with hyphenation."

4. "I am not anti-American," Diefenbaker said in 1958. "But I am strongly pro-Canadian."

5. During the 1965 election campaign, Diefenbaker was speaking off the record when he attacked a political ally turned foe: "The papers say Dalton Camp is revolting. I cannot disagree."

6. Of Pierre Trudeau, the prairie populist asked, "Have you ever seen him kiss a farmer?"

7. The eroding value of the Canadian dollar in 1975 inspired this Diefenbaker quip: "I'm disturbed because the doctors tell me I'm as sound as a dollar."

8. In 1970, Diefenbaker told *The Toronto Star,* "I would never have been Prime Minister if the Gallup poll were right."

9. In his article "The Last Best Dief," journalist Larry Zolf wrote about a Diefenbaker few Canadians knew about: "This was Dief the unifier, the pacifier, the holistic magician."

10. Diefenbaker, the deaf canine sidekick on the Canadian police drama *Due South,* was named after Canada's thirteenth prime minister.

EXERCISE 5

1. P.L. Travers wrote the book *Mary Poppins* about a magical English nanny who defies the laws of physics and alters the lives of everyone she meets.

2. Asked about the character of Mary Poppins, Travers said, "I never for one moment believed that I invented her. Perhaps she invented me."

3. Travers believed "A writer is only half a book—the reader is the other half."

4. Travers never felt comfortable in the spotlight following the success of *Mary Poppins.* "I never talk about personal matters," she said, "only ideas."

5. And Travers had firm ideas about the audience for her stories: "[T]hey were never in the first place written for children, but for everybody—or maybe to ease my own heart."

6. When *Mary Poppins* was made into a movie that differed in many ways from the book, Travers felt extremely uneasy.

7. "The characters are entrusted to you," Travers commented; "I don't want it ever to be possible that somebody could take [Mary Poppins] and write a story about her that wasn't mine."

8. Travers also found it difficult to convey to Mary Shepard, the illustrator of the original Mary Poppins books, just exactly how Mary Poppins should look.

9. "Finally," Travers explained, "I went out and found a little Dutch doll and showed it to her. But even then there were disagreements."

10. In an essay entitled "Lively Oracles," which Travers wrote for the journal *Parabola,* she shared her thoughts about time: "Where the center holds and the end folds into the beginning there is no such word as farewell."

PROOFREADING EXERCISE

I've been reading the book *How Children Fail* by John Holt. I checked it out to use in a research paper I'm doing on education in North America. Holt's book was published in the early 1960s, but his experiences and advice are still relevant today. In one of his chapters, "Fear and Failure," Holt describes intelligent children this way: "Intelligent children act as if they thought the universe made some sense. They check their answers and their thoughts against common sense, while other children, not expecting answers to make sense, not knowing what is sense, see no point in checking, no way of checking." Holt and others stress the child's self-confidence as one key to success.

CAPITAL LETTERS (PP. 188–91)

EXERCISE 1

1. I have always wanted to learn another language besides English.

2. Right now I am taking English 1204 in addition to my writing class.

3. The course title for English 1204 is Basic Grammar.

4. English 1204 is a one-unit, short-term class designed to help students with their verb forms, parts of speech, phrases, and clauses.

5. I hope that learning more about English grammar will help me understand the grammar of another language more easily.

6. Now I must decide whether I want to take a Spanish, French, Italian, or American Sign Language course.

7. I guess I could even take a course in Greek or Russian.

8. When I was in high school, I did take French for two years, but my clearest memory is of the teacher, Mlle. Gauthier.

9. She was one of the best teachers that Walkerton High School ever had.

10. Unfortunately, I did not study hard enough and can't remember most of the French that she taught me.

EXERCISE 2

1. Sir Laurence Olivier was one of the most famous British actors of the 20th century.

2. He was well known for playing the leading roles in Shakespeare's plays.

3. He performed in London, on such stages as The Old Vic Theatre and St. James's Theatre, and for several years, he was director of the National Theatre.

4. Of course, Olivier also played to audiences in cities around the world, such as Montreal, Los Angeles, Moscow, and Berlin.

5. Among Olivier's most celebrated roles were Henry V, Othello, Richard III, and King Lear.

6. Although we can no longer see him on stage, we can still watch the film versions of his classic performances.

7. Olivier also directed many plays and some of his own films.

8. He directed the 1948 black-and-white film version of *Hamlet* and received the Academy Award for Best Actor for his performance in the title role.

9. One of Olivier's most treasured memories was of a single live performance of *Hamlet* in Elsinore, Denmark; it was scheduled to have been played outside but had to be moved inside at the last minute, causing all the actors to be especially brilliant under pressure.

10. North American audiences might remember Sir Laurence Olivier best for his portrayal of the tempestuous Heathcliff in the movie *Wuthering Heights,* but he was a Shakespearean actor at heart.

EXERCISE 3

1. My mom and dad love old movie musicals.

2. That makes it easy to shop for them at Christmas and on other gift-giving occasions.

3. For Mom's birthday last year, I gave her the video of Gilbert and Sullivan's comic opera *The Pirates of Penzance.*

4. It isn't even that old; it has Kevin Kline in it as the character called the Pirate King.

5. I watched the movie with her, and I enjoyed the story of a band of pirates who are too nice for their own good.

6. Actually, it is funnier than I thought it would be, and Kevin Kline sings and dances really well!

7. Dad likes musicals, too, and I bought him tickets to see the revival of *Chicago* on stage a few years ago.

8. He loved all those big production numbers and the Bob Fosse choreography.

9. There aren't many musicals made these days, but my folks did say that they would like a copy of the 1997 movie *Evita,* starring Madonna.

10. *Evita* is the Andrew Lloyd Webber musical about the former first lady of Argentina, Eva Peron.

EXERCISE 4

1. Keanu Reeves was born in Beirut, Lebanon, on September 2, 1964.

2. His father, Samuel, is of Hawaiian and Chinese descent.

3. Growing up in Toronto, Ontario, Keanu attended Jesse Ketchum Public School and four high schools, including the Toronto School for the Performing Arts, before dropping out at age seventeen.

4. After moving to Hollywood, he considered changing his name to K.C. Reeves.

5. Keanu had his first starring role in the 1986 movie *River's Edge.*

6. The actor has since appeared in such films as *Something's Gotta Give, Bill and Ted's Excellent Adventure, My Own Private Idaho,* and *Sweet November* with South African actress Charlize Theron.

7. Of course, Keanu is best known for his role as Neo in *The Matrix* and its two sequels, *The Matrix Reloaded* and *The Matrix Revolutions.*

8. In the early 1990s, Keanu was rejected by the Stratford Festival at an audition.

9. He captured the attention of the North American press in 1995 when he played the title role of Hamlet at the Manitoba Theatre Centre in Winnipeg.

10. In addition to acting in films, Keanu has done TV commercials for Kellogg's Corn Flakes and played bass guitar in the bands Dogstar and Becky.

EXERCISE 5

1. In 1999, New York's American Museum of Natural History featured an extremely popular exhibit.

2. The title of the exhibit was "The *Endurance:* Shackleton's Legendary Antarctic Expedition."

3. The *Endurance* was a British ship that set sail for Antarctica in 1914.

4. Ernest Shackleton was the ship's captain, and Frank Hurley was the photographer Shackleton took along to document the expedition's success.

5. Shackleton and his crew were attempting to be the first to cross Antarctica on foot and to claim this accomplishment for Britain.

6. Having nearly reached its landing site, the *Endurance* got stuck in the ice, and the crew lived on the icebound ship for nearly a year before it was crushed by the ice and sunk.

7. The crew escaped the sinking ship but were forced to live on the ice and eventually to travel to an uninhabited island.

8. Realizing that they could not survive much longer on their supplies, Shackleton took five men with him in a lifeboat named the *James Caird* and covered 1300 kilometres before they reached another ship.

9. Shackleton made it back to rescue the crew members he left behind, and all of them returned home safely.

10. The New York exhibit's displays, which included the *James Caird* itself and Frank Hurley's pictures, brought the voyage of the *Endurance* and the heroic efforts of Shackleton and his crew to life for all of the visitors who saw them.

REVIEW OF PUNCTUATION AND CAPITAL LETTERS (P. 192)

1. The cross on Mount Royal is a famous landmark in the city of Montreal.

2. Have you ever seen David Cronenberg's early films, such as *Rabid* or *They Came from Within?*

3. They've remodelled their house, and now they're ready to sell it.

4. "How much will the final exam affect our grades?" the nervous student asked.

5. We have reviewed your policy, Mr. Martin, and will be sending you a refund soon.

6. The two students who earn the most points for their speeches will face each other in a debate.

7. Ms. Thomas, the new English 1200 professor, recently received a national poetry award.

8. Even though I enjoy my French class, I believe I should have taken Spanish first.

9. You always remember Valentine's Day and our anniversary, but you forget my birthday!

10. His favourite part in the original *Toy Story* movie is when Buzz Lightyear shouts, "To infinity and beyond!"

11. My sister subscribes to *Canadian Geographic* magazine, and my whole family loves to look through it when she's finished reading it.

12. Finding low airfares takes time, patience, and luck.

13. My friend is reading the novel *Thousand Pieces of Gold* in her English class.

14. I wonder how much my art history textbook will cost.

15. Bill Gates, founder of Microsoft, is one of the richest people in the world.

COMPREHENSIVE TEST (PP. 193–94)

1. (pro ref) She asked her sister, *"May I go to the store?"*

2. (shift in time) Instructors break their classes up into groups when they *want* the students to learn on their own.

3. (p) I wonder if the real estate agent has called yet.

4. (apos) A *man's* overcoat lay in a corner of the bus shelter near my house until someone finally took it away.

5. (sp) The teacher's lecture had an *effect* on all of us.

6. (sp) We don't know which of the events *occurred* first.

7. (wordy) *Parking is a complex problem on campus.*

8. (cap) My favourite high-school teacher moved to *Vancouver* when she retired.

9. (pro) The school awarded scholarships to my roommate and *me,* and we're both so happy.

10. (// and wordy) Cranberries can be harvested *dry or wet.*

11. (wordy) Do the dishes and take out the trash before you leave the cabin.

12. (mm) *By going to museums,* children can learn about dinosaurs.

13. (frag and awk) *The room required a deposit,* but my cheque had not arrived.

14. (cs) I haven't finished my term paper; the library has been closed for the long weekend.

15. (s/v agr) Each of the branches *is* covered with lights.

16. (dm) *After we took a long vacation,* our house didn't seem as small as it did when we left.

17. (ro) The hills were steeper than we thought; none of us had worn the right shoes.

18. (cliché) *I often eat too much junk food.*

19. (wordy) I *returned the library book;* it had been overdue for a long time.

20. (pro agr) *The townspeople* turned their porch lights on in support of the proposition.

PART 4 WRITING

ORGANIZING IDEAS

EXERCISE 1 THESIS OR FACT? (P. 211)

1. FACT
2. THESIS
3. FACT
4. FACT
5. THESIS

6. FACT
7. THESIS
8. FACT
9. THESIS
10. FACT

EXERCISE 2 ADDING TRANSITIONAL EXPRESSIONS (P. 213)

When I moved into my own apartment for the first time last month, I discovered the many hidden expenses of entering "the real world." *First of all*, I had no idea that utility companies needed a security deposit from anyone who hasn't rented before. Each utility required a $30 to $50 deposit. *Therefore*, my start-up costs just for gas, electricity, and phone used up all the money I had saved for furnishings. *Next*, I found out how expensive it was to supply a kitchen with the basic staples of food and cleaning supplies. My initial trip to the grocery store cost $125, and I hadn't even bought my curtains at that point. *Finally*, I was able to budget my money and keep a little aside for any other unexpected expenses of living on my own.

WRITING ABOUT WHAT YOU READ

ASSIGNMENT 17 WRITE A 100-WORD SUMMARY (P. 229)

100-Word Summary of "Why Write?"

These days, writing well is a necessary skill for those who want to succeed—not only in business but also in personal life. In business, people who communicate well generally do well. Men and women have always looked for mates who had the skills that allowed them to thrive in their environment. Since writing well is such a predictor of success in the 21st century, it is one of the qualities people now seek when looking for a mate. So correct grammar, good sentence structure, and an appealing writing style are among the things that can make you sexy.

Index